KAIROS

In ancient Greek philosophy, *kairos* signifies the right time or the "moment of transition." We believe that we live in such a transitional period. The most important task of social science in time of transformation is to transform itself into a force of liberation. Kairos, an editorial imprint of the Anthropology and Social Change department housed in the California Institute of Integral Studies, publishes groundbreaking works in critical social sciences, including anthropology, sociology, geography, theory of education, political ecology, political theory, and history.

Series editor: Andrej Grubačić

Recent and featured Kairos books:

Between Thought and Expression Lies a Lifetime: Why Ideas Matter by Noam Chomsky and James Kelman

Taming the Rascal Multitude: Essays, Interviews, and Lectures 1997–2014 by Noam Chomsky

Beyond State, Power, and Violence by Abdullah Öcalan

Building Free Life: Dialogues with Öcalan edited by International Initiative

The Sociology of Freedom: Manifesto of the Democratic Civilization, Volume III by Abdullah Öcalan

The Art of Freedom: A Brief History of the Kurdish Liberation Struggle by Havin Guneser

The Battle for the Mountain of the Kurds: Self-Determination and Ethnic Cleansing in the Afrin Region of Rojava by Thomas Schmidinger

Mutual Aid: An Illuminated Factor of Evolution by Peter Kropotkin, illustrated by N.O. Bonzo

Revolutionary Affinities: Toward a Marxist-Anarchist Solidarity by Michael Löwy and Olivier Besancenot

Global Civil War: Capitalism Post-Pandemic by William I. Robinson

For more information visit www.pmpress.org/blog/kairos/

The State Is the Enemy
Essays on Liberation and Racial Justice

James Kelman

ISBN: 978-1-62963-968-0 (paperback)
ISBN: 978-1-62963-976-5 (hardcover)
ISBN: 978-1-62963-983-3 (ebook)
Library of Congress Control Number: 2022931961

Cover by Drohan DiSanto
Interior design by briandesign

10 9 8 7 6 5 4 3 2 1

PM Press
PO Box 23912
Oakland, CA 94623
www.pmpress.org

Printed in the USA.

for
Estelle Schmid and Suresh Grover

You must insist on living.
There may not be happiness
but it is your binding duty
to resist the enemy,
and live one extra day.
          —*Nâzım Hıkmet*

Contents

Introduction   1

Oppression and Solidarity   19

The Freedom for Freedom of Expression Rally,
Istanbul 1997   29

A Press Conference in Turkey   50

Em Hene!   52

The University of Strathclyde Students' Association
Grants Honorary Life Membership to Kurdish Leader,
Abdullah Öcalan   61

But What Is It They Are Trying to Express?   70

Who's Kidding Who?   79

Nobody Can Represent a Grieving Family   86

The Evidence Provides the Pattern. The Pattern *Reveals*
the Crime.   92

Pernicious Fabrications   98

A Notorious Case   105

Murder in the Line of Duty   119

Arise Ye Torturers-to-the-Crown   134

Home Truths   160

A Brief History   170

ADDENDUM
The 1997 Gathering in Istanbul for Freedom of Expression   180

NOTES   207

SELECTED BIBLIOGRAPHY   225

INDEX   226

ABOUT THE AUTHOR   231

Introduction

In the United Kingdom the effects of imperialism and colonization are inescapable. People of other races and classes are an easy target, and they are targeted. The most basic forms of racism and elitism are practised. Some of us see it and some of us don't; sometimes we fight and sometimes we don't. Those of us who belong to victimised communities also have choices, but far fewer. A few years ago, a young Kurdish refugee managed to escape from Turkey. There was no sanctuary in Scotland. He was murdered in a racist attack on a Glasgow street. His name was Firsat Yildiz and this was 2001, the year the British State criminalised the Kurdistan Workers' Party (PKK). The *Guardian* newspaper carried a feature, "He Fled from Hell in a Turkish Prison, Only to Die a Bloody Death in Glasgow."[1]

The day after the murder a Turkish football club arrived at the city airport to play a European football match, while on the same afternoon a demonstration against the Turkish State by over a thousand Kurdish refugees took place in the centre of the city. Many wore the colours and insignia of their outlawed party, their outlawed culture, and they spoke in their outlawed language. Any such public demonstration in Turkey would have brought them severe punishment and imprisonment by the Turkish police and military.

A BBC news bulletin reported briefly on the demonstration then cut to Glasgow Airport, showing the arrival of the

Turkish team and the football supporters who had travelled to cheer them, displaying the flags and colours of their club and country. The context presented by the BBC was that of a typical European country engaged in a typical international football competition. There was also the BBC silence on the situation in the southwest of the country, which was then a war zone.

More than twenty years later it remains a war zone, though the context here has shifted. Kurdish people are still being targeted in the United Kingdom. In September 2017 one heavily subsidised attack was carried out in Edinburgh by the British State. A broadsheet newspaper carried reports of Police Scotland "probing alleged 'fundraising for a proscribed organisation' and wider criminality by a number of unnamed individuals across the capital."[2] But this was more than that. A feature of the report was an unattributed photograph that had nothing to do with Police Scotland's attack on the community centre in Edinburgh. Instead it showed a partly destroyed bus following a bombing incident in which six Turkish soldiers died. The actual incident took place in Turkey several months earlier. Somebody must have dug it out of the archive library. Why did they choose a several-months-old photograph of something that happened in Turkey involving the Turkish military? What had that to do with an attack on a Kurdish community centre in Edinburgh? Once the focus is on the photograph further questions arise: Who wrote the caption?

> Scottish anti-terror police are probe alleged links to the PKK terror group in Edinburgh. It was behind this attack on a mini-bus in southern Turkey that killed six soldiers in February.

No self-respecting journalist would ever write such stuff. Who was responsible for "Scottish anti-terror police are probe alleged links"? Was it the work of a professional journalist?[3] Would a Police Scotland spokesperson refer to their special "counter-terrorism" unit as "Scottish anti-terror police"? The caption may be a grammatical mess but unless we unpick the bad grammar, we are given to understand that an "Edinburgh-based PKK terror group [was] behind the attack." What does this mean? Did a group of people travel from Edinburgh to southern Turkey in order to bomb "a mini-bus" used by the Turkish military? It is ludicrous. This photograph, complete with caption, has found its way into Glasgow's *Herald* newspaper—no doubt from a Turkish source—in order to justify the 2017 attack on the Kurdish community by a network of British State departments.

The use of such disinformation by mainstream British media can reach the level of farce. In this same article there is a link offered to an article they published way back in 1994. The older article is such fantastic and sleazy nonsense that I cannot quote from it. But it could be used by first-year students on a Spot the Spook course designed by MI6. The journalist reported to have written the 1994 article shares the name of a journalist nowadays based in Washington, DC, and a member of the Reuters team on World Affairs.[4] The one thing established by the *Herald* is how little respect they have for their own journalism, never mind their own readership.

Police Scotland clarified the matter of the attack on the community centre:

> Executive action in collaboration with several partnership agencies was conducted in the East of Scotland within the reporting period. Locations were searched under the Customs and Excise Management Act, Common Law Fraud and the Terrorism Act. Subsequent investigation identified additional Immigration act offences, with a significant sum of money potentially eligible for Proceeds of Crime Act confiscation. This operation has provided investigative opportunities to allow continued collaboration with Her Majesty's Revenue & Customs, Trading Standards and Home Office Immigration Enforcement.[5]

Now we have it. It was a coordinated assault, putting into practice British State policy on minorities. "Police Scotland's counter-terrorism officers ... have long developed close working relationships with other law enforcement agencies including those with a UK-wide remit," and this was the result. This outrageous assault on the Kurdish community was authorised by the British State, at executive level.

There was no fixed objective other than to strike fear into the Kurdish community. Every last one of the people gathered there was guilty until proven otherwise. Guilty of what, is the question. Of being Kurdish, is the answer. As it is in Turkey, so too in the United Kingdom. Such is the depth of the shameful collusion between British and Turkish State authorities. Kurdish people are guilty until proving themselves not guilty. Proving you are not guilty is the best you can do. It is impossible to be innocent.

The stuff on the PKK was a pretext. Membership of a proscribed political party counts as a crime, and displaying the colours of Kurdistan may be produced in evidence of that, but here in Edinburgh "were several partnership agencies." Plenty of other criminal charges could be laid against the Yilin Kurds relating to "Customs and Excise Management," "Common Law Fraud," issues on Immigration Control. Anyone on the premises "with a significant sum of money" was liable to have it confiscated under the "Proceeds of Crime" legislation. Empty your pockets! Define "significant"!

The Police Scotland "counter-terrorism officers" attacked the Kurdish community knowing that on the balance of probability they would find something wrong. They have been at liberty to do this at least since the 1980s, thanks to a piece of racist legislation introduced by the Whitehall Parliament.[6] British State authority is at liberty to attack at any time of the day or night, and this is what they do, any time, any day. Young black people gave a name to something similar which operated in England and Wales as far back as fifty years ago: they called it "Sus Law." It was designed to the same effect. Anyone who was black was liable to be stopped and searched. Racial identity was the only ground necessary.[7]

Those of us who are not Kurdish but express our solidarity with the Kurdish struggle are also guilty of going to the support of someone who is under suspicion of criminal behaviour which may be connected to a terrorist organisation. We see here not only the relationship between the British State and that of Turkey but also an indication of the road ahead and the extent to which the UK is drifting into the kind of society we associate with fascism.

My first involvement with the Kurdish community was back in 1991, and I haven't finished yet.[8] This book falls within that category. Half of it concerns the plight and courage of the Kurdish people. The more I learned the more obvious it was that if Kurdistan was not a country then it should have been— and would have been, all things being equal. But things were far from equal and we need not fix attention on Turkey alone, but discover the seminal role of France, the USA and the United Kingdom. Many of the essays are derived from talks I delivered at solidarity events. Perhaps the authorities will buy up batches and burn them, and people ordering one online will be traced and prosecuted. Be warned.

Within the Kurdish liberation movement, activists were aware of Scotland's struggle for independence. But like most people in Scotland I knew nothing, even as a young writer. I had become acquainted with the work of Yaşar Kemal before I was published but I did not know he was Kurdish. I used to browse the Ks in the local library and this was where I came upon his name: Kafka, Kemal, Kerouac, Kersh. I wondered whereabouts I would land when my first book came out. I didn't expect to go to jail, which is where so many writers wind up in the Republic of Turkey. I discovered Yaşar Kemal was Kurdish in 1995 when he "was tried in Istanbul's No. 5 State Security Court" on a charge of "thought crime."[9]

He was convicted of "inciting hatred," for which he received a twenty-month suspended sentence. A campaign was organised in solidarity with him by Turkish writers and activists, which was supported by foreign humanitarian groups. In 1997 I attended the Freedom for Freedom of Expression Rally in Istanbul, part of a delegation of twenty writers. Our purpose was to present ourselves to the State Prosecutor with a "declaration of crime" in solidarity with Kemal and very many writers and activists then being prosecuted by the Turkish State Security Court for doing precisely the same thing several months earlier.

Inside Turkey the presence of twenty foreign writers was a major media happening. In the UK nothing was reported. There was no interest from any British media.

Demonstrations and protests in Turkey were banned by the National Security Council (the military). The way activists got round it was to call a press conference and then throw it open to all. At the rally the organisers called one such and three to four thousand people turned up, including two thousand troops.

At that same period the sociologist İsmail Beşikçi had spent many years of his life in prison for exercising the freedom to think. The exploration of the identity of the Kurdish people has been his lifetime work. His thirty-three publications were banned as "thought crimes." In 1999 solidarity events took place in Glasgow and Edinburgh to raise awareness of his plight. His publisher, Ünsal Öztürk, had been released from prison and came to Scotland to take part. He spoke at both events. No doubt the authorities were attuned to these events, but at that time the Kurdistan Workers' Party had yet to be criminalised by the British State.

Other events were held and the musician and activist Şanar Yurdatapan travelled to the UK from Turkey just to be there at these solidarity events. Neither Beşikçi nor Öztürk nor Yurdatapan is a Kurd; all three are Turks and all three were targeted by the State authorities. The Turkish National Security Council does not concede such "freedoms" to its general population. People have to fight for them. In Turkey expressing a thought is a crime. Democratically elected politicians are imprisoned for the slightest reason.

The Turkish State regarded Beşikçi as its second most dangerous man. The man occupying prime position was Abdullah Öcalan, president of the PKK. They belong to my own generation, coming to adulthood during the 1960s and early 1970s. Their interest in external struggles and liberation movements in general were influenced by the politics and intellectualism of the day. Nowadays this would be termed "extreme left"; then it was merely "radical" or "alternative," or "humanitarian." People across the globe saw it was possible to challenge hegemony, whether in London, Grenada, Diyarbakır, San Francisco, Santiago, Johannesburg, Paris or Chicago.

In those days the PKK was one more liberation group and as happens in their situation the plight of other disenfranchised people is significant. The British State had granted my country a wee sort of government of its own. Scotland is a country, but only within the UK. Outside of the UK Scotland does not qualify as a country. I identify as Scottish but officially I am forced to be a British citizen. The PKK were interested in the politics of such a position, and how devolved power might work. At a press conference relayed by his lawyers, Abdullah Öcalan spoke of the need to form "democratic alliances between political parties in Turkey not simply [towards] an election [but as] developed between various parties while Europe was in transition to democracy.... A lesson must be learned from the solution of Scotland, Ireland, and Wales."[10]

In Turkey the advocacy of something as puny as "the Scottish solution" means a person is an "evil terrorist." Even to conduct a dialogue towards the creation of a devolved parliament requires a change in the law; in Turkey it is a crime. "Not one sentence can be uttered in defence of the Kurds, or of the

Kurdish leader, without the charge of 'separatism' or 'terrorism' being levelled." This suppression of all discourse around
the subject exemplifies the farcical nature of that so-called trial
at which Öcalan was tried as a criminal, found guilty and sentenced to death, betrayed in particular by the governments of
Greece, Italy and Germany.

For several decades people have detailed atrocities, massacres, rapes and tortures, even genocide. Petitions are presented.
Analyses are performed, statistics and algorithms formulated.
Meanwhile the tyrants do what tyrants always do: whatever
they like. It happened yesterday, and the day before, and the
day before that too, and will continue tomorrow and the next
day and the next day, and on and on and back and forth and
will not stop, not until forced. For those of us with no personal
connection to Kurdistan the danger is being overwhelmed.

There is much to learn, much to discover. I once gave
Creative Writing students an essay delivered by Mehmed
Uzun to State Security Court No. 5 in Istanbul.[11] I was trying to
give them an idea of the situation facing writers and publishers and the extreme danger they confront on a daily basis, for
nothing other than doing their best, writing the truth. Uzun's
essay does not offer a list of names, any of that kind of thing.
His essay offers himself. From this we make an inference:
where there is one there are two, perhaps four, or sixteen, or
256, or 65,596. How many writers, musicians and artists are
there in Kurdistan? How many people? How many children?
What languages do they speak? What do they do and how do
they live, and where do they come from? And is it mountains
and flatlands they have? Are there rivers and lochs? What are
their songs and their stories?

Some older maps picture an entity by the name of
"Kurdistan." I used the image of the neck and head of a horse
to remember the shape. I could draw a line enclosing southeast Turkey, northern Syria, northern Iraq, northwest Iran
and note how the northeastern section of Turkey "linked"

into southern Georgia and Armenia. This line is an unbroken outline and may be described as a border. It was straightforward to visualise such a territory as a country. If people called it a country who would have disagreed? Why would people call it a country if it was not a country? Why would they have to?

In the last interview given by Öcalan before his imprisonment he was asked to account for "the PKK's bad image." At the time fifteen Kurds were on trial in France, "accused of being terrorists." Deals were being done by the powers, and everybody knew it. Öcalan was matter-of-fact in his reply: "France is making a lot of concessions to Turkey. Politics are often based on material interests. We, the Kurds, we have nothing to give."

Except themselves, and for several generations the people of Kurdistan have been giving themselves. Soon after that interview Öcalan was betrayed and captured. He is imprisoned on the island of İmralı. There is nothing else on this island except this prison. There is only one prisoner.

How he landed there is a complicated story.[12] According to an unnamed representative of Turkey's most powerful supporter, the USA, "We spent a good deal of time working with Italy and Germany and Turkey to find a creative way to bring him to justice."[13] Öcalan gave his own account: "NATO central headquarters had played the essential role." When he landed in Kenya, which he had thought a safe destination, he was captured and taken to Turkey. The Greek ambassador met Öcalan in Nairobi and confided to him: "I was leading the NATO unit which had been after you for twenty years; while searching for you in the sky I found you in my hands."[14]

On the few occasions that I've talked with young Kurds there seems a hunger for their own history, not from all but for some. Their history, as with the history of my own people, is radical history. I see this sensibility in my own country, where many young people love the Gàidhlig language, hearing the songs, the stories. But very many don't. They can barely cope with hearing the voice.

Oppression begins at home. We learn of the effects of imperialism on our own doorstep. When I was a child of around seven or eight years of age a schoolteacher asked my class to name their clans. I was able to say Mackenzie, my father's middle name. I told him when I got home and he said, Oh you've got more than that, but he didn't tell me any. Maybe he didn't know of them. I doubt if he ever discovered that when his mother was born in 1881 the family were squatting on marshland on the outskirts of a village. One side of her family were descendants of Clan Macleod and their associate clans. They had lived on the island for a thousand years or more, perhaps since the Viking invasions of the tenth century. The other side were descended from Clan Mackenzie and their associate clans. They had been there for two hundred years, relative newcomers to the island. They landed from mainland Scotland in the earlier part of the seventeenth century. They were there to root out the indigenous population and to take the island on behalf of King James, first Monarch of the United Kingdom.

King James had learned that wiser "conquerors tend not to drive out or exterminate the conquered race, but to form a landed aristocracy, with more or less servile occupiers of the land under them."[15] He negotiated with one powerful mainland clan and sponsored their invasion and possession of the island. The Clan Chief was transformed into a scion of the British ruling class and the clan lands transferred into his personal possession. Henceforth he did as he was told until he no longer needed to be told. His interests were class interests. By the end of the seventeenth century the clansfolk had been evicted and cleared off the land to make way for deer forests and lodges which now were properties owned by himself.

By the end of the eighteenth century more generations of islanders were evicted and cleared to make way for sheep farms and other profit-making enterprises. By now the Clan Chief was a full Peer of the Realm and assisting the British Army to capture and conscript local boys and men on behalf of the Crown, posting them overseas to do or die on behalf of British business interests. One of the kilted warriors who went by the name of Murdo Mackenzie spent many years abroad, fighting on behalf of Crown enterprises and the British State Co. Ltd. Murdo survived to make it home. By the end of the nineteenth century his grandson and family were squatting with his wife and children on a piece of bog. My grandmother was second eldest of the children. After a thousand years on the island of Lewis the family had no "entitlement" to live anywhere at all. She moved to Glasgow and her siblings to North America.

My grandmother knew no English until she went to school. No Gàidhlig was allowed in the classroom. My father had three surviving brothers. None could speak their mother's language. I have four brothers. None of us can speak the language. None of us knew the culture. It was all slightly ridiculous, embarrassing, and always irrelevant.

People from other cultures know the reality of the British State. The more the working class and lower orders experience such power, the less likely they are to harbour delusions on fair play, truth and justice, and never ever to confuse their own interests with that of the State, nor their own communities with that of the ruling elite. Communities are forced to negotiate with the imperialist. They split and remain separate, each with its own history; bonds of families, clans, religious ties; its own heroes and martyrs to the cause.

Those whose language has been suppressed or outlawed will recognise this form of oppression. It is part of the dehumanising process we confront as victims of the State's demand for unity. People are locked into prejudicial states of mind; the original cause of the enmity is lost in time. Soldiers fight to the death because of what happened five minutes ago to their friends and comrades whose legends and exploits remain as personal memories. Our kinsfolk die for "the wrong cause."

This too is radical history. An awareness of how it operates gives us the chance of escaping isolation: struggling together, culture through culture, community and community. Struggle creates solidarity.

The resistance to racism, sectarianism and other forms of discrimination is where the struggle remains. But the experience of those who know the workings of empire is there to be taken, explored, adapted and used. This surely begins with the war on racism, of taking courage from those who are forced to deal with it in every area of society, offering support and solidarity, and learning the depth of the struggle, and the need to develop methods of defence appropriate to that.

By the late 1960s the ruling elite wanted to rid themselves of any dissident deemed dangerous, without being held accountable. A British soldier or policeman couldn't just shoot to kill British citizens. But why not? Members of the colonial police could kill indigenous civilians in other parts of the Empire. Why not here? There were parts of Great Britain that seemed like a foreign country to the ruling elite. Why not treat it as such? What would it take to define sections of its own population as the enemy? What if the local population were defined as the enemy? All it required was a different set of rules, principles and procedures being put into place. The rest would follow.

The colonial experience of the military and legal wings of the British Empire were especially crucial. Throughout the 1970s the British Army and the British police targeted particular areas of its own population in the north of Ireland: the traditional enemies, the indigenous Irish and Roman Catholic communities. On the mainland the target areas were the black and Asian communities, later adapted to include all immigrants, asylum seekers, radicals, activists, dissidents and anyone else who refused to acknowledge the supremacy of British State authority. The three most powerful unions were those of the steelworkers, the miners and the railway workers. They were the chief targets, and that original, basic project culminated in 1984–85 when the British State went to all lengths necessary to destroy the National Union of Miners, and in so doing inflict a blow to the working class from which it has failed to recover.

In the early 1970s a spate of strikes brought a strong reaction by the State. They targeted the procedures and methods that defined trades unionism, challenging legally, illegally, overtly, covertly. State authorities attacked the picket line, isolating individuals and individual branches. They blocked decisions by consensus, forced through voting by ballot, attempting to put an end to the so-called unofficial strike. Workers were criminalised for defending one another against the worst kinds of shop-floor abuse. No matter how badly an employer victimised and mistreated a worker their fellow branch members could not put down their tools and walk off the job.

Trade unionists were reluctant to identify too closely with people from other cultures and traditions. It was easier to support liberation movements in Africa and South America than align themselves too closely with the struggle of local minorities. The mainstream left align themselves with political parties and cultural formations who will not challenge at that foundational level. Every member of every mainstream political party in the UK bows or curtseys to the Crown. If they don't, they get thrown out. The struggle in Northern Ireland leads to confrontation of a sort that ultimately excludes all of the Parliamentary left. It can only end in disunity and finishes off the United Kingdom.

The hatred of the Celtic race has its basis not in working-class or lower-order prejudice and sectarianism. It belongs to the war waged against the race by the ruling elites of England and later by Britain, whose perception of the Gàidhealtachd was expressed by King James himself, who saw

> two sorts of people: the one that dwelleth in our mainland, that are barbarous for the most part, and yet

mixed with some show of civility: the other, that dwel-
leth in the Isles, and are utterly barbarians, without any
sort or show of civility. For me the first sort, put straitly
to execution the laws made already by me against their
overlords and the chiefs of their clans; and it will be no
difficulty to danton [subdue] them. As for the other sort,
follow forth the course that I have intended, in planting colonies among them of answerable inland subjects,
that within short time may reform and civilise the best
inclined among them: rooting out or transporting the
barbarous and stubborn sort, and planting civility in
their rooms.[16]

He set out to rid the UK of the Celtic people and the culture.
This was the project at the formation of the United Kingdom
back in 1603, and it has remained a project.[17]

But there were other projects to be resolved by the ruling
elite. How were they to ensure that those among them whose
properties included raw resources open to mining would have
access to the cheaper forms of labour? That was straightforward. Within a year "the worst bondage began." The law of the
land was changed. By 1606 the Crown had enslaved its entire
mining community: the men, the women and the children of
the three kingdoms, England, Wales and Scotland. The workers
were born slaves and died slaves, so too the grandchildren of
their grandchildren for almost two hundred years, right until
the end of the eighteenth century. This inhuman horror did not
end until the end of the eighteenth century, known as the Age
of Enlightenment in mainstream history.

During that same period the British State authorities did
not allow "Roman Catholics [to] purchase land, hold civil or
military offices or seats in Parliament, inherit property, or
practice their religion freely without incurring civil penalties.
A Roman Catholic in Ireland could not vote in Parliamentary
elections and could be readily dispossessed of his land by his

nearest Protestant relative."[18] The people of the three kingdoms were advised to remember the Crown's original project
by the man in charge of the British Army in Northern Ireland.
Soon after he took command authority was imposed cynically,
and with immediate effect,[19] using strategies associated with
a colonial police and imperialist army of occupation. Under
his control communities in West Belfast and Derry were dev-
astated, and some of those who got in the way were murdered.

Soon after the 2017 raid by Police Scotland on the Kurdish
community centre, I was in a library and overheard a conversa-
tion going on between three staff members. The name Turkey
cropped up, and I eavesdropped. The library staff were not
discussing fascism, censorship and suppression; police brutality, the destruction of historic sites, of cities and towns; the
links between gangsterism, the far right and government; the
imprisonment of writers, foreign journalists, student activists, trade unionists, even elected members of their own parliament. None of that. The library staff were discussing sand
castles, sunny beaches and the cost of return flights to the sun-
kissed shores. They were extolling the virtues of Turkey as a
holiday destination.

I considered saying something but what was there to say?
I would have tried not to be sarcastic, not to be angry, neither
to condescend nor to patronise. I hope I might have tried to
inform them in some way. But where to begin? I didn't say anything. I wish I had. We cannot continue to gather information
forever. There comes a point where we have to move with what
we have.

Three thousand years ago Miletus was a major international port. People passed through here connecting to all parts
of the ancient world. Nowadays the region is part of southwest Turkey: tourist friendly, full of properties, marinas
and resorts. Miletus is long gone. The nearest coastal town is
Didim. "British people have [been buying] holiday homes [here
for years], establishing themselves as a visible community of

many thousands, to the extent that utility bills in the district are now printed in English as well as Turkish."[20]

I checked out a company who specialises in advice for western tourists. Somebody wondered if it was safe to visit this part of Turkey because of the "terrorist activities in Syria." Somebody else advised them "to relax and enjoy their holiday … in the company of 40 million other tourists [who were] travelling to Turkey in 2015."[21] I checked a little further and discovered that most everything in this fun-filled holiday region is owned by Doğuş Holding A.Ş., "one of the largest private-sector conglomerates in Turkey, with a portfolio of 250 companies in 7 industries, including high-end car dealerships, retail stores, restaurants, cafes, construction companies, radio stations, TV channels and tourism businesses."[22] The holding company had previously owned Garanti Bank, one of Turkey's largest private banks, which is now part of BBVA, "one of the largest financial institutions in the world … present mainly in Spain, South America, North America, Turkey and Romania.… In 2019 the Bank changed its name to BBVA, dropping local brand names in Argentina, Mexico, Peru, and the United States.… [Then] in 2020, BBVA USA was sold to PNC Financial Services for 11.6 Billion dollars."[23]

The distance from Didim to Kobani is roughly the same as the one from the east to west Texas border. Fighter jets and other airborne machinery do it in the flick of a switch. Further information is available from suppliers of global war and defence implements. A leading member is a neighbour of my own here in Scotland. Lockheed Martin UK Ltd. have an office twenty miles far from where I live. This is the home of missiles that destroy the world in the flick of another switch. We're used to it. They've been here since the end of the Second World War. Their office is across the road from Faslane Cemetery.

Lockheed Martin UK Ltd. works closely with the UK and Turkish State authorities, and more than fifty other state authorities throughout the world, including Indonesia, Saudi

Arabia, Israel, India, Canada, Japan, Australia, Chile, Argentina and so on and so forth. Most of the world powers and their allies are either at war or assisting one side against another. A Lockheed Martin Ltd. copywriter advises us that the company is helping all these worldwide nation-states to "protect their national interests while strengthening their economies, industries and communities from within."

In Scotland the company has embarked on a space exploratory programme in partnership with the Shetland Islands Council and its other "partners at the US Space Agency, ABL Space Systems and SaxaVord Spaceport." The people of the Shetland Islands have applauded their local politicians for securing this extraterrestrial project, and applauded Lockheed Martin for considering the needs of the local community.[24] School pupils have been promised pizza-delivery jobs, supplying the needs of the technical staff and ground-area cleaners employed at the Spaceport. Early interviews are promised for optional weekend opportunities on Mars should maximum operational potential be fulfilled.

"The defence giant" reminds potential investors, notwithstanding their diverse charitable enterprises, that they have so far "gathered nearly \$8 billion worth of contracts including a multi-billion dollar contract to provide satellites for what will eventually be replacing the Space-Based Infrared System, as well as contracts valued hundreds of millions for air-to-surface missiles, anti-ship missiles and the VH-92 Presidential Helicopter Replacement Program."[25] Meantime, global clients should expect suppliers to honour all contracts in partnership with themselves in the advancement of necessary ground, air and supersonic space-implements designed to maximise clinically effective genocidological forms of population reduction at its most democratically acceptable levels.

We see reality when we do some basic research on these global giants. None of it depresses me. It is the opposite. What we discover is what we always knew. It is up to us.

Three thousand years ago in the city of Miletus, a group of people formed a community who engaged in the most fundamental of questions: what is reality, and how do we deal with it? This is such an extraordinary quest that we not only know the names of three men centrally involved in the quest, but that their work remains every bit as significant. The three men were Thales, Anaximander and Anaximenes. A little later, only a few miles farther north, Xenophanes and Heraclitus were working along the same lines. In those days this region was an outpost of the Greek Empire. Then it belonged to the Persian Empire. Before modern Turkey we had Ottoman Turkey and way way back we had the Assyrian Empire, the Babylonian Empire, the Chaldean Empire, then all the barbarians; barbarians from everyplace under the sun. People moved and returned from Tibet, Mongolia, Africa, India and Europe too. And I'll hazard a guess: there were ruling elites and authorities in every one of them. And people were having to deal with it, fighting to survive, challenging and dying in the attempt. The men named above learned and listened to everything they could and they made sense of it as best they could.

What we have is our own capacity as human beings. Communities and individuals interact. We learn from one another, from the past, from other cultures and dynasties. What is this and what is that and what goes on between them. Empathy is one of the primary relationships between human beings. It is species driven. We distinguish human beings from other life forces, other species. Solidarity begins from empathy. Empathy takes us into any human situation, and solidarity helps us deal with it. We learn to share one another's perspective. The only worthwhile support is from within the movement itself.

Oppression and Solidarity

Certain ethnic groups are well treated by the dominant nations only to the extent that these groups accept abandoning their culture, their mother tongue, their history and their literature, in other words to the extent that they accept assimilation. We have a duty to encourage these ethnic groups to oppose assimilation, to develop and enrich their mother tongue, their literature and their culture. Only in this way can world culture develop, enrich itself and serve humanity.

—Article 18 of the Statutes of the
Human Rights Commission

This is fine as far as it goes, but I wonder who are the "we." The one thing I do know is that this "we" never refers to the oppressed and suppressed groups under discussion. They are not so much the subject of Article 18 as the object. They do not get a say in the matter. Things get done to them. The "we" of Article 18 have a choice: they can treat oppressed groups well or not well; they can encourage or not encourage. But no matter what that "we" decide, it is their decision. The rest of the world have to put up with it.

Article 18 of the Statutes of the Human Rights Commission is as good a definition of western liberalism as you will find. From pronouncements such as this you can tell why European civilisation has produced so much theology and philosophising

on action and non-action, ethical debates on duty and obligation, individual and collective; reasons for and against taking
responsibility. An entire edifice of educational, ecclesiastical
and social structures exists, designed not to change society for
the better but to establish if "we" have any such obligation in
the first place.

People and communities under attack never have these
ethical worries; they just find ways of defending themselves.
The "we" of Article 18 acts to exclude the vast majority of
the world's population. It may be the voice of a benefactor
but it talks in the voice of power, of control: the voice of the
imperialist.

It should go without saying that any culture, history or
literature is valid. Or any mother tongue. Let's call it language;
even using the term "mother tongue" in this imperial context
somehow renders it invalid, an inferior "salt-of-the-earth" type
thing. It should be an obvious point that we can't use terms
like *superior* or *inferior* when we speak about cultures and
languages, not unless we're willing to use these terms about
actual people. If we feel happy describing persons or peoples
as inferior, then by all means we can use these terms when we
speak of their cultures or languages.

Of course, in our part of the world these so-called obvious
points aren't recognised as obvious at all. Not only are they
not recognised as obvious but our society is premised on the
opposite view, that one culture is superior to another, that one
language is superior to another, one literature superior to
another, one class superior to another: that one people is superior to another. That's the fundamental premise which sets the
structural basis of our society; it's endemic to it, it informs
everything within it, from law and order to education, from
health to housing to immigration control. And because of that
when for example a racist violation takes place on the streets
it is entirely consistent that it should do. If the State is racist,
why should we act as though racism on the street is some sort

of aberration? We live in a racist state, so it's consistent. Why should we act as if it's a kind of social phenomenon?

But when we talk about the hegemony of English culture we aren't referring to the culture you find down the Old Kent Road in London, we aren't talking about the literary or oral traditions of Yorkshire or Somerset; we are speaking about the dominant culture within England and within the UK as a whole, the culture that dominates all other English-language-based cultures, the one that comes from within the tiny elite community that has total control of the social, economic and political power bases of Great Britain. And leaving aside the USA's sphere of influence this is also the dominant culture throughout the majority of English-speaking countries of the world.

There is simply no question that by the criteria of the ruling elite of Great Britain so-called Scottish culture, for example, is inferior, as the Scottish people are also inferior. The logic of this argument cannot work in any other way. And the people who hold the highest positions in Scotland do so on that assumption. Who cares what their background is, whether they were born and bred in Scotland or not, that's irrelevant, they still assume its inferiority. If they are native Scottish, then they will have assimilated the criteria of British ruling authority. If they hadn't, they wouldn't have got their jobs. Exceptions do exist but exceptions only make the rule.

So of course Scotland is oppressed. But we have to be clear about what we *don't* mean when we talk in these terms: we don't mean some kind of "pure, native-born Scottish person" or some mystical "national culture." Neither of these entities has ever existed in the past and cannot conceivably exist in the future. Even when arguments involving these concepts are "rational," they can only be conducted on some higher plane. And it's always safer for human beings—as opposed to concepts or machines—when this higher plane is restricted to mathematics, theoretical physics or logic (or else religions that insist on a fixed number of gods). The logic of this "higher plane" generates a never-ending stream of conceptual purity to do with sets and the sets of sets. In earlier times we might substitute "set" for "god," insert a capital letter and seek the God of all gods.

Entities like "Scot," "German," "Indian" or "American"; "Scottish culture," "Jamaican culture," "African culture" or "Asian culture" are material absurdities. They aren't particular things in the world. There are no material bodies that correspond to them. We only use these terms in the way we use other terms such as "tree," "bird," "vehicle" or "red." They define abstract concepts, "things" that don't exist other than for loose classification. We use these terms for the general purpose of making sense of the world, and for communicating sensibly with other individuals. Especially those individuals within our own groups and cultures. When we meet with people from different groups and cultures we try to tighten up on these loose, unparticularised definitions and descriptions.

If you happen to be a Scotsman in a Scottish pub and you get talking to another Scottish man and you ask where he comes from, you don't expect him to say "Scotland," you expect him to say "Glasgow" or "Edinburgh" or "Inverness." And if you're a Glasgow woman in a Glasgow pub and you meet another Glasgow woman and ask where she's from, you expect her to say "Partick" or "the Calton" or "Easterhouse" or some other place local to the city.

Once in my company a white working-class guy got into an argument with a black middle-class guy, a writer who had been doing a reading then during the follow-on discussion spoke of the historical culpability of white people in relation to black people. It was quite brave because this was in Glasgow and the audience was 95 percent white. The white working-class guy lost his temper and called him a black bastard. He was out of order to do so and there isn't any excuse. But the black guy was also out of order. Both were wrong. There is a simplistic, generalised version of history which offers a sweeping account of the inhuman savagery perpetrated on black people by white people. There is a tighter version wherein the inhuman savagery is perpetrated by white peoples. An even tighter version concerns the inhuman savagery perpetrated on black peoples by white peoples. And so on. There is also the daily abuse and violation experienced by black people that is beyond anything white people can comprehend. There is also the day-to-day horror of existence experienced by a great many white Glaswegian people that a great many black people, including this particular black guy (who is an academic as well as a writer), have no conception of, and his blanket use of black and white, in context, served only to indicate his intellectual myopia about the everyday brutalities the British State perpetrates on sections of its own people, its so-called white brothers and sisters. White nationalism or black nationalism, it always missed the point.

Wherever you look either at home or abroad you find cultures under attack, communities battling for the right to survive—often literally, where the fight for self-determination means not only putting your own life on the line, it's risking and endangering the lives of your people and your family and your friends and your children. This is a war that's being waged and engaged on countless fronts. And these heavy defeats will continue until authentic and meaningful honest dialogue starts occurring between the countless communities and peoples under attack.

In an interview with İsmail Beşikçi—held while he was awaiting trial in a Turkish prison in 1990—he referred to the prosecution of the Kurdistan Workers' Party (PKK), which took place in Germany the same year, and reported on the "secret agreement between the NATO alliance and Turkey in relation to Kurdistan." Covert deals are always being done of course. This one means the Ankara government is entitled to do anything it likes under the heading "Rooting Out the PKK." For the actual people in Turkish Kurdistan it means they would rather flee across the Iraqi border than remain at home, they would rather confront Saddam Hussein's forces than stay and face the Turkish authorities.

About fifteen years ago a group of Kurdish students published a tract demanding that incitement to racial hatred be made a punishable offence and were charged with having claimed that there was a Kurdish people, thereby undermining national unity.[1]

They had published the tract in response to various anti-Kurd threats made publicly from right-wing sources, including one nationalist journal implicitly threatening the Kurdish people with genocide. Meanwhile for the past seventy years the authorities have sought to destroy everything which might suggest a specific Kurdish identity, not just in Turkey but in Iraq, Iran and Syria. Different theories about nationhood have been constructed, essentially "to prove" the non-existence of the Kurdish people, that they are not and never have existed.

The plight of the Palestinian people derives from similar historical factors, following the breakup of the Ottoman Empire and the end of the 1914–18 war. Like the Kurds, they have witnessed the theft of their land and resources, their very identity; the mass slaughter of countless human beings. The people of Asia, Australasia and Africa have their own stories: the horrors of imperialism and the continuing effects of this.

The black and immigrant communities in the UK need no reminder of the primary role of the British State. Here too other home communities are under attack. In Glasgow the incidence of asbestos-related terminal disease is nearly eight times higher than the UK average. Fifteen members of the Clydeside Action on Asbestos group have died since the turn of the year. I'm talking about ordinary working people in so-called ordinary working conditions, conditions that ultimately killed them.

There is constant pressure on this support group. They receive no help from the official labour movement, not the

Scottish Trades Union Congress (STUC) and not the Labour Party, not from any left-wing party or group. They exist on donations from victims and sympathisers. Their major battles are against lawyers and the legal system, doctors and the medical profession, insurance companies and the asbestos industry, and one primary arm of state control, the Department of Social Security (DSS). The British authorities always deny that the asbestos these victims were exposed to is at the root of their various, essentially fatal diseases, contracted through no one's fault but that of their employers who knew the danger but didn't tell them, often in direct contravention of government legislation, knowingly and cynically.

Even in Glasgow where around twenty thousand people have contracted asbestos-related terminal diseases since the end of 1945 very few people are aware of the reality of the nightmare faced by their neighbours and relatives, a nightmare that will become worse and is not reckoned to hit a peak for at least another generation. The State distorts and disinforms. Side by side with the asbestos industry and the big insurers the authorities stop the information process, dishing out their propaganda. So most victims die of a disease the State says they haven't got. And as long as they deny the disease that's killing these thousands of people throughout the country the DSS avoids having to pay out the disablement allowances and entitlements due to the victims. They avoid the people of the country knowing the full horror of a tragedy that could have been averted, given that those who perpetrated the tragedy—the asbestos multinationals—have been in full cognisance of the deadly nature of asbestos fibre, at least since the 1890s, while continuing to stuff our schools, factories and hospitals full of it.

Activists within black and immigrant communities here in Britain will soon pick up on the general form of the asbestos struggle. It's only in the last ten years, in the wake of the New Cross Massacre (as John La Rose and others point out) that the State has conceded racism might be a motive in violent assault and murder. Even so they fight tooth and nail to deny it on each and every occasion. Just as each and every victim of asbestos-related industrial disease must fight to demonstrate the cause of their imminent death, so too must a victim of racist violation fight to demonstrate that the people responsible for the violation were motivated by race hatred.

No life-or-death struggle takes precedence over another.

Speaking with folk from different parts of the colonized and otherwise oppressed world, and with folk from within the different black communities and the different groupings here in Britain, one crucial problem lies in being honest with one another.

At some point people from overseas have to appreciate why many left-wing, sympathetic people in this country just look nonplussed, embarrassed or depressed when asked to send off letters and petitions to Labour Party MPs and councillors and trade union officials. It's not that making representation to our elected and constitutionally attested representatives might not be a good move, as far as *your* particular struggle is concerned, but within my struggle, here in Glasgow, within the context of its culture(s), such a move is absolutely worthless, a waste of time and resources. That's my opinion, though it rarely gets expressed, for at least two reasons, the first of which is dubious: I don't like being presumptuous. The second reason is that *you* have said such a move is crucial. And I'm aware, or should be aware, that a decision made by those involved in one struggle is determined ultimately by its own context, that one solitary compromise, even with ruthlessly brutal states like that of the British, South African, Turkish, Israeli or USA, may save hundreds, even thousands of lives. When a compromise like that needs to be made it cannot be made outwith the context of that struggle and that struggle alone. This doesn't mean only those born and bred within the culture of that struggle have the right to make such decisions.

But generally it does mean that. So when an outside group or community seeks support in an approach to our domestic ruling authority, generally, we have an obligation to go along with the request, no matter our reservations.

It is fundamental that the general struggle for human rights is shown solidarity by those engaged in other struggles. A too-rigid adherence to one line or idea or theory is a hindrance. More often than not this rigidity just indicates an unwillingness to accept that particular struggle in itself—an unwillingness to accept what should be the inalienable rights of those engaged within that struggle, the right to fight as they see fit, in a context that ultimately is theirs and theirs alone.

There's nothing more ridiculous than these so-called radical left-wing parties coming along to some demonstration or protest apparently in solidarity, then spending their time arguing with the people out doing it on the street, about the theoretical incorrectness of their ideological approach, their lack of awareness of "the international context." I'm reminded of that one about the guy selling—I can't remember—*News Line* or *Militant* or the *Morning Star* or *Living Marxism* or *Socialist Worker* or the *Workers' Hammer* or whatever the hell, at the time of the printworkers' battle with Rupert Murdoch (and the British State) a couple of years ago. A small group of workers had overturned a car in preparation to defend themselves against the forces of law and order, the comrade boys-in-blue, and this guy goes up and tries to tell them the Tories are the class enemy while at the same time forcing his newspaper down their throats.

But that doesn't mean we give up discussion and go in for blanket gestures of solidarity. Every struggle has a context. Every struggle has its own culture. The mistake we make is not discussing our differences, at the right time and the right place. For our part we have to take the bit between our teeth and make sure refugees and exiles don't confuse the official labour movement with the authentic left. They need to know why many of us don't turn up or don't get invited to demonstrations organised by the official labour movement. We all assume too much. We don't like being presumptuous. But we have to risk it. This doesn't mean making decisions for other people and criticising them when they make a move that doesn't square with our own perspective; if we continue on that path then all talk of solidarity remains just that—talk, the sort of humbug you hear from party hacks everywhere.

I remind people here this evening, especially the ones who've got a copy of a recent *Glasgow Keelie* in their pocket, that the police confiscated as much of this issue as they could get their hands on.[2] Everyday suppression of this nature is part of the reality of contemporary Glasgow, part of what we take for granted. The first thing to acknowledge is what's happening under your nose.

(1991)

The Freedom for Freedom of Expression Rally, Istanbul 1997

The arrogance of [the Iranian King] Jamshid had set his subjects in revolt against him, and a great army marched towards Arabia from the highlands of Iran. They had heard that in Arabia there was a man with a serpent's face that inspired terror and to him they went in order to elect him as their king. Zuhak eagerly returned with them and was crowned.... Jamshid fled before him, and for a hundred years was seen by no man, till Zuhak fell upon him without warning in the confines of China and put him to death. Thus perished [Jamshid's] pride from the earth.

For a thousand years Zuhak occupied the throne and the world submitted to him, so that goodness died away and was replaced by evil. Every night during that long period two youths were slain [whose brains provided food for the serpents that grew from Zuhak's shoulders].... It happened that [there remained two men of purity, of Persian race who] succeeded in entering the king's kitchen. There, after no long time, they were entrusted with the preparation of the king's meal, and they contrived to mix the brains of a sheep with those of one of the youths who was brought for slaughter. The other one they saved alive and dismissed secretly, saying to him: "Escape in secret, beware of visiting any inhabited town; your portion in the world must be the desert and the mountain."

In this manner they saved two hundred men, of whom is born the race of Kurds, who know not any fixed abode, whose houses are tents, and who have in their hearts no fear of God.

—Abul Kasim Mansur Firdawsi (ca. 935–1025 AD)

This three-day event, the Freedom for Freedom of Expression Rally, was organised and hosted by the Freedom of Thought initiative, a two-hundred-strong group of artists and activists. There is a multiple trial in progress in Istanbul: writers, musicians, actors, journalists, lawyers, trade unionists and others are being prosecuted by the State Security Court. Twenty international writers attended the rally; most are members of PEN but three travelled at the invitation of Amnesty International, including myself.

More writers are imprisoned in Turkey than in any other country in the world but "the real question [is] not that of freedom for a writer. The real question is that of the national rights of the Kurds."[1] The annexation of Kurdistan, the attempted genocide and the continued oppression of the Kurdish people are three of the major scandals of this century. Historically, the British State, if not the prime mover, has had a pivotal role.[2] At one point "we" needed a client state "to secure ['our'] right to exploit the oilfields of Southern Kurdistan," and so "we" created a country, gave it a king and called it Iraq.[3] "Our" active participation in the assault on the Kurdish people continues to the present where "we" retain a leading interest in diverse ways, e.g., client state of the USA, member of NATO, member of the European Union etc. Turkey itself "is now the number two holiday destination for UK holidaymakers thanks to superb weather, great value for money accommodation, inexpensive eating out and lots to see and do."[4]

Prisoners are routinely tortured and beaten in Turkey, sometimes killed. Rape and other sexual violations occur constantly. In the Kurdish provinces the mass murders, forced dispersals and other horrors practised by the security forces are documented by many domestic and international human rights agencies. People have been made to eat excrement. From Kurdish villages there are reports of groups of men having their testicles tied and linked together, the women then forced to lead them round the streets. There are files held on children as young as twelve being subject to the vilest treatment. This from a sixteen-year-old girl detained not in a Kurdish village but by the police in Istanbul:

> They put my head in a bucket until I almost drowned. They did it again and again.... They tied my hands to a beam and hoisted me up. I was blindfolded. When I was hanging I thought my arms were breaking. They sexually harassed me and they beat my groin and belly with fists while I was hanging. When they pulled down on my legs I lost consciousness. I don't know for how long the hanging lasted.... They threatened that they would rape and kill me. They said I would become paralysed. The torture lasted for eight days.[5]

The young girl was later charged with being a member of "an illegal organisation." Germany, the USA and the UK compete to supply war and torture implements to the Turkish security forces who learned about the efficacy of the hanging process from their Israeli counterparts. A student we were to meet later at Istanbul University was once detained for twenty-four hours and during that period she too was tortured.

There exist "152 laws and about 700 paragraphs ... devoted to regulating freedom of opinion." The Turkish Penal Code "was passed in 1926 ... [and is] based on an adaptation of the Italian Penal Code.... Its most drastic reform was the adoption in 1936 of the anti-communist articles on 'state security' from the code of Mussolini. Only in April 1991 were some changes

made through the passage of the Law to Combat Terrorism."
Before then, and up until 1989

> court cases against the print media had reached a record
> level with 183 criminal cases against 400 journalists ... at
> least 23 journalists and editors in jail with one of them
> receiving a sentence of 1,086 years, later reduced to
> 700 on appeal. The editor of one [well-known journal,
> banned by the Özal dictatorship] was prosecuted 13 times
> and had 56 cases brought against her. She was in hiding
> at the time the journal appeared in July of 1990. One
> of her sentences amounted to six years, three months.
> Despite international appeals and protests the Turkish
> Government refused to reverse her sentences. No left-
> wing or radical journal was safe from arbitrary arrest,
> closure or seizure of entire editions. Police persecution
> extended into the national press and included daily
> newspapers. Authors and publishers of books were vic-
> timised. In November 1989 449 books and 25 pamphlets
> were burned in Istanbul on the orders of the provincial
> governor.... [Until] 1991 189 films were banned ... [and
> during the following two years came] the liquidation
> of journalists, newspaper sellers, and the personnel of
> newspaper distributors, as well as bombing and arson
> attacks against newspaper kiosks and bookstores.... [In
> 1992] twelve journalists were murdered by 'unknown
> assailants' [and] in most cases, the circumstances point
> to participation or support by the state security forces.
> [In 1994 writers and journalists were sentenced to] 448
> years, 6 months and 25 days.... There were 1162 violations
> of the press laws [and] a total of 2098 persons were tried,
> 336 of whom were already in prison.... The security
> forces interfered with the distribution of press organs,
> attacked their offices, and arbitrarily detained publish-
> ers, editors, correspondents and newspaper salesmen.[6]

Shortly before the military coup in the spring of 1991, I took part in a public meeting organised by the Friends of Kurdistan.[7] I looked at parallels in the linguistic and cultural suppression of Kurdish and Scottish people, and that was a mistake.[8] Parallels between the two may be of some slight functional value from a Scottish viewpoint but when we discuss the Kurdish situation now and historically we are discussing the systematic attempt to wipe from the face of the earth a nation of some thirty million people. It is doubtful if any form of oppression exists that has not been carried out on the Kurdish people and I think the scale of it overwhelmed me. I combined some of the elements of my 1991 talk with those of others of the same period and published an essay.[9] I now give an extract from my notes for that talk, taken from a fine collection of essays published by Zed Press in 1979, which may act as a brief introduction to how things were for Kurdish people before the September 12 military coup back in 1980.[10]

> The Turkish Republic set up its apparatus for the repression of the Kurdish people soon after it was founded. Following the War of Independence, during which they were acclaimed as "equal partner" and "sister nation," the Kurdish people found their very existence was being denied. The authorities have since sought to destroy everything which might suggest a specific Kurdish identity, erecting an entire edifice of linguistic and historical pseudo-theories which supposedly "proved" the Turkishness of the Kurds, and served as justification for the destruction of that identity.
>
> These theories have become official doctrine, taught, inculcated and propagated by the schools, the universities, the barracks and the media. The authorities banned all unofficial publications that tried to even discuss the subject. Historical or literary works, even travellers' tales published in Turkish and other languages, were

all removed from public and private libraries and for the most part destroyed if they contained any reference to the Kurdish people, their history or their country. All attempts to question official ideology were repressed.

It is estimated that twenty million Kurds dwell in Turkey and the Kurdish language has been banned there since 1925. In 1978, of all Kurdish people over the age of six, 72 percent could neither read nor write. The publication of books and magazines in the language is illegal. The Turkish authorities purged the libraries of any books dealing with Kurdish history, destroyed monuments and so on.[11] All historical research into Kurdish society was forbidden. An official history was constructed to show the Kurdish people were originally Turks. Until 1970 no alternative research could be published. Thus officially the Kurds are purest Turk.

The Turkish authorities have systematically changed the names of all Kurdish towns and villages, substituting Turkish for Kurdish names. The word *Kurdistan*, so designated from the thirteenth century, was the first to be banned; it is regarded as subversive because it implies the unity of the scattered Kurdish people. Kurdistan is colonized not by one country but by four: Turkey, Iran, Iraq and Syria whose Chief of Police published a study [in November 1963 which] set out to "prove scientifically" that the Kurds "do not constitute a nation," that they are "a people without history or civilisation or language or even definite ethnic origin of their own," that they lived "from the civilisation and history of other nations and had taken no part in these civilisations or in the history of these nations." [He also] proposed a twelve-point plan:

1) the transfer and dispersion of the Kurdish people;

2) depriving the Kurds of any education whatsoever, even in Arabic;

3) a "famine" policy, depriving those affected of
any employment possibilities;

4) an extradition policy, turning the survivors of
the uprisings in Northern Kurdistan over to the
Turkish Government;

5) a divide and rule policy; setting Kurd against
Kurd;

6) a cordon policy along the lines of an earlier plan
to expel the entire Kurdish population from the
Turkish border;

7) a colonisation policy, the implantation of pure
and nationalist Arabs in the Kurdish regions to
see to the dispersal of the Kurds;

8) military divisions to ensure the dispersion;

9) "collective forms" set up for the Arab settlers
who would also be armed and trained;

10) a ban on "anybody ignorant of the Arabic language exercising the right to vote or stand for
office";

11) sending Kurds south and Arabs north;

12) "launching a vast anti-Kurdish campaign
amongst the Arabs."[12]

Media organs are the property of the official language in Turkey, and the Kurdish people are kept
starved of outside news. Kurdish intellectuals are
expected to assimilate, to reject their own culture
and language, to become Turkicised. A person from
Kurdistan can not be appointed to fill a post without
the prior approval of the political police. Kurds are
not nominated for jobs in the Kurdish provinces; the
authorities try always to separate them from their own
country.

All business conducted in the language of state and Kurdish speakers must use interpreters. Literature produced in exile, beyond the Turkish borders, is not allowed into the Republic. Kurdish writers and poets have had to write in Turkish, not simply to ensure publication but because they were unfamiliar with their own forbidden language and culture.

For a brief period a group called the Organisation of Revolutionary Kurdish Youth (DDKO) was tolerated by the authorities; this group set out to inform public opinion about the economic, social and cultural situation; organising press conferences and public briefings, publishing posters, leaflets etc., focussing attention on the repression within Kurdish areas; its monthly ten-page information bulletin had a print run of thirty thousand, which was distributed amongst Turkish political, cultural and trade union circles, as well as in Kurdish towns and villages. Eventually "news" about what was happening to the Kurds filtered through to the media and the public and there were protests against the repression. Six months before the military coup of March 1970 the leaders of the organisation were arrested and after that all "left-wing parties and organisations were outlawed."

But from 1975 new youth organisations formed, known generally as the People's Cultural Associations (HKD), concentrating on educating their members and helping peasants and workers who were in conflict with the authorities in one way or another. A policy of terror and ideological conditioning was implemented by the Ankara government which in the words of Turkish sociologist İsmail Beşikçi managed to "make people believe he who announced 'I am Kurdish' was committing a crime so heinous that he deserved the death penalty." Dr

Beşikçi was put on trial for the crime of "undermining national feelings" and "making separatist propaganda."

In the same talk I drew attention to the interview İsmail Beşikçi had given while in prison awaiting yet another trial. He had remarked of the German prosecution of the Kurdistan Workers' Party (PKK) that the one thing established was the existence of a "secret agreement between the NATO alliance and Turkey, in relation to Kurdistan." Germany has now fallen into line with the Turkish State and has declared the PKK an illegal organisation: even to sport their colours is a criminal offence. The victimisation of Kurdish people has spread outwards; we are witnessing the attempted criminalisation of the entire diaspora.[13]

Throughout Europe there are incidents being reported by monitoring agencies. In November in Belgium "100 police and members of the special intervention squad ... raided a Kurdish holiday centre.... The Ministry of Justice claimed [it was] used by the PKK as a semi-military training camp." Nobody at all was arrested. But forty people were deported to Germany. On February 2 of this year [1997] "the Danish television station, TV2, revealed that the Danish police intelligence service (PET) had written a 140-page report on meetings of the Kurdish parliament in exile which took place in Copenhagen in March 1996 [and the] transcript ... ended up with the Turkish authorities."[14]

Here in the UK, Kani Yılmaz is halfway into his third year in Belmarsh Prison, London. He came from Germany in October 1994 at the direct invitation of John Austin-Walker MP, to meet with British MPs and discuss cease-fire proposals between the PKK and the Turkish armed forces.[15] In a shameful act of betrayal the British State responded by arresting him. Germany wants him extradited and Turkey waits in the wings. Sooner or later they will find a way to sort out "the extradition problem," thus the British can hand him back to Germany, who can hand him back to Turkey. Or else they might just cut out the middleman; this would be their ideal situation.

Olof Palme of Sweden was assassinated more than ten years ago; it so happens he was also the only European leader who ever confronted the Turkish State at the most fundamental level, by "recognising the Kurdish people as a nation and [committing] himself to attaining recognition of their rights."[16] It would be comforting to suppose that the British and other European governments and state agencies act as they do through sheer cowardice. Unfortunately I doubt this is the case. The Turkish State has the means of authoritarian control for which many Euro-state authorities would cut off their left arm. In certain areas they draw ever closer, for example in matters relating to asylum and immigration; their punishment of the most vulnerable of people; the torture that takes place in prisons and police cells, the beatings, the killings. And not too long ago, "on 14 February 1997, the [British] government attempted to introduce a private members' bill, the Jurisdiction (Conspiracy and Incitement) Bill, which would have had the effect of criminalising support for political violence abroad. It was only defeated when two left Labour MPs, Dennis Skinner and George Galloway, unexpectedly forced a vote on the third reading and caught the government unawares, as they were relying on cross-party support for the Bill."[17]

In October 1996 came the report on Lord Lloyd of Berwick's Inquiry into Legislation Against Terrorism, published "with very little publicity and only a brief press-release, an inquiry into counter-terrorist legislation ... set up jointly by Home Secretary Michael Howard and Secretary of State for Northern Ireland Sir Patrick Mayhew. Such is the terrorist threat," says the report, "that not only is permanent legislation desirable to combat terrorism, but past powers need to be further widened and strengthened." The expert commissioned by Lord Lloyd "to provide 'an academic view as to the nature of the terrorist threat' [was] Professor Paul Wilkinson of St Andrews University." His "academic view" provides Volume 11 of the report whose "new definition of 'terrorism' is modelled on the working definition used by the FBI: 'The use of serious violence against persons or property, or the threat to use such violence, to intimidate or coerce a government, the public or any section of the public, in order to promote political, social or ideological objectives.'"[18]

No later than one month after its publication, "amid allegations of financial losses" the *Mail on Sunday* named the professor as a "terrorist expert in college cash riddle." Then came the more interesting information, that Professor Wilkinson was "believed to work for the British security services and the CIA." There is one thing established by the fact that Wilkinson is still commissioned for work as sensitive as the Lloyd Report, this is the contempt held by the British State not just towards the public but its elected representatives.

His connections were something of an open secret before this; readers of *Lobster* magazine have known of his pedigree for at least ten years, in particular his "inept role in the state's attempt to discredit Colin Wallace in the 1980s."[19] This was when "disinformation was run into the Channel 4 News office" by Wilkinson, two members of the UDA plus "a former colleague of Wallace" at the Information Policy Unit in HQ Northern Ireland.[20]

Notwithstanding any of this, the "terrorist expert's" credibility is undiminished, and as I write, following the day of transport stasis in London,[21] one of Scotland's two "quality" daily newspapers, the *Glasgow Herald*, again features the Professor's "academic view"; on this occasion he proposed that "to defeat their terrorist tactics, British and Irish security must target the godfathers of the IRA's crimes" and not give in to such tactics as "bringing a complex transport system to a halt.... Any group of clever dicks in an open society could achieve that."

The juridical system in Turkey may be complex but its central purpose seems straightforward enough: it sanctifies the State and protects it from the people. Following the 1980 coup and throughout the next decade changes in the law took place, the mechanisms for the suppression of Kurdish people altered. For the Kurds it became one nightmare after another. The level of state-sponsored terrorism degenerated to a point where sometime between 1981 and 1983, in Diyarbakır Prison, forty Kurdish youths were tortured to death for refusing to say, "I am a Turk and therefore happy."[22]

We have to respect the fact that it was not until 1984 that the PKK began its armed struggle. If we do not then we play into the hands of the Turkish propaganda machine. The new constitution had come into existence in November 1982 and an indication of the potential repression is available there, e.g., this from the opening preamble: "No thought or impulse [may be cherished] against Turkish national interests, against the existence of Turkey, against the principle of the indivisibility of the state and its territory, against the historical and moral values of Turkishness, against nationalism as defined by [Mustafa Kemal] Atatürk, against his principles, reforms and civilising efforts." Not only is the possibility of democracy denied at the outset, it is illegal even to think about something that might be defined by the constitution as "against Turkish national interests." The system is so designed that any Turkish government, courtesy of the constitution, is in thrall to a higher authority: the National Security Council (i.e., the military).

Some might argue that "Turkish democracy" is designed solely to suppress the Kurdish population and it would be presumptuous of me to argue the point, especially with Kurdish people. But if justice is ever to be achieved by the Kurds in Turkey, perhaps it will come about through the will of the majority of the people, and the majority is Turkish. Münir Ceylan, one of the contributors to the *Freedom of Expression* publication, makes the point that "if you analyse the Anti-Terror Law carefully, it is obvious that [it] is intended to destroy the struggle for bread, freedom and democracy not just of the Kurdish people but by our entire working class and working masses."

It seems that among Turks there has been an increase in solidarity with the Kurdish people, and also a willingness on the part of many to confront one of the world's most ruthless state-machines. The courage and perseverance of Beşikçi surely have been crucial in this. Next to Abdullah Öcalan, president of the PKK, the National Security Council appears to regard the sociologist and writer as its most dangerous enemy. Beşikçi is not Kurdish but Turkish. Since 1967 he has been in and out of court and has suffered "arrest, torture, jail, ceaseless harassment and ostracism."[23] Now fifty-seven years of age he has spent nearly fifteen years of his life in prison. Each time an essay, book or booklet of his is printed he is given a further term and so far the aggregate stands at more than one hundred years. Under Turkish law his publisher is prosecuted simultaneously and to date has received sentences in the region of fourteen years. Less than two years ago the two men "were abused [and] physically assaulted while being conducted from prison to the court … [and their] documents … rendered useless."[24]

There is a distinction between the people of a country and its ruling authority. The Turkish State is not representative of the Turkish people and neither is the British State representative of myself or Moris Farhi from England, who was there in Istanbul on behalf of PEN International Writers in Prison Committee. My invitation to the Freedom for Freedom of Expression Rally came from Amnesty International (UK), by way of Scottish PEN. Although not a member of either body I was glad to accept. There were twenty-one foreign writers present and each of us would have been conscious of the relationship to Turkey held by our individual countries: the Netherlands, Germany, the UK and Sweden supplied two apiece; one each from the USA, Mexico, Canada-Quebec, Finland and Russia; one writer represented Palestinian PEN, whereas six writers came from Israel.[25] The multiple trial of writers, artists and others which is now in process derives from January 1995 when

> Yaşar Kemal was tried in Istanbul's No. 5 State Security Court regarding one of his articles which was published in *Der Spiegel* magazine. On the same day, intellectuals gathered outside the court in support [and] decided to collude in the "crime" by jointly appending their names to [that and other] articles and speeches alleged to be "criminal." The "Initiative Against Crimes of Thought" was born [and] a petition started. Within a short time the signatures of 1080 intellectuals from various fields had been collected [and they] co-published a volume of articles entitled *Freedom of Expression*. Under the Turkish Penal Code Article 162: republishing an article which is defined as a crime is a new crime, and the publisher is to be equally sentenced.... On 10 March 1995 the "co-publishers" voluntarily presented themselves before the State Security Court to face charges of "seditious criminal activity."[26]

Thus the state authorities were challenged at a fundamental level, leaving the Turkish government "with the old dilemma: either democratise the law and the constitution or face the opposition of Turkish and world democratic opinion, and the stench of another major scandal."[27]

There is scarce room for bureaucratic manoeuvring in the Turkish system and if a "crime" has been committed there is little option but to prosecute. If not then the prosecutor himself is open to prosecution.[28] So far the *Freedom of Expression* initiative has forced the hand of the authorities to the extent that the State Security Court has had to bring to trial 184 people. It is known as the "Kafka Trial" and has been described as "the most grotesque farce in Turkish legal history." Even so, the State makes use of its power and "for the accused [it is] likely to result in twenty months' prison sentences." Some of them are already in receipt of suspended sentences for earlier "criminal" thoughts or statements and their periods of imprisonment will be even longer.

The next step taken by the campaign organisers was to produce an abbreviated form of the *Freedom of Expression* publication and then invite international authors to sign up as "co-publishers." In principle the repressive nature of the Turkish legal system does not allow foreigners to escape the net, even on foreign soil. By using a network based on PEN International Writers in Prison Committee and other human rights agencies the campaign's organisers managed to obtain the signatures of 141 writers as co-publishers of the booklet. But this time the State Security Court declined to prosecute "on the grounds that [they] would not be able to bring [the international writers] to Istanbul for trial ... because such an 'offence' does not exist in US or English law." (Perhaps not yet. I take nothing for granted.)

So the campaign organisers moved a stage further: they invited some of the international writers to come to Istanbul in person and present themselves at the State Security Court. Again using the network of PEN and other human rights agencies they asked that invitations be issued on their behalf. The twenty-one of us present included poets, filmmakers, novelists and journalists. Interest in the "Kafka Trial" had escalated within Turkey; at each public engagement there was a full-scale media presence.

On Monday morning more than half of us were in court to witness the trial of an actor, one of the 1,080 Turkish writers, artists and others who signed as "publishing editors" of the original *Freedom of Expression*, the collection of writings by authors either already in prison or due to stand trial. Yaşar Kemal has received a twenty-month suspended sentence for

his own contribution to the book. But the actor's trial was postponed until May, presumably when no international observers
will be present. Meantime he continues rehearsing a joint production of Genet's *The Maids* and Kafka's "In the Penal Colony"
and hopes to be at liberty to take part in the performances.

Following the postponement some of us were due at Bursa
Prison; the authorities were allowing us to visit Beşikçi and
his publisher, Ünsal Öztürk. Others were scheduled to meet
Ocak Işık Yurtçu, a journalist imprisoned at Adapazarı. Then
permission was reversed by the authorities; we could make
the journey if we wanted but we would not be allowed to speak
to the prisoners. It was decided we would send a "symbolic"
delegation. A majority of us volunteered to make the journey
but places were limited to three, and two went to Bursa Prison.
Louise Gareau-Des Bois was nominated to visit Adapazarı.
She is vice president of Canada-Quebec PEN and also speaks
a little Turkish; seven years ago the Quebec centre seconded a
Kurdish PEN resolution concerning Beşikçi. When she arrived
at the prison the authorities reversed their previous reversal
and she was allowed to talk with Yurtçu through a fenced area
for nearly twenty minutes. What disturbed her most was the
great number of young people behind bars, some little more
than boys.

We were in court for a second occasion with Moris Farhi
who was signing his name to the abbreviated version, *Mini
Freedom of Expression*. The State Prosecutor dismissed his declaration out of hand. The third time we arrived at the State
Security Court a dozen of us were there on our own behalf. But
a heavy contingent of police had been instructed not to let us
enter the gate. The prosecuting authorities were refusing to
accept our statements, not even if we sent them by registered
post. We held a press conference outside on the main street
and signed our statements in front of the television cameras.
Münir Ceylan was there with us. He is a former president of
the petroleum workers' union and from 1994 served twenty

months' imprisonment for making statements such as the one quoted above. Recently he received a further two-year sentence and expects to be returned to prison any day now. His case has been taken up by Amnesty International, supported by the Scottish Trades Union Congress. He and others walked with us to the post office, in front of the television cameras, where we sent our signed statements by registered mail.

If the authorities continue to refuse our names alongside those of the Turkish writers and other artists who have been on trial, then the initiative's organisers will attempt to have the State Prosecutor charged with having failed "to fulfil the constitutional commitment to equality of treatment." It is a bold campaign and puts individuals at personal risk; some have been threatened already, some have experienced prison, others expect it sooner or later. On the same afternoon we had a public engagement at Istanbul University. A forum on freedom of expression had been organised by students and a few sympathetic lecturers. About twenty young people came to meet us then escort us to the campus; four of their friends are serving prison sentences of eight to twelve years for "terrorist" activities.[29]

Every day at Istanbul University between one hundred and two hundred police are on campus duty, and the students have their bags searched each time they enter the gate. Along with us on the bus came Vedat Türkali, a famous old writer who spent seven years in prison for political activities.[30] He remains a socialist and is now domiciled in England. When we arrived we discovered not only had the forum been cancelled by the security forces, they had shut down the actual university. More than two thousand students had gathered in protest outside the university gates. We were instructed to link arms and march as a body, flanked by students on either side, straight to the gates of the university.

Hundreds of police in full riot gear were also present. The cancelled forum on freedom of expression had become the focus of a mass student demonstration, the underlying concerns being the current withdrawal of subsidised education and the continued victimisation of the student population. I could not see any tanks although occasionally they are brought in on student protests. When we got to the gates at the entrance to the university the riot police circled and sealed us off. Some student representatives, lecturers and the media were allowed into the circle with us. A few held banners, an act of "terrorism" in itself, and were requested to fold them away, not to provoke the situation.

After negotiations with the security forces it was agreed that an abbreviated press conference could take place with the international writers and that statements might be broadcast to the students via a loudhailer. Demonstrations are illegal in Turkey unless permission has been granted by the security forces. Most people have given up seeking permission; instead they organise a press conference and invite everybody. A female student opened the meeting, then Şanar Yurdatapan spoke,[31] calling for everyone to stay calm, no blood should be spilled under any circumstances. Next to speak was the lawyer of the four imprisoned students, Pelin Erdal, one of whose own relatives was raped during a period of detainment. Only about a dozen of the twenty-one international writers were present at this press conference and each one was introduced. The situation was extremely tense and time restricted. Joanne Leedom-Ackerman (vice president of PEN International) and Alexander Tkachenko (president of Russian PEN Centre) were delegated to speak, and they were given a great ovation by the students. Then we had to leave at once, linking arms to stay as close together as possible, returning quickly the way we had come.

There was no news of any bloodshed although we did hear that a disturbance and arrests had taken place in the area of the post office, after we had left the scene earlier in the day. That evening we attended a reception held for us by the Istanbul Bar

Association. A few lawyers are among those openly express-ing their opinions on the issue of freedom of thought and expression. We met Eşber Yağmurdereli, lawyer, writer and playwright, at present "appealing against a 10-month sentence [for referring] to the Kurdish minority." He is also under sus-pended sentence from an earlier case; if he loses the appeal he will face "imprisonment until 2018."[32]

It was at the same reception we heard that Ünsal Öztürk, Beşikçi's publisher, had just been released from prison. He came to our last official engagement, described as "a meeting of writers and artists, organised by Turkish PEN Centre, the Writers' Syndicate of Turkey and the Association of Literarists." However, there was little opportunity of a meeting as such. Twelve or more people spoke from the platform during the two hours, including some of the international writers. For some reason Öztürk was not invited to speak. Nor for that matter was Türkali. I mentioned to a member of Turkish PEN that it might have been worthwhile hearing what Türkali had to say and was advised that in Turkey there are "thousands like him," whatever that might mean.

I thought it also of interest that Şanar Yurdatapan was not invited to speak. Yurdatapan and his brother, his secre-tary and a translator were our four main hosts and escorts throughout the four- to five-day visit, ensuring we remained together in the various awkward situations. He is one of the central organisers of this campaign and has served previous terms of imprisonment. He also led an international delega-tion to probe the notorious Güçlükonak massacre of "11 men travelling in a minibus." According to official sources they were killed by the PKK, but the "investigations left little doubt that government security forces carried out the killings."[33]

We also met Ünsal Öztürk and his wife socially on the last night. They sat at our table for a while, giving information through an interpreter to Soledad Santiago of Mexico's San Miguel PEN Centre who was hoping to take up his case through the PEN International Writers in Prison Committee, although he is a publisher and not a writer. Like Münir Ceylan and others, Öztürk is liable to be re-arrested at any moment and I found it difficult to avoid watching his wife, who seemed to be doing her best not to watch Ünsal too often and too obviously.

The next morning it was time to fly home to "freedom and democracy." For the flight into Turkey I had been advised to take nothing that might be construed as political—especially "separatist"—propaganda. For the flight to Glasgow via Amsterdam on Thursday afternoon I was also careful. During the past days students had given me diverse literature to take from the country but the situation by this time had become extremely sensitive. In the lounge of our hotel that morning only four of the twenty-one remained, passing the time before being driven to the airport. People there were showing more than particular interest in us, and doing it in shifts. I thought it better not to take chances, and so I dumped the diverse literature.

When we left I bought three English-language newspapers. One carried a report on the introduction of torture in USA prisons; the other had a front-page lead on the arrival of a new prison ship off the south coast of England—which may prove opportune for Turkey's justice minister who recently complained of "a negative atmosphere about Turkey. But now we will monitor human rights in Europe. The only thing Europe does is criticise Turkey. However, from now on we will criticise Europe."[34]

In Article 18 of the Statutes of the Human Rights Commission the language itself is exclusive, where "we" have "a duty to encourage ethnic groups" whose culture is under attack but the "ethnic groups" under attack are somehow left out of the equation. Perhaps "we" do have a duty, but it is to stand aside and let "them" fight back in whatever way "they" deem necessary. Perhaps the real duty "we" have is not to interfere when "they" resist oppression.

I also accept the significance of the distinction between democratic rights and human rights: democratic rights—unlike civil liberties or human rights—"assert the rights of the people to struggle against exploitation or oppression"; the right to defend yourself under attack, it allows of empowerment, of self-determination. I accept the right to resist oppression and that this right is inviolable. The people of Turkey and/or Kurdistan will resist oppression in whatever way they see fit. I can criticise the form this resistance sometimes takes but I am not about to defend a position that can only benefit their oppressors.

Almost nothing of contemporary Turkish writing is available in translation via English-language UK or USA publishing channels. As far as I know, not even Beşikçi's work has managed to find a publisher.[35] At Glasgow's version of a press conference, organised by Amnesty International (Scotland) and Scottish PEN on the morning after my return from this extraordinary event in Istanbul, only one journalist turned up. This was an embarrassed young guy from *List* magazine, a fortnightly entertainment listings magazine. A couple of weeks before my visit to Istanbul the *Scotsman* newspaper had included the following snippet in a rare UK report on Turkish domestic affairs: "Turkey's armed forces have intervened three times in the past 37 years to restore law and order in the country and to safeguard its secular nature."

(1997)

A Press Conference in Turkey

At the gates to Istanbul University, surrounded by riot troops. Şanar Yurdatapan is on megaphone.

Some writers from PEN International were here in solidarity for the Freedom for Freedom of Expression event. The writers are surrounded by riot troops. James Kelman stands two back from Şanar Yurdatapan and behind him is one of the riot troops. This was a "press conference," the only method the citizens had available in Turkey to hold a public meeting. The other writers here include Alexander Tkachenko (front row second left) and Joanne Leedom-Ackerman (front row far right).

Among Turks at this period there was an increase in solidarity with the Kurdish people, and also a willingness on the part of many to confront one of the world's most ruthless state-machines. The courage and perseverance of Beşikçi was crucial in this. Next to Abdullah Öcalan, president of the PKK, the Turkish National Security Council appeared to regard Dr Beşikçi, a sociologist, as its most dangerous enemy. Beşikçi is not Kurdish, but Turkish. Since 1967 he had been in and out of court and suffered "arrest, torture, jail, ceaseless harassment and ostracism."

Here writers from the PEN delegation are awaiting a visit to Bursa Prison to meet with İsmail Beşikçi.

Beşikçi's thirty-three books were banned and he had received sentences totalling more than one hundred years in prison [by 1997] for "thought-crimes," his advocacy of the national rights of the Kurdish people. The visit to meet him was cancelled by the authorities. Other writers with Kelman in this photograph include Louise Gareau-Des Bois (vice president, Quebec PEN Centre, Canada), Joanne Leedom-Ackerman (vice president, International PEN), and Soledad Santiago (San Miguel PEN Centre, Mexico).

(1997)

Em Hene!

Some people find it possible to support campaigns on behalf of writers imprisoned for their political beliefs without worrying about the substance of these beliefs, why the writers are imprisoned in the first place. They know next to nothing about the writer's culture, community or society and manage not to regard such knowledge as fundamental to the campaign. It follows that they agitate for the cessation of human rights abuses without inquiring why the rights of these particular human beings are being abused in the first place. At the time of writing [2001] in Turkey there are many writers in prison but if one writer is being victimised for daring to give expression to a "dangerous thought" it is likely that tens of hundreds are in the same plight, perhaps tens of thousands, with none but their family and friends to fight and campaign on their behalf. The writer and sociologist İsmail Beşikçi has spent nearly fifteen years of his life in prison. He argues that those who campaign on his behalf must recognise that the campaign cannot be about one writer; it is about the existence of Kurdistan, it is about justice for Kurdish people.

Abdullah Öcalan is president of the Kurdistan Workers' Party (PKK) and until his capture in Italy was one of the most wanted men in the world.[1] For the majority of the Kurdish people he is a hero. Beşikçi has maintained that Öcalan is a legitimate leader of the Kurdish people. In the first report I read of Öcalan's capture the pro-Turkey bias was blatant, straight from the public relations department of the National Security Council. It is still a surprise when distortion and propaganda of this magnitude come unchallenged in the mainstream media. This example arrived via Associated Press (AP) thus would have appeared not only in the US but in the UK and elsewhere in the "free" world. One comment sticks with me: that there have been "no executions in Turkey since 1984." That kind of rubbish is just disgraceful. Who knows the number of executions committed in Turkey since 1984? State executions are also "extrajudicial," defined as the "unlawful and deliberate killings of persons by reason of their real or imputed political beliefs, ethnic origin, sex, colour or language, carried out by order of a government or with its complicity [and] take place outside any legal or judicial process."[2]

Human rights organisations will have approximations of the number. There can only be approximations. It is estimated that between 1991 and early 1997 there were "more than 10,000 'disappearances' and political killings."[3] Each Saturday in Istanbul women and girls gather in the famous old thoroughfare of Galatasaray to bear witness to the "disappearance" of husbands, boyfriends, fathers, sons and brothers. The courage of these women and girls is quite something; there are hundreds of them. Most are Kurdish but a few are Turkish. Sometimes the police just wade in and batter them with riot sticks, whether observers are there or not.

Football fans will recognise Galatasaray as the name of a leading Turkish football club. The stadium is not too far away and this area is at the heart of Istanbul's tourist quarter. Holidaymakers and football fans are surprised that the women are battered right out in the open. Some look the other way. This is encouraged by the British political authorities who, when they are not supporting the Turkish State in a less passive manner, take care not to look themselves. It is only a few months since the end of that other sorry saga, the

British government's cowardly, but ruthless, treatment of Kani Yılmaz.

The man was arrested on his way to address a meeting in London. It was not until the summer of 1997 that he was finally extradited to Germany to face charges of organising attacks on Turkish businesses and properties. The Labour government's Home Secretary was Mr Jack Straw who

> ignored campaigners' pleas and upheld the court order for his extradition. Yılmaz had spent almost three years in detention in Belmarsh prison. The decision, following the House of Lords' rejection of his petition against the extradition, was a slap in the face to supporters who believed that Straw would carry his opposition convictions into government; Straw was one of several Labour MPs who protested strongly when Yılmaz was arrested and detained for deportation on "national security" grounds on his way to a meeting at Westminster in October 1994.
>
> That arrest had caused embarrassment to the Tory Government because Yılmaz had been allowed into the country freely days beforehand: the German Government's action in seeking his extradition was widely seen as *too convenient*, particularly since Yılmaz, a refugee from Turkey, had spent much time in Germany, where he had stayed quite openly and there was never any attempt to charge him with criminal offences.... [The original intention of Yılmaz, John Austin-Walker and others was] to discuss finding a peaceful solution to the war in Kurdistan and self-determination for the Kurdish people. He [later] said he will not seek judicial review of the Home Secretary's decision, having had his confidence in the British judicial system severely undermined by the courts' passive endorsement of the extradition request. But he will use the German courts

as an opportunity to present the case of the Kurdish people and to expose the collaboration of Europe's governments with the Turkish State.[4]

In the AP news item where this extract was taken, mention was made of the German authorities "seeking Öcalan on a 1990 warrant." This refers to the time the German State prosecuted the PKK which up until then was a legal political party. The Turkish State was doing its utmost to have the PKK criminalised throughout Europe as a terrorist organisation. Its deputy chief of staff in 1995 stated, "We'll finish terrorism but we are being held back by democracy and human rights."[5] Around that time there had been a horrible massacre "in the village of Geri [when] 30 people, mainly women and children, were brutally killed." This massacre was reported as the work of PKK "terrorists" and the Turkish authorities "showed video footage for days to members of the European Parliament," in an attempt to discredit the PKK and to have its leadership outlawed as "terrorists." Subsequently a delegation from a human rights association went to the village of Geri itself and came up with somewhat different findings. Members of the delegation "included the President of the now banned Socialist Party" and also Hatip Dicle, "ex-MP of the Democracy Party (DEP), currently serving 15 years imprisonment alongside Leyla Zana and three other DEP MPs."[6] In Dicle's opinion, "shared by all the members of our delegation ... this massacre was an act of the contra-guerrillas." But even though discredited the Turkish State would regard its work of that period as highly successful, given that the German prosecution of the PKK at that period resulted in its being banned. Dicle also makes the point that whenever anything sympathetic to the Kurdish struggle is happening "on the eve of important international gatherings," the Turkish State will move to undermine and subvert the Kurdish case.

Beşikçi was awaiting trial in a Turkish prison that same year. In an interview with Amnesty International he commented on the German prosecution that the one thing it did establish was the existence of a "secret agreement between the NATO alliance and Turkey in relation to Kurdistan."

The Turkish State resorts to terrorism to achieve or maintain its ends and one large area of Turkey, the southeast, has been under martial law for years. The southeast of Turkey is the northwest of Kurdistan. Kurdish people have been executed summarily in this area for decades. The savagery of the Turkish military has been such that Kurdish people have crossed the Iraqi border. They would rather face Saddam Hussein than the monstrosities of the Turkish military.

During the 1960s there was a strong student movement in Turkey as in different parts of the world and Öcalan emerged from this. The political system of that time has been described as "democratic fascism." Even that was too liberal for the military and they conducted a coup in 1971. The young Beşikçi had been doing his own sociological research from the early 1960s, coming up with certain findings in relation to the Kurdish people that did not suit the establishment, academic or political. He was by turn marginalised, victimised, excluded from academic work, had his work censored and suppressed; later he was brought before the law and imprisoned. It is ironic that a couple of the present Turkish government were also rebellious students of the period, to the extent that they were imprisoned.

If Beşikçi was Kurdish and not Turkish he would be dead already. In the western "democracies" he would be neither imprisoned nor murdered, just marginalised. There are different ways of suppressing the work of writers and it is doubtful if even one country in the world exists where freedom of expression can be taken for granted. Beşikçi's writings are suppressed by the Turkish authorities but people also need to pay attention to the fact that his work is not available to the English-speaking public of the world. None of his thirty-three books has so far been published in the English language.[7]

There is a block on information about Kurdistan. The UK media are either silent or party to the different forms of propaganda issued on Turkey's behalf. The situation is epitomised by the UK travel industry who, under the nose of HM Government, try to sell us "Summer Sunshine Holidays" in a war-ravaged police state. The Turkish propaganda is often blatant but masquerading as news, as in the notorious article run by the *Observer* in September 1997, attacking "the PKK in particular and the Kurdish community in general [which] consisted of a series of unsubstantiated allegations ranging from the perverse to the bizarre made by a young Kurd who had either been terrorised or disorientated or compromised by Turkish intelligence." Harold Pinter and Lord Avebury were among those who condemned the newspaper publicly and many people were outraged to discover that such blatant disinformation circulates in one of the top "quality" newspapers. It was important that the *Observer* should have been condemned but those who were too outraged might be suffering delusions about the UK media; it indicates the depth of untruth to which they have become accustomed.

Of course this is a time when the public receives images of starving children in Africa as adverts for national charities; the images themselves are structured on disinformation, much of it racist. These charities are headed by a vanguard of millionaire celebrities: members of the aristocracy, rock stars and movie stars; twenty-nine football stars, dashing young captains of industry, and so on. In their wake the public is supposed to donate money as a moral duty—or perhaps not quite, the money is to be given on the understanding that the suffering experienced by the starving children has to do with the inherent nature of Africa itself. It has nothing to do with politics, nothing to do with the foreign policy of external forces, not interest rates and not the movement of capital, nothing to do with "guidelines" that may be enforced by the IMF or the World Bank. None of that. Instead the suffering is to be seen as a sort of physical attribute of the African continent, perhaps of the "African character." If the African adult population could learn to plan more efficiently and devise better strategies then they would take better care of their children. Until that indefinite point in the future the charities of the western democracies have to do the job for them; self-determination is not an option, not yet, and *you* can help! Such is the nonsense fed to the British people.

The peculiar relationship the UK media have with the public was in evidence a few weeks ago [April 26, 2001], again in the *Observer*; this time it was a feature article by Norman Stone, "renowned Oxford historian." It was little more than a public relations exercise on behalf of the Turkish State. Professor Stone is currently at the Department of International Relations, Bilkent University, Ankara. Stone's views are of the far-right variety and he is open in praise of those he describes as the "true heroes" of our time, e.g., Brian Crozier.[8] For very many years Professor Stone's "hero" was an "operative of the CIA" and a leading figure "within the whole panoply of right wing... intelligence and propaganda agencies," including straight CIA-funded projects such as the Congress for Cultural Freedom and Forum World Features.

Crozier was also a founding member of the secretive but highly influential Pinay Circle, "an international right-wing propaganda group which brings together serving or retired intelligence officers and politicians with links to right-wing intelligence factions from most of the countries in Europe."[9] In the UK he founded the Institute for the Study of Conflict, "part of a network of right wing bodies ... lecturing on subversion to the British army and the police."[10] This network included Common Cause, the Economic League and bona fide agencies of the British State such as MI5, much of whose "intelligence work was inspired not by the demands of security but by extreme right wing political ideas."[11] Another colleague was Brigadier Frank Kitson who in 1969 "was seconded to Oxford

University for a year to read and synthesize the literature on counter-insurgency. His thesis was published in 1971 as *Low Intensity Operations*, and a year later he was given command of a brigade in Belfast to test his theories."[12]

Crozier is one of an international group of "terrorist experts" who argues for "the concept of internal war ... and the parallel ... between the situation of a country at war with an external enemy, and the country faced with a situation like Ulster, or Vietnam, or Turkey or Uruguay." If the general public in these countries can swallow the idea that they are at war then all kinds of "emergency regulations" can be introduced.[13] As with Professor Stone he is an apologist for the brutalities of the Turkish military. The year 1971 was a crucial period in recent Turkish-Kurdish history, "when the army overthrew the Demirel government ... and thousands of people were arrested and tortured in counter-insurgency centres which had been set up by Turkish officers trained by the US in Panama."[14] This is interpreted by Crozier as a "military intervention to force the creation of a government determined to restore order." In response to an article critical of "allegations of ill-treatment during interrogation in Ulster" he wonders why people were "so distressed [by such] relative mildness.... What if it [had extended] to the grim horrors reported during ... the early 1970s in Turkey?" Then he justifies the barbarism of the Turkish State security forces on the grounds that it "undoubtedly helped to provide the security forces with the intelligence they needed [to smash the Turkish People's Liberation Army] as an effective instrument of revolution."[15]

I think if I was Kurdish I would have become a wee bit tired hearing European writers and others urging the Turkish State to change its ways. It is difficult to think of one country in Europe that does not collude with Turkish ruling authority in one way or another. "Turkish ruling authority" is just another name for Turkish National Security, which is just another name for the Turkish military. Beyond the *Observer* and the mainstream media in general the contempt for the UK public is in evidence elsewhere, including at the highest levels of government as when the previously discredited academic Professor Paul Wilkinson was commissioned by Lord Lloyd "to provide an academic view as to the nature of the terrorist threat."

It would be of more value to the people of Kurdistan that we let our own governments know that we are aware of the reality, that we know what is happening behind the closed doors of power, we know of the cowardice of our own politicians and academics and of their complicity, both at the present time and historically. We should accept responsibility and challenge those who hide in the shadows. If we expect media coverage of this "dirty war" and the atrocities being perpetrated against the Kurdish people, we do so in the knowledge that weapons and torture implements used by the Turkish State are supplied by the Scottish and British business community, as well as those of the USA, Germany and France.

While Professor Stone praises Turkey as the "fastest-growing economy in the European region" another academic has now spent nearly fifteen years of his life in prison. Beşikçi is being punished as an example to other writers, to other activists, to other academics, to other sociologists, to other scientists and—most crucially—to other Turks. During one trial speech he made the basic point that it was not he who was on trial but science itself. How can the science of sociology exist as a valid field of study until he is released from prison and his work made freely available? Until then the entire subject is contaminated, not only in Turkey and in Kurdistan but elsewhere throughout the world.

(2001)

The University of Strathclyde Students' Association Grants Honorary Life Membership to Kurdish Leader, Abdullah Öcalan

Bestowing an honour such as this makes it not just a meeting but a special occasion. It is marvellous that the students of Strathclyde University should honour Abdullah Öcalan in this way. As former students here, both myself and my wife, Marie, I am very pleased personally to see it happen.

Of course I am also aware of the pitfalls in honouring one individual in this way. It could tie us into that notion of "the Great Leader," the one without whom we would all be Lost. I find such a notion not only unacceptable, I find it repugnant. People here will feel the same. But there are those who fall for it and there are those in whose interest it is to enforce the falsification.

And what a terrible disservice it does to those hundreds of thousands of courageous Kurdish people who have fought and died in the struggle towards liberation, towards self-determination. Those who are opposed to a people's right to self-determination will use any means at their disposal to undercut and oppose that struggle. A typical method is to transform the liberation movement into the political project of one tiny group of foreign extremist fanatics. Ringleaders! The Vanguard! Without these ringleaders and vanguards the masses would be content to know their own place in the scheme of things, be content with their lot and a belief system grounded in the hereafter, looking forward to a glorious Life after Death, if they are religious, and the docile masses are always portrayed as religious. In the case of Kurdistan it gives the idea that these millions of people are a nomadic lumpenproletariat who would be content to chase goats up and down mountains, ignorant of their own history, living in abject poverty, kowtowing to their political and cultural superiors, if it wasn't for these foreign left-wing infiltrators who are all atheists and communists.

Even better when the authorities can lay the blame for the discontent on the shoulders of one individual. It is a strategy used by corrupt rulers to cling onto power. They strive to establish that there is no liberation movement without the Great Leader. No mass struggle, only the Great Leader.

Once the ruling authorities and their allies have this established their chore is straightforward. To destabilise the struggle they need only "expose" the Great Leader. They transform the Great Leader into a greedy and power-hungry charlatan whose overriding impulse is self-interest and self-glorification. Ruling authority will use their propaganda to "reveal" the Great Leader as a contemptible coward who enters into acts of betrayals with all and sundry to achieve his own evil end. They will lie and distort the truth to portray the Great Leader as a weak and selfish coward who has sold out his closest comrades in a last-ditch attempt to save his own skin.

This is not to say that greedy and self-glorifying Great Leaders do not exist. Of course they do. Typically we find that most such individuals are not really leaders at all, they are tyrants, placed into power by the so-called western democracies. This has been the case in Europe, Asia, Africa, Australasia and the Americas. It is a strategy we associate with imperialism. These so-called Great Leaders lead no movement at all. What they have is a paid army, a fascist administration, and the financial, material and human resources of these same western democracies. This has been the case in both Iran and Iraq and an example is the Shah of Iran.

The Turkish authorities want to reach a position where they can say: if not for Öcalan there would be no Kurdish liberation movement. It is only through his evil machinations that such a thing exists at all. This is not just a lie, it is an offensive lie and it dishonours the Kurdish people. Those who make use of the lie are engaged in destabilising the liberation movement. And this is the context to which we should pay heed when we hear these dark rumours about Öcalan doing secret deals that will sell out his Kurdistan Workers' Party (PKK) comrades, compromise the liberation struggle and deal a death blow to the birthright of the Kurdish people.

These dirty tricks and double-dealings are predictable and people should be strong enough to treat them with contempt. It happens during periods of negotiation. The ruling authority who holds power will undermine any bargaining counter from the other side. It is quite simple. They refuse to negotiate until they have absolutely no choice. They will drag out the process for as long as they can. The Turkish State is being dragged to the negotiating table and they do not like it one bit. Thus they will postpone it and postpone it and postpone it for as long as it takes and for as long as they can, in the hope that it all blows over and is forgotten about. Nobody cares about the long term. It is basic: those who hold power will cling onto power.

The question of Kurdish liberation and the exercise of self-determination is very complex. A look at maps of the Middle East will give some idea of the complexity. A highly unusual thing occurs in an old one I have of the Middle East. There is an entity that is Kurdistan. Now to carry such a map in Turkey before 2002 was a criminal offence. Yes, even to carry the map! The name *Kurdistan* was against the law. Even to utter the word: Kurdistan!—a criminal offence. To sing a Kurdish song: a criminal offence. To give your children a Kurdish name: a criminal offence. In Turkey to use the Kurdish language in any way at all was a criminal offence. The Turkish authorities jailed Kurdish people, they tortured Kurdish people and they put Kurdish people to death because they refused to lie down and accept such iniquitous and anti-human legislation.

The Turkish constitution entered existence in November 1982. The very possibility of democracy was denied. This from the opening preamble: "no thought or impulse [may be cherished] against Turkish national interests, against the existence of Turkey, against the principle of the indivisibility of the state and its territory, against the historical and moral values of Turkishness, against nationalism as defined by [Mustafa Kemal] Atatürk, against his principles, reforms and civilising efforts."

Mustafa Kemal Atatürk was the major Turkish figure of the First World War period. The struggle for the liberation of Kurdistan returns us to the end of the First World War, when the deals were being done, when the land spoils and plunder were being divvied up by the Allies and when Turkey, given the okay by Britain and America, cheated the Kurdish people out of their right to nationhood. Whether nationhood is ultimately a good or a bad thing is not the concern. The issue is that at the end of the First World War nation status was on the cards and it was denied. Kurdistan was partitioned, the land divided between the surrounding countries: Turkey, Syria, Iraq and Iran, and it happened to the benefit of foreign interests, led by the UK, by France and by the USA.

The annexation of Kurdistan and the attempted genocide and the continued oppression of the Kurdish people are three of the major scandals of this century; a fourth was the genocide in Armenia. The British State has had a pivotal role. During the 1920s Britain needed a client-state "to secure [British capital's] right to exploit the oilfields of Southern Kurdistan." What did they do? Basically they created a country, gave it a king and called it Iraq. Britain has continued to collude in the terrorist assaults on the Kurdish people from then until the present. The British State has held great influence and could have tried to aid the cause of justice. They have never done so. But why should anyone be surprised by that? There is no place for such naivety. We have to pass beyond a position that confuses the procedures of state with a value system centred on ethical standards and moral principles.

Abdullah Öcalan wasn't born until after the end of the Second World War. He is of my own generation. In fact he is two years younger than me. Fifty years ago during our teens and early twenties it was a very different time. Public protest was common. The Vietnam War raged in all its horror. Liberation struggles were taking place in different parts of the world: class struggles and pan-nationalist struggles. Within the western democracies themselves such things were happening. But there was a heavy reaction to that and assaults on freedom took place in most every region of the world.

Back then there was a sense of solidarity that nowadays seems from another world. It even spread across class lines. Middle-class students engaged, and many academics also engaged, and some were jailed for their part in "fomenting student unrest"—as though the students were incapable of their own "unrest." There was a very strong student movement also in Turkey during the mid to late 1960s and Öcalan emerged from this. The political system in Turkey at that time has been described as "democratic fascism," although even that was too liberal for the Turkish military who conducted another coup in 1971.

People may see the award of this honour to Öcalan as symbolic. Fair enough. Öcalan may well be a symbol for millions of people but first and foremost he is a living, breathing human being who has been locked up in a Turkish prison since 1999. It was a very difficult period. Öcalan had been in Syria, where he had lived on the run for a long number of years. Until he was betrayed by the usual suspects, the so-called western democracies—Britain, America, Italy, Germany and so on—who blanked out any reportage deemed negative towards the Turkish State and sought to normalise everyday life in the country. The southwest coast was portrayed as a safe haven for European tourists. The farther in and farther east more adventurous visitors strayed, a different country was being discovered, one they had known nothing about. Their holiday brochures had forgotten to explain to them that beyond the holiday resorts most of the country was akin to a police state, that it was dangerous to stray too close to the border, and that the southeast of Turkey was something else altogether: it was a war zone.

Their home governments had omitted to advise them that this was not identified as the southeast of Turkey by millions of people throughout the world, it was Northern Kurdistan. There was no context in which the words *Kurd*, *Kurdish* and *Kurdistan* were to be mentioned. The Turkish State lawyers had managed to wangle that within their 1982 constitution. Young Kurdish people and their Turkish comrades were being imprisoned for daring the authorities by unfurling Kurdish flags in the law courts and by singing Kurdish songs.

What these young people were witnessing was the criminalisation of the entire Kurdish people. Once criminalisation is "allowed," anything is possible: barbarism, mass murder, genocide. Once a political party is outlawed it means anything at all except dialogue and negotiation. People are ignored, ghettoised, marginalised, jailed, tortured and killed. There are no rules and no mercy. Who cares what happens to a bunch of "terrorists," never mind that up until the day before they were a community of women and men who advocated a particular politics and way ahead for their culture and community.

I mentioned earlier how back in 1995 "in the village of Geri 30 people, mainly women and children, were brutally killed." This massacre was reported as the work of PKK "terrorists" and the Turkish authorities "showed video footage for days to members of the European Parliament, in an attempt to discredit the PKK and to have its leadership outlawed as terrorists." Subsequently a delegation from a human rights association went to the village of Geri itself and came up with a different finding, "shared by all the members of our delegation … this massacre was an act of the contra-guerrillas."

But even though discredited the Turkish State propaganda worked; the German prosecution of the PKK resulted in it being banned as an illegal organisation. The Turkish State humiliated the European Parliament by serving them a complete fabrication about the PKK. In fact they themselves may well have held ultimate responsibility for the massacre.

While awaiting trial in a Turkish prison during that period the great Turkish sociologist İsmail Beşikçi was interviewed by Amnesty International and commented on the German prosecution of the PKK. He said that the one thing it did establish was the existence of a "secret agreement between the NATO alliance and Turkey in relation to Kurdistan."

In 1953 Dr Mohammad Mosaddeq headed the government in Iran. Mosaddeq was detested by the Turkish, US and the British states. One of his most blatant criminal acts was to put a check on monarchy and ruling authority by making it subject to the democratic control of the Iranian people. A similar plan was suggested four hundred years earlier, in sixteenth-century Scotland, by the writer George Buchanan. He argued that all monarchs should be subject to democratic control and that none should exercise an absolute God-given authority.

In sixteenth-century Scotland this was anathema to the monarchy and the financial interests of the ruling class. So too in twentieth-century Iran the financial and business interests of the ruling class were endangered by these dangerous notions of democratic control. The British State acted quickly alongside the USA to get rid of the danger by destabilising the government, criminalising and occasionally assassinating intellectuals and activists. Mosaddeq was captured, imprisoned and detained under house arrest until his death in 1967. Thus he avoided execution. But no ruling authority wants to create a martyr—perhaps a factor in why Abdullah Öcalan remains alive.

Britain and America installed their own Great Leader in Iran: the Shah. By means of the terrorism he practised on the

Iranian people, aided and abetted by Britain and the USA, the Shah managed "to hold onto Iran" for the next twenty-five years, acting on behalf of the so-called western democracies, who themselves were acting on behalf of global financial and business interests. The revolution that ousted the Shah brought to power an Islamic republic headed by Ayatollah Khomeini.

During the twenty-five years of absolute rule by the Shah one place of freedom was the mosque. A general problem for tyrannies and dictatorships is religion and the problems effected by religious belief and belief systems. It is difficult to attack religious institutions at fundamental levels and virtually impossible to criminalise entire religions, although down through the centuries both have been tried by ruling authorities.

In some societies it is the only indoor public space left. Across Kurdistan restrictions on freedom of movement have existed in one place or another for decades while in Turkey martial law has been established on many occasions. Places of religious worship are all-important within tyrannies and dictatorships, not just for expressions of religious faith but as meeting places. People chat to one another. It happens in mosques, churches, temples and synagogues.

While the Shah ruled there was a powerful irony at play for the Kurdish peoples. In their efforts to contain the Kurdish population in Iran the State's propaganda unit broadcast Kurdish programmes in Kurmanji, the Kurdish language. It didn't matter that this was right-wing, pro-authoritarian propaganda; the crucial factor was that it took place in the Kurds' own language. Kurdish people could listen and hear their language in this public arena, traditional Kurdish songs, snippets of Kurdish history: what an extraordinary experience.

I mentioned earlier the inaugural Freedom of Expression event in Istanbul in 1997. Perhaps there should be room for another event, the Freedom to Know. This event could deal with our ignorance of our own history, the denial of our right to learn where we are, who we are, who we were, where we were; to know the stories, languages, songs and traditions of our own people.

It is very hard for people to determine their own existence when they don't even know who they are nor to which communities, groups and even families they might belong.

Abdullah Öcalan has spent most of his life either on the run or in prison. He and others are arguing in favour of a different way ahead taking into account the most awkward questions, including the relationship of armed warfare to the liberation movement and the place of the nation-state in regard to self-determination in the twenty-first century. If I read this correctly this vision is anti-state and validates ideas on group and community autonomy. I approve of that! Fascism attacks communities and leaves us stranded as individuals, attempting to make sense of the world in the most isolated manner.

Kurdish history, as with Scottish history, belongs to radical history, like that of any marginalised people or community. It is suppressed as a matter of course. The people of Kurdistan have been struggling for decades for the right to determine their own existence. This honour that Strathclyde students are paying to Abdullah Öcalan represents more than an honour to one individual; it recognises the justice of the struggle. From Scotland the message is one of support and solidarity. Let the politicians in this country heed the students.

(2015)

But What Is It They Are Trying to Express?

I need to say that the views I express here are my own, derived from my own perception, the result of my own reading, my own knowledge and my own observations, and if I go wrong I apologise in advance. This evening is entitled Remembering Turkish Voices of Dissent.[1] I see a need to take this a step beyond if we are to come to terms with what is happening in Turkey, and most especially in the southeast, Turkish-Kurdistan, not only at present but for several generations. To describe the "voices of dissent" as Turkish is something I can only do with major qualification. I have to make reference to Kurdistan and the plight of the Kurdish people. If not, then the danger is that we miss the most fundamental factors. When we say "Turkish voices," do we mean to include Kurdish voices? If we say, "yes, of course," then we may have fallen into a trap, that we allowed the Turkish State to set the agenda, that the name "Turkish" embraces Kurds.

Oppression in Turkey goes through periods of severity, then tails off. For the past couple of years it's been nightmarish. People here will have followed events and be familiar with the name of another writer now imprisoned, Gültan Kışanak. She is also Co-mayor of Diyarbakır, which is the main city in Turkish-Kurdistan. "After months of armed conflict in the city center that ended in March 2016 ... [she and her male Co-mayor] Fırat Anlı were detained by Turkish police on 25

October 2016.... Just after the detention, the internet connection across the Kurdish region was cut. As of 27 October 2016, millions of people still have no internet access. This blackout attempt aims at silencing the voice of people in the region as well as to prevent them from exercising their right to be informed about developments."[2]

Kışanak has been an activist all her life:

> In the 1980s [I] was imprisoned ... in notoriously brutal conditions, with torture and killings. To be Kurdish, to be a woman and to be leftist created triple difficulties for me. I was kept in a dog kennel for six months because I refused to say "I am not a Kurd but a Turk." Our older women friends, our mothers' age were tortured because they could not speak Turkish. I still have signs of torture from those days on my body.[3]

What we have to understand is that the Turkish State has done all in its power to convince the world, including its own population, that there is no such thing as Kurdistan, no such people as Kurdish people, no such culture, no such language, no such anything; nothing. The Turkish State has attempted to extirpate every last vestige of Kurdishness and put into its place Turkishness. The Turkish State would discuss Turkish voices of dissent forever and ever, but if we exchange Turkish for Kurdish, it's another story.

A deal was done at the end of the First World War between the major western powers. Kurdistan was divided into four and became part of Turkey, Iraq, Syria and Iran. For almost a hundred years now these millions of Kurdish people have been without a country, and for many of them it's been a form of hell on earth. But from the ashes of that the Kurdish people have refused to die out, they have refused to become extinct. It is estimated that there are twenty million Kurdish people in Turkey—add another twenty million in the Middle East and Europe.

Much of the campaigning material I see about the current situation connects directly with Freedom of Speech and Expression but when campaigns stop and start on Freedom of Speech and Expression, I am not *necessarily* sympathetic. Also, I don't see arrests and imprisonments in Turkey as "arbitrary" at all. I think we need to be very cautious on that one.

Nor has it much to do with general principles concerning Freedom of Speech and Expression. It is a mistake to insist that it is about general principles. When you do this you fail to take into account the reality of the Turkish constitution and the Turkish penal code. These are not ethical issues. The far right in Turkey which is bringing its own pressure on Recep Tayyip Erdoğan and the Turkish government has a very solid foundation within the Turkish legal profession. These people are lawyers by profession. General principles don't apply. They don't give two hoots about general principles. What matters is what exists in the constitution and how best that can be applied in civil society. In other words what they can get away with, and they will push that as far as it goes, and when that fails the lawyers and the rest of them will step aside and leave it to the military. That's what happens. I'm not a lawyer and I'm not a soldier. I'm making general observations based on my own understanding.

I once wrote against a campaign which concerned Freedom of Speech and Expression, or at least it so appeared. I didn't see it as that at all. I just thought it was an elitist kind of thing, at best silly, but essentially crap. It laboured under the misapprehension that here in the UK we have a long tradition of Freedom of Speech and Expression which is inviolable and that we should do all in our power to maintain these freedoms against the forces of ignorance. I beg your pardon? What a joke. One point I tried to make was that it was ludicrous to say that Freedom of Speech and Expression existed in the UK. I also said that when you attack people, don't be surprised when they attack ye back. Self-Defence Is No Offence.

English literature attacks all sorts of people, and this is a general rule if not principle. English literature is the expression of a value system. If a writer fails to challenge values within this system then he or she is guilty. Guilty of what? Guilty of failing to challenge these values. Which values? You tell me. Are there values in this society that we should attack? Come on, I'm talking to you writers. Are there any values that we cannot help but attack in order to write honestly and truthfully?

Freedom of Speech and Expression. Freedom to speak about what? Freedom to express yourself about what?

Forget the general principle. To see this as a general principle plays into the hands of despots, dictatorships and every other authoritarian regime.

They don't give a damn about Freedom of Speech and Expression. It is irrelevant. They already have Freedom of Speech and Expression. Even better: they have freedom of action. They say and do what they like. Right is might. They have the power and they have the might.

And they will let us say and do what we like, as long as they don't disapprove.

What is it that the Turkish State is trying to stop people saying, or thinking, or expressing? This meeting is also in support of Aslı Erdoğan, and to demonstrate solidarity with her. Aslı Erdoğan is not Kurdish but Turkish. İsmail Beşikçi, sociologist, anthropologist, historian, spent seventeen years of his life in prison. Why? Why are so many journalists and writers and artists and trades union organisers and politicians and members of the judiciary, and every kind of people you care to mention, languishing in prison right now?

It has nothing to do with general principles of Freedom of Speech and Expression. It has everything to do with speaking on behalf of Kurdish people, of expressing our horror and condemnation of the Turkish State's barbaric assaults on Kurdish people. Speaking freely on the situation in Kurdistan is to break the law, not to breach a principle of natural justice.

Aslı Erdoğan is in prison for her support of the Kurdish people, for the fact of her solidarity and where this has taken her, like many other heroic and courageous Turkish people. Some are Christian, some are Muslim; some hold other religions, some are atheists. In common is their humanity, their hatred of injustice; their inability to stand aside and pretend they don't see what is happening.

In Turkey in the great majority of cases it is not so much Freedom of Speech and Expression that is the problem, it is speaking on behalf of Kurdish people, it is expressing your horror and absolute condemnation of the Turkish State's soul-destroying inhumanity. I am arguing that speaking freely on the situation in Kurdistan is to break the law, not breach a principle.

When we look at the Turkish constitution we see that by using certain elements of language we are breaking the law, and there is no freedom enshrined in any place in the world that allows us to break the law. This is part of the difficulty in talking about campaigns concerning so-called Freedom of Speech and Expression. They aren't worth a damn when they come up against State laws. These campaigns on behalf of Turkish writers and issues around Freedom of Expression are crucial; I'm not saying they are not important. Of course they are. But they only take us so far.

It is not Freedom of Expression that matters so much as the subject matter. I want to shout out my support and my solidarity with the Kurdish people, those people who have been carrying a life-or-death struggle for decades.

It doesn't matter if the Turkish State "grants" me the Freedom to Express my solidarity. I have to grab that opportunity when I can, with or without any concessions. Freedom is not a concession. Am I supposed to request of a brutal dictator that he grants me Freedom of Speech and Expression? It is ludicrous.

Courageous Turkish people must be supported but the reasons why they are being punished must also be supported.

We cannot support Turkish dissidents blindly. We cannot conduct campaigns on their behalf and ignore why it is they are in that horrendous position.

There is a war going on in Turkey. I'm not 100 percent surprised if people in this room don't know about this. The UK and most of the western so-called democracies are either cowed into silence by Turkey or find it in their interests to remain silent. In 2014 Gültan Kışanak was elected Co-mayor of Diyarbakır. She and her colleague and Co-mayor, Fırat Anlı, were arrested and imprisoned less than two years later. Fırat Anlı was released in 2017 but Gültan Kışanak remains in prison. She was sentenced to more than fourteen years for being a member of the Kurdistan Workers' Party:

> In the 1990s there was no sign of freedom—just like now—I worked for newspapers where Kurdish and women's rights were the main issue. These were alternatives to the mainstream newspapers. The conditions for journalists, especially for Kurdish journalists were harsh—just like today. Some of our journalist friends were killed while they were doing their work. I worked as a journalist for 13 years and published sections focusing on women's issues within the newspaper.
>
> After 2007, women became more visible and powerful. The 2007 elections were revolutionary for both Kurdish and Turkish women. Eight out of 26 Kurdish MPs were women. Women became more confident as co-chairs and men had to accept them as equals. Other political parties were embarrassed and started to introduce a co-chair system as well.
>
> The state's military operations in the Kurdish regions during the last year have destroyed all city life. The Turkish Human Rights Organisation has published a report about what has happened between 16 August 2015 and 18 March 2016 in 7 cities and 22 towns

in the Kurdish regions. A total of 1,642,000 people were affected by the state's operations and curfews. Among the 320 people who have lost their lives were 72 children and 62 women. Tens of thousands of houses were destroyed. At least 250 thousand people are homeless now. Women and children have been especially affected by this damage. Most now living in uncivilised conditions in tents without water and electricity for months. They cannot find enough food and clean water to keep them alive. They don't have access to any health system. Although women have tried to protect themselves and their children from illnesses, the rates of premature birth, neonatal deaths, stillbirth, and child deaths have all increased. Children are traumatised and most have lost their normal lives and trust.

[About the coup in July this year] we can see that the high ranking military generals and personnel who carried out a very brutal war against Kurdish people were directly involved ... these [same] generals, who have carried out crimes against Kurds and violated all human rights in Kurdistan, are not blamed for this reason. They are only blamed for [their failed] coup attempt ... the generals who organised the coup, are claiming the significant role they played in the war against Kurds as part of their defence. They try to justify themselves by proclaiming what big Turkish nationalists they are.

After the coup Erdoğan started a dialogue with most of the opposition political parties [but excluded] the HDP.[4]

Some of you will know of the Peoples' Democratic Party (HDP), "the pro-Kurdish Peoples' Party which is the third largest party in Turkey." This party has been operational for less than two years in which time it has gone on to unite different people, groups, communities and the Turkish left. For HDP "the first step is the establishment of democratic and autonomous local governments." Ayla Akat Ata, another women's rights activist now in prison, has explained that

> From the beginning, the Kurdish movement has had three main aims: national struggle, class struggle and gender struggle. All ... three are as important as each other if we are to find a real solution for our people ... The Kurds will create a democratic autonomous system against the centralist, barbaric and corrupt state system. To create something better for people might not be easy, but Kurds will succeed and this will benefit Turkey and the entire Middle East. We want to create a strong parliamentary system with more power given to the regions. The existence of a one-man system of rule is destroying the democratic legitimacy of parliament and has significantly weakened it.... [It] doesn't matter how many elections you have, democracy is merely reduced to a rubber stamp for dictatorship. Sadly a Turkish nationalist block exists and supports this type of dictatorial rule.[5]

There is one essential campaign that we might wage, for the release to freedom of a man who, with others, has been trying to work out a way to resolve the situation, that might bring a meaningful way ahead for Kurdish people, and not only in Turkey but in Syria and Iraq, and Iran too. This man has spent the last few years working his ideas out on the page and for a brief period he was in direct negotiation with the Turkish government. I refer to Abdullah Öcalan. We might begin by requesting that Mr Erdoğan and the Turkish government resume negotiations with Mr Öcalan and other Kurdish politicians—yes, resume, even while he was in prison he and senior Kurdish politicians were talking together, but that came to an abrupt end roundabout 2012.

You must surely be aware that Öcalan has been imprisoned since 1999. He lived on the run for a long number of years, until betrayed by the usual suspects: Britain, America, Italy and Germany. He was one of the most wanted men in the world. How come? Only a few years before he was simply a high-profile Kurdish politician, a founder member and president of the Kurdistan Workers' Party (PKK). How did he get from there to being such a monstrous criminal? In the first report I read of his capture the pro-Turkey bias was blatant. From Associated Press one comment stood out, that there have been "no executions in Turkey since 1984." This was a disgraceful distortion of the truth. Who knows the number of executions committed in that country since 1984. What we have had there are summary executions. In the same news item was a reference to the German authorities "seeking Abdullah Öcalan on a 1990 warrant." Up until then the PKK was a legitimate political party. The Turkish State had done its utmost to have this political party criminalised as a terrorist organisation.

And it succeeded. Once criminalisation is "allowed" anything is possible. There are no rules, no mercy. People are ignored, ghettoised, marginalised; jailed, tortured, killed. Who cares what happens to a bunch of "terrorists," never mind that up until the day before they were a community of women and men who advocated a particular politics and way ahead for their culture and native lands.

PEN International can begin by offering our support and solidarity with Kurdish writers and artists and sending a strong message of support and solidarity to the Kurdish PEN Centre, if it hasn't been bombed out of existence already. The last I heard it had been broken into and ransacked.

(2016)

Who's Kidding Who?

Following the end of the 1914–18 War and the breakup of the Ottoman Empire, the newly formed Turkish State had many enemies from within. These included reactionary right-wing forces, people who would have been more at home with the Allied Military command. In the early years Kemal Atatürk and the Young Turks

> changed a monarchy into a republic ... closed the monasteries, dissolved their organisations [and] destroyed the whole religious basis, the old laws and social life ... saluting superiors and the acknowledgment of salutes by inferiors were changed. The salaam was forbidden [and he] made it a punishable offence to laugh at the mad, eccentric or crippled.... [They] set out to change the whole mentality of the people—their old ideas, their habits, their dress, manners, customs, ways of talking.... For four hundred years the priests had forbidden all delineation of the human form.... [Kemal] opened a mixed school in Ankara to study the nude ... revolutionised the status of the family and the rights of ownership, forbade polygamy and the harem ... radically adjusted the position of women, who ceased to be chattels owned by their husbands [and] became individuals and free citizens.... [He] encouraged women to shed their veils

and come out into the open, made them members of his political party with equal footing with men, helped them become doctors and lawyers; two became judges, four elected to the municipal council [and] produced the Children's Bill, regulating the employment of children, forbidding them to be taken to bars, cafes-chantants and uncontrolled cinemas.[1]

Social change as radical as this would have been seen as very dangerous. People are suffocated by various layers of authority; cultural, religious, communal and in the home. The State is built on population control. Under Kemal's drive for ultimate power crucial areas of authority were being subject to challenge, even dismantled. People may have been cast adrift from tradition but control is exercised by tradition. They were learning to think for themselves. If this was Kemalism it was dangerous. Some would have seen it as a form of socialism, which would end in communism. Others would have seen it as naive. A dictatorship won't work. Here on earth higher powers must exist. Supreme power is exercised when people work together.

The British State doesn't have a constitution and doesn't want one. It functions by consensus, by class interest. Whatever lies in the best interests of the ruling class is the only way. No challenges to authority. It hardly matters the authority, so long as it controls areas of thought, the more the merrier.

Kemal "had studied the English [political] system and approved of it." It is important to understand this. As far as the Great British public is concerned the political parties are forever "attacking each other," said Kemal. But this only happens within "'office hours': 'out of office hours' they must be best of friends [and] should dine together in all friendliness … working for the good of [England]."[2]

With the British model in mind he needed a docile opposition. He created one. It was not a serious enterprise. He based his idea of a democratic opposition on the Whitehall model, something akin to the British Labour Party, where the State infrastructure is never under threat, where the politicians sing "God Save the Monarch" and are ejected from government buildings for untoward behaviour.

This was ideal, exactly as Kemal desired. No matter what the politicians got up to, the Turkish State would remain in control; Kemal was the Turkish State, and intended so to remain. His created party of opposition was designed "not for any kind of libertarian or democratic purpose, he did it to teach his politicians a lesson, that he alone was in charge. [It] didn't work. Turkish officialdom couldn't cope. They saw their duty to silence all opposition," and they cracked down far too severely.[3] Authentic voices of opposition were now heard and further action followed on from that. People started driving "government officials ... out of villages.... Religious leaders were aiding and abetting the [struggle]. Threats [came] in Armenia [and] the Kurds were fighting fiercely. [They] had invented the Blind Man's Court Martial. [Every] Turk captured was summarily tried and brutally mutilated."[4]

It was all too much. Kemal sent in the army. "Martial law was declared, censorship reimposed, newspaper editors punished severely [and] the Turkish troops retaliated cruelly on the Kurds, hanging and imprisoning the leaders, crushing revolt, ejecting every Armenian possible, wiping up the Communists, hanging those who had plotted against him, arrested, bastinadoed and imprisoned a thousand Turks, hung twenty eight of their leaders. The frontiers were cleared, the revolts crushed. Every class, every man and woman—felt and knew the master's hand."[5]

Before the breakup of the empire, Ottoman Turkey was composed of different societies, different cultures, different peoples: Turks, Kurds, Arabs, Persians, Azerbaijanis, Assyrians, Iraqis and others. But the empire had gone. This was 1932 and from hereon the cry was purity, national unity:

Turkey for the Turk. This led to the political system we nowadays equate with fascism. Difference became suspect; other cultures and minorities were targeted, criminalized: surely inevitable from the point of enforced assimiliation, when Atatürk changed

> the Arabic characters of Turkish into Latin to revolutionise all thought in Turkey, all Turkish literature.... The Koran and New Testament were translated into Turkish.... All prayers in the mosques [had to] be in Turkish. Foreign schools [were] discouraged [and] must omit all reference to religion. Teachers must teach Turkish.... Arabic and Persian [must] be eliminated.... Tartar words and phrases must be discovered out of old books, documents and songs, revived and used to replace the foreign words. [Kemal] called in European experts ... adopted the German Commercial [Code], the Italian Penal [Code] and the Swiss Civil Code.[6]

After the breakup of the empire the western powers were in at the kill, stealing and grabbing what they could, and nation-states came into being. Even during the height of the First World War, while millions of young men and women were fighting and dying, the state authorities were in cutting deals, assigning one another future shares of the plunder, and the

> French and British reached a secret agreement in 1916 dividing Mesopotamia into zones of British and French influence. This division of spoils included a share for Tsarist Russia. A proclamation was issued shortly after British troops captured Baghdad in 1917. "Our armies do not come into your cities and lands as conquerors or enemies, but as liberators.... You are free to participate in your own civil affairs ... in collaboration with the political representatives of Britain who accompany

the Army."[7] Then they imposed colonial rule, ignored the secret agreement and seized the oil-rich province.[8]

Plans changed soon enough, following the October Revolution in Tsarist Russia in 1917. In the UK the reaction from military hawks such as Winston Churchill was loud and clear. He wanted to bomb Russia immediately. After that he thought to use the same or more deadly weapons "against the rebellious tribes of northern India ... 'I am strongly in favour of using poisoned gas against uncivilised tribes,' he declared in one secret memorandum [and] criticised his colleagues for their 'squeamishness.'"[9] This was in reference to "the top secret M Device," an exploding shell containing a highly toxic gas. "Among other reactions" the effects of the "M Device" were "uncontrollable vomiting, coughing up blood and instant, crippling fatigue."[10]

The British State were stamping out liberation struggles at home as well as abroad. Ireland had not yet broken free of the imperial yoke. In the same year as the Sykes-Picot spoils of war agreement with the French, British military command bound fourteen of their own citizens, set them in front of a firing squad, and shot them dead in Dublin.[11]

In those days Churchill was not portrayed by the establishment as an eccentric upper-class English duffer who saves nations and suffers little children to grow within a freedom-loving democracy. His disregard for the lives of ordinary men, women and children was a byword at the higher levels of state bureaucracy. Churchill "saw Iraq as an experiment in high-technology colonial control [and] pacified the country using airplanes, armoured cars, firebombs and mustard gas. Air attacks were used to shock and awe, to teach obedience and to force the collection of taxes."[12] He made "officials in London" uneasy, the few who "sometimes had qualms about the violence." Other "colonial administrators expressed enthusiasm for the power of his military enterprise."

These included Gertrude Bell, "sole woman at the British top table wrangling over the future of the Middle East [and] instrumental in the creation of modern Iraq." Here is Ms Bell's personal appreciation of Churchillian strategies in a letter home to daddy, Knight of the Realm and Second Baronet, Sir Thomas Hugh Bell:

> The RAF has done wonders bombing insurgent villages. It was even more remarkable than the display we saw last year ... much more real ... wonderful and horrible.... They dropped bombs all round it, as if to catch the fugitives and finally fire bombs which even in the brightest sunlight made flares of bright flame in the desert. They burn through metal and water won't extinguish them. At the end the armoured cars went out to round up the fugitives with machine guns.[13]

What exactly is "an insurgent village"? As with Winston Churchill, the British State has developed a place for Gertrude Bell in their pantheon of heroes. No matter that her "involvement has been debated ever since [what] isn't questioned is her love of the Arab people and their culture." Here we are. Gertrude Bell "set up a museum to house some of Iraq's cultural treasures—it is still there today; now known as the National Museum of Iraq."[14] There is good and bad everywhere. It's the nature of the world. In the last resort everybody must agree with the British State. That would be a point to raise with the Kurdish and Iraqi descendants of the hundreds of thousands of people whose lives were deemed worthless, whose massacre she approved so graphically.

It is this Brit-speak gobbledygook that people must heed: the language of the imperialist apologist. This is classic Brit-speak and employs the "two-sides-to-every-story" argument as a means of defending the indefensible. Yes, Hitler and the Nazis were inhuman but at least the trains ran on time. Yes, slavery was wrong but the slaveowners built mighty churches, opera houses and art galleries—and also museums wherein the ruling class donated 0.0001 percent of the treasures they had plundered, then tithed a similar percentage of their profits to vouchsafed religious and charitable enterprises.

The British State tells the public to ignore Gertrude Bell's admiration of the cynical barbarism practised by Churchill and the military on their behalf, and forget that the supreme goal was to steal and secure for British-based capital "the oil-rich provinces" of Iraqi-Kurdistan.[15] Leave to one side the genocidal massacres and horrors perpetrated on the civilian population: deep down, in her heart of hearts, Gertrude Bell not only loved the people but the culture too. The BBC further advises young folk everywhere that Ms Bell "was into archaeology, map-making, photography [and] with her awe-inspiring skills … travelled across Arabia, mapping it as she went … inform[ing] the world's understanding of the Middle East and the various peoples who lived there."[16] Therein a message of hope, especially for young women. Not that you too can be a fascist bastard, but that first and foremost Gertrude Bell "sat at the top table" and, by definition, struck a blow for female emancipation.

Perhaps meaningful pressure can be brought to bear on the contemporary Turkish State by the people of the United Kingdom and like-minded liberal democracies. But not at the expense of historical reality. People from elsewhere in the world have a different perception of the British way. This is a system structured on hierarchy and on privilege, boasting of a monarchy and an aristocracy whose focus on the unity of the United Kingdom is unswerving. The idea that Turkish people should seek to aspire to this will produce little more than a horse laugh.

(2018)

Nobody Can Represent
a Grieving Family

Many years ago a march against racism in Scotland took place in memory of another asylum seeker murdered here, this time in Edinburgh by a gang of white racists. The police and legal authorities had denied the attack was racially motivated, a common response. The march was organised by the Lothian Black Forum, a group formed by black and Asian people and others in solidarity with the struggle.

Around 1,500 people marched that day. Far-right groups were rumoured to be turning up to disrupt things. Such rumours usually fly about. How justified they are is another question. But rumours of this nature help justify a large police presence. Were the cops there to escort and protect the marchers, control and impose order on the marchers, or to show the world who's boss? In this instance attempts at neutrality were soon given the lie. Minutes before the march began police command advised the organisers that this march in memory of Ahmed Shekh,[1] the Somali man murdered in the capital of Scotland by a gang of white racists in 1989, could not go ahead unless certain banners were withdrawn.

People looked about to find the guilty banners. Police command had to point them out. They belonged to local branches of the Transport and General Workers' Union, as I recall, and the schoolteachers' trade union, the Educational Institute of Scotland (EIS). Displayed on the guilty banners were portraits of James Connolly, who was born about a mile from where this march against racism was due to begin. Connolly was one of Scotland's greatest Marxist scholars and political activists, an official of the Irish Transport and General Workers' Union and the first full-time secretary of the Scottish Labour Party.

In a healthy society the memory of such a man would be cherished. Here in Scotland the majority of the population has never heard of him: of those who have the majority are unaware he was Scottish; they presume he was Irish therefore Roman Catholic or Roman Catholic therefore Irish, and attached to the IRA. The police were very clear. The banners were unacceptable.

The local trade unionists were prepared to withdraw their banners on the orders of the police. They left the decision to the organisers. After a brief discussion the organisers of the march returned the decision to the police. If they had a problem with the trade union banners it was up to them what they did about it; they could make their own decision. They were the authorities. The people marching were the people marching. Trade unionists marched under their own branch banners and would not be asked to remove them. Nobody offering support and solidarity in the struggle would be turned away. This was a march against racism, in memory of the Somali refugee murdered by white racists, and if the police wanted to stop the march then that was up to them. The organisers of the march were adamant. There was more discussion. A compromise was reached. The march went ahead and the trade unionists marched with their local branch banners aloft; the compromise was that they marched at the rear.

But I appreciated that compromise. In Scotland, respect for authority is the norm. People are not scared to take the initiative, they just aren't used to it; they tend to do as they are told. On protest marches and demonstrations the police say where they want marchers to march and generally the marchers comply. It rarely occurs to people to say no. If the authorities say to Scotland's radicals, "Go down that street over there instead of this street," then Scotland's radicals tend to go down that street over there instead of this street. If the authorities advise the protesters to keep their voices low and not to blow any whistles, then the protesters behave accordingly and march peacefully, blending with the scenery. And during the march the police stopped individuals from collecting money in cans.

The marchers assembled and the public meeting began. The first speaker was a guest from London. He said hello to everyone. And he meant everyone. He extended his greetings to the police, then extended his greetings even further: he included the ones in plainclothes, he said hello to them too.

Some gasped, some laughed. But it was so essentially political, and bold, and such an aid to the confidence and even self-respect of the people who had come to this anti-racist rally in memory of Ahmed Shekh, the man from Somalia who sought refuge in Scotland and met such a violent death. The white racist murderers escaped justice. More than thirty years on and no one has been charged with the murder.

Professor Gus John was the guest speaker and a veteran in the struggle against racially motivated crime and violation. He was one of the authors and compilers of the Burnage Report in the 1980s, following the killing of a thirteen-year-old schoolboy.[2] The British State authorities were horrified at the outcome of this report. It was not the murder of the Bangladeshi boy in the playground that horrified them, it was the public exposure of the situation in schools. Racism was rampant: the school playgrounds were not the problem; it was the staffrooms and the classrooms of the education authority; it was here the racism was rampant. Once again, it wasn't the racism the authorities found so upsetting, it was the fact that it was being brought to the attention of the public.

People who should have been attuned to what was happening remained in ignorance. This march in Edinburgh took place in 1989, only four years after the end of the miners' strike, after more than a year of struggle and hardship. So much working-class resistance had been battered into submission by British State forces. Special police units and undercover units of the army worked together, backed to the hilt by the legal, the political and media establishment. Now in 1989 when the Scottish police authority tried to block trade unionists from carrying a trade union banner featuring an image of James Connolly, an elite unit of the British Army walked into a lawyer's office in Belfast and shot dead Pat Finucane, a civil rights lawyer. They shot him dead in front of his wife and three children.[3]

Meanwhile campaigns organised in the old-style main-stream tradition mosey along on the assumption that State authorities are in ignorance. Campaigners believe that their task is to put the evidence in front of the proper authorities. Once the authorities realise what is happening they will correct the injustice and do all in their power to alleviate the suffering of the bereaved family. This, of course, is non-sense. The authorities are well aware of the reality. They are manipulating the conditions towards that end, employing law enforcement agencies to ensure that accountability is avoided. Whether or not criminals escape prosecution is not relevant. The primary concern is escaping liability.

Those campaigns are well intentioned but generally they operate as a means to an end. The suffering of the bereaved family becomes a means to that end. The people who speak from the platform deliver a political programme designed by their party strategists. Typically this involves finding a place within government and working to bring about change. Once they succeed in bringing about change, apparently, racism and racial injustice will cease.

It is difficult to avoid sarcasm. It appears that the public must understand that the ways and workings of government are mysterious and only those used to their operations have a hope in hell of altering the process. Of course the human suffering caused by State policies and strategies is a horrible effect of this, and very much regretted by many State officials. It is important to recognise this. People may be doing their level best to avoid all of that. It is important to address the proper authorities. Human suffering and the pursuit of justice are matters dealt with by particular agencies, not all of whom are under direct governmental supervision. These include government agencies and non-government agencies, charities, religious groups and others too. The public should understand that a grasp of these subtleties are of great assistance. This is why people attuned to the workings of government are to be respected and relied upon in certain situations. This is why, at some public meetings and demonstrations organised in mainstream campaigns, a bereaved family might sit with the public while campaign organisers speak "on their behalf."

How is such a thing possible? How can anyone speak on behalf of a family whose child, parent or grandparent has been murdered in a racially motivated attack and who see the police and legal system doing nothing to find and prosecute the killers? Instead of that the grieving families are being treated as hostile witnesses, as enemies, perhaps spied upon by the police authorities?

A different approach may be learned. No one can "represent a grieving family." Nobody can act on our behalf. We are the family, the friends, the community. Any campaign must begin from ourselves. People should know what they are talking about, and be used to talking to people who do not. People will support us; people will be in solidarity with us and will demonstrate alongside us but it must begin from us and be sustained by us. What is reality in this country? What rights do we have? What is possible? Can this be achieved? Are the police and legal authorities entitled to act in this manner? If not then we must challenge them. We have to begin from that. We must say to them that we will not accept it. And we do not accept it. They must account for their actions. They must account for themselves to us. We are not to be represented. Where? The Westminster Parliament? What is that, a joke? A joke at our expense.

The struggle against racism and racial injustice offers an aid to understanding on the operations and the functions of the State. In the United Kingdom people directly engaged in these struggles have a different perspective from the activists of the old-style labour and socialist movement who appear more comfortable offering solidarity to folk in faraway countries. They have failed to learn from black and Asian activists that the struggle against racism and racially motivated crime and violation is a direct effect of imperialism and colonization, and the struggle begins on their own doorstep.

(2019)

The Evidence Provides the Pattern.
The Pattern *Reveals* the Crime.

Genocide is the end of imperialism but the imperialist marches on, unless stopped, so too the racist. Many of those who commit racist crimes trumpet their identity. People are "proud of being white." They want to "stand up and be counted." They are "us," not "them." This has a place in "anti-racist studies" but is of little consequence to those who are targeted in racially motivated crimes. The crucial thing is to stop it happening, not work out why it happens and why it is that the perpetrators commit the crimes.

Murder is the conclusion of the racial harassment of one human being. People who commit aggravated racially motivated crimes will have a history of racist attitudes, racist behaviour and innumerable instances of racist practice. Past activities will include forms of intimidation and provocation.

The authorities use the difficulty of establishing racial motivation in these crimes to deny the evidence that will reveal it. When the evidence is not allowed the crime cannot be established. The authorities dismiss the evidence and deny the crime. If a crime did take place it was another crime altogether. It may well have been murder but not racially motivated.

Families see the police failing to investigate crimes properly and are forced to seek evidence on their own initiative. They discover indisputable evidence of racist behaviour and racist practises by the criminal. They find previous racially motivated crimes committed by the suspect. They find this being dismissed by the authorities as circumstantial. And when the family tries to reveal the evidence publicly, the authorities threaten to charge them with breaking the law. The family are said to be interfering with the case such as to prejudice the outcome.

In the United Kingdom "the struggle to get such attacks accepted as racial only succeeded after 1981."[1] That was in the wake of the New Cross Massacre in London, when "the lives of 13 black youths, all between the ages of 15 and 20 years old, were snuffed out on Sunday 18th January 1981 by [what appeared to be] a racist fire-bomb." An action committee was formed and immediately organised a "protest against the racial massacre, the indifference of the government and the media, and the inadequacy and bias of the police investigation." The families of the dead and their friends and supporters had to fight all the way to stop the "police and coroner [proving] that the massacre had *not* been the result of a racist attack."

That last sentence has to be read twice. The campaign itself succeeded to the extent that the coroner was obliged to return an open verdict. It is an indictment of the British State and it continues to stand guilty, in 2021, forty years after the outrage, "not a single person has been charged and brought to account."

Kuldip Singh Sekhon was a father of seven daughters aged ten and under and he was murdered in the most savage of attacks.[2] He drove taxis part-time in the evenings and worked the days full-time at Heathrow Airport, one of the legions of low-paid workers. The post-mortem revealed he had been stabbed fifty-eight times. His money and gold watch were still there when his body was found. His killer was a known racist and had been convicted of racially motivated crime in the past. Before this man came to trial the Sekhon Family Support Group stated that the killing would be "shorn of any racial motivation."[3] They were castigated for this by the police. Yet it proved to be the case.

The Detective Superintendent who led the investigation in West London was fully convinced, right from the very beginning, that the attack was not racist. How was such a thing possible? The statement he made was a curious jumble of elitist prejudice and general ignorance:

> Racial motivation was never a factor, right from the start. If I had found one piece of evidence, I would have investigated it to the hilt…. Let's be honest, ninety per cent of kids like him in that sort of area are going to be racist. They're not of high intelligence, they're poorly educated, ignorant of the history of ethnic minorities in this country and the emergence of a multiracial community. It wouldn't surprise me if he was a racist.[4]

What it amounts to is an *a priori* denial of racial motivation as a material factor at all. This is what the police investigation team have "ruled out right from the start"? "If I had found one piece of evidence," said the Detective Superintendent, that might have suggested the possibility of "racial motivation."

The killer of the man was known to the police. He was identified as a white racist within the local community. Now he had stabbed to death an Asian man. Fifty-eight times he struck into him with a knife. He did not rob him of his night's takings or of his gold watch. He stole none of the dead man's personal belongings. The police and legal authorities accepted that the killer "in all probability" was a racist but this had no bearing on the crime.

How was such a thing possible? Forget the reprehensible ignorance and elitist prejudice of the Detective Superintendent, the easy equation of education with intelligence, of education with non-racism. The incidences and occurrences of racist behaviour were everywhere, all the evidence of racially motivated harassment. He already had been convicted of racially motivated crime, known to be involved in other racially motivated abuse. Now, finally, he had killed a member of the race he was known to hate. But none of it had a bearing, as far as the authorities were concerned. Neither the police nor the judge saw it as relevant.

Every human being who dies at the hands of racists has been at the receiving end of innumerable incidences of racially motivated assault and behaviour which have gone unrecorded, rarely witnessed, never punished. Examples of racially motivated activity include spitting at people in public, shoving excrement into their bags and coat pockets; name-calling in the street, elbowing elderly people in a shop queue; stamping on the home ceiling, kicking the bedroom walls where children sleep; blaring the volume of television and music centres; pushing lighted newspapers through letter boxes; slapping babies in prams; urinating on doorsteps; knocking over elderly women on the pavement, beating up elderly men, sexually abusing girls; attacking solitary young people at bus stops, smashing up stores and gang-shoplifting; driving towards groups of people and forcing them to jump to safety.

Many of these incidents if taken in isolation are not classified as crimes at all. If they are in breach of any law it will be "civil" rather than "criminal." The crucial factor here is that in civil law the person who suffers the outrage must prove the case against the perpetrator. This becomes a horror in itself. Victims are confronted immediately by an inquisitorial procedure that can hardly be other than hostile: Prove to us that these occurrences have happened, says the official. Prove to us that such occurrences are racially motivated. Prove to us that the perpetrator is racially motivated.

Why do you think that you are being abused? There are two sides to every story, say the officials. Why do you think the negative behaviour exhibited towards you and your family is racially motivated? Are you sure it wasn't a disagreement between neighbours? What do these people you describe as racist thugs have to say about you? What you call racist abuse may be incidents between two sets of feuding neighbours.

Have you considered that? Are you sure it wasn't a misunder-
standing? You are new to our culture and don't know much
English. Perhaps if your neighbours knew you better these
misunderstandings would not occur. Show them your presence is not a threat, say the officials. Is it tea you people drink?
Why not invite them in for a cuppa.

No civilised society should stand for any of it. In the United
Kingdom minorities have been putting up with it for generations. Survivors of the vilest forms of racial harassment have
had to convince authority that crimes have been committed
against them. If the police are allowed the benefit of the doubt
then, clearly, they fail to grasp the nature of the crime. What
is harassment? Police officers look for one particular incident.
They fail to grasp that harassment is not one particular incident or occurrence at all, it is a *set* of incidents and occurrences.
This *set* consists of an indefinite range of actions and activities,
ranging from civil disagreements through pitiless bullying to
the worst criminal activities. The crime is racially motivated
harassment. The evidence provides the pattern. The pattern
reveals the crime.

Two months after the murder of Kuldip Singh Sekhon a
day of remembrance took place. It had taken that length of time
for the authorities to release the body to the bereaved family,
and by then it had decomposed badly. No proper respect or
consideration was accorded at a point when such a thing was
possible. Instead was that typical sense of hostility underlying the British State's attitude towards the victims of racially
motivated violation. Nevertheless the family of Kuldip Singh
Sekhon were within their religious tradition and tended to
that as best they could. The coffin remained open during the
period of mourning. Many of Kuldip's former work colleagues
came along. Every shop along Southall main street closed as a
mark of respect.

The Monitoring Group had coordinated the Sekhon
Family Support Group. In the days following Suresh Grover

"was informed by a number of local labour councillors that an intelligence report was being compiled on the Group by local police."[5]

There was nothing new in that. All the police authority had to do was check through their own filing cabinets and data bank. A year earlier the Metropolitan Police had branded the Monitoring Group "a pernicious organisation spewing out lies and propaganda in pursuance of their own ideological aims."[6] This was when they were supporting yet another family who were suffering the vilest racial harassment. No support was being given to this family by the authorities and they were being called upon to account for their lack of action.

In April 1989 a benefit night was held on behalf of Kuldip Singh Sekhon's family. This day had an additional significance. It marked the tenth anniversary of the killing of Blair Peach. The Monitoring Group had come into existence and developed from the campaign to bring his killers to justice.

The extreme hostility of the Metropolitan Police towards the Southall activists derived from that. It was not because the Monitoring Group were accusing the police of not doing their job. It was because the killers of Blair Peach were police officers. His murderers were members of another elite unit. This one wasn't a clandestine formation of the British Army; it was one working for the Metropolitan Police.

(1993)

Pernicious Fabrications

A movement of the authoritarian right had been in place in both the US and UK from the 1960s. In the UK, the victory of the 1979 Tory government set the conditions for its consolidation. All manner of nazis, racists and fascists crept out of the woodwork. Each time the brutality of the police entered the public domain the wider British public were witnessing what minorities were having to confront on a regular basis. The affairs of the Special Patrol Group (SPG), a so-called elite unit of the Metropolitan Police, were laid bare for public scrutiny. Although formed in the mid-1960s it was not until "1973 the public first really became aware of [its] existence when two young Pakistani men, holding toy guns, demonstrated at India House and were shot dead." This was an extraordinary response by a unit of London's Metropolitan Police.

Further "community concerns [were raised] throughout the 1970s: around, for example, raids on the Mangrove restaurant and Metro club in Notting Hill, [then] about mass operations in Lewisham ... over a spate of 'muggings.'" By 1975 the SPG had stopped 65,628 people, of whom only 4,125 were arrested. Even so the "complaints came from within the Black community.... No one [else] was really prepared to listen."[1]

How to criminalise a people in one fell swoop. "65,628 people [stopped] to arrest only 4,125." Black communities were well-versed in that, so too certain other minorities. The shift to military-style policing had begun, noticeably, from the end of the 1960s. Then in 1969 the British Army invaded one of its own so-called countries and committed another atrocity, this time targeting a large section of its own population. In Northern Ireland, in August 1971, the British Army shot dead nine innocent people and were directly responsible for two more deaths related to the incident.[2]

During that same month in England the Metropolitan Police authority sent in 500 police and sundry plainclothes operatives to deal with a demonstration by 150 black people in the heart of London. Here was another case where an incident condemned for an "over-reaction" may be construed as more than that. The black community was being taught a lesson.

The demonstration was to protest "long-term police harassment of the popular Mangrove Restaurant [and] led to nine arrests and 29 charges [ranging] from making an affray, incitement to riot, assaulting a policeman, to having an offensive weapon." Only minor charges were brought against the nine and five were "completely acquitted."

The trial lasted two months, but "the case made legal history when it delivered the first judicial acknowledgement of 'evidence of racial hatred' in the Metropolitan police force."[3] The State authorities retaliated. They sought and found an excuse to finish off the owner altogether. They barred him from entering his own restaurant—a restaurant whose customers had included internationally renowned figures "such as Bob Marley, Nina Simone, Sammy Davis Jr., Diana Ross, Marvin Gaye, Jimi Hendrix ..."[4]

The Metropolitan Police had taught the public yet another lesson. How many were required before a proper appraisal was made of the situation?

Before her 1979 election Prime Minister Margaret Thatcher had wanted to give a speech to the Tory Party in which she referred to the Labour Party as "the enemy within." She was advised against it by some of the wiser heads. In other chambers of the Westminster Parliament the reaction to this nonsense ranged from muffled chortles to outright guffaws. But there were many within the upper reaches of the British State who agreed with her assessment. She was giving voice to the considered opinion of the authoritarian right. This group had gained control of the Tory Party.

One of her early advisors on State security was Brian Crozier, director and founder member of the Institute for the Study of Conflict, an operation part funded by the CIA.[5] Crozier prided himself on being confidant and advisor to both Margaret Thatcher and Ronald Reagan. He gave his assessment of the situation:

> The problem was subversion: the deliberate undermining of the State and society. Subversion is an insidious man-made disease, a creeping paralysis in which the State's defensive organs are invaded and neutralized, until they cease to function: the political equivalent to AIDS. In Britain, as in other affected countries, the ultimate aim was to turn the country into a "people's democracy" on the East European model.... In Britain ... the Labour Party had been largely taken over by the subversive Left. Many other areas of life were affected: the schools and universities, the media, the Churches.[6]

This was consistent with Margaret Thatcher's own opinions, expressed at a meeting with her and other members of another far-right formation, the Freedom Association. The "enemy within" embraced all manner of people and communities within the United Kingdom. Anyone at all had become suspect, particularly those who refused to hide their beliefs and put justice and truth to the fore.

Under her leadership of the Tory Party and from before, during the 1960s, all manner of slimy far-right creatures were escaping the can, wriggling and sniffing their way around. By the late 1970s the Tory Party had moved so far to the right that it won most all of the votes reserved for fascists, ultra-nationalists, white supremacists, neo-nazis and others of that ilk.

In May of 1979 a General Election was scheduled. Mainstream political parties were canvassing across the United Kingdom. A group of racists had formed a party known as the National Front (NF) and registered officially to take part in the process. This gave the appearance of political legitimacy. If unchallenged it allowed the racists to engage in further behaviour of the worst sort. All of it might have been recorded towards the crime of "racially motivated harassment." This was during the last days of a Labour government. The Labour Party easily could have confronted the NF by denying them the use of a meeting room at the local town hall. But they lacked the will for that. They preferred not to antagonise the populist right-wing vote. Already they had shown their lack of fight and willingness to mollify the racists with the introduction of anti-immigrant legislation. Now, two weeks before the General Election, they permitted the white supremacists to travel to Southall and host a public meeting at the town hall.

Clearly, the NF had chosen the location deliberately, as a provocation. It was left to the people of Southall to express their outrage.[7] They organised a demonstration in the town centre. They discussed the matter with the local police authority and appeared to have reached an understanding. But on the day itself those discussions were ignored. The Metropolitan Police invaded Southall as an army; they occupied the town in an almighty show of strength:

> 2,756 police, including Special Patrol Group Units, with horses, dogs, vans, riot shields and a helicopter [were] sent to crush the protestors.... The evidence of hundreds of eye-witnesses shows that by late afternoon the police ... went berserk. Police vans were driven straight at crowds of people, and when they scattered and ran, officers charged after them, hitting out at a random ...

"hitting people over the head with truncheons." "Police horsemen were charging [using] their long batons to hit people." A Daily Telegraph reporter saw "several dozen crying, screaming coloured demonstrators ... dragged bodily ... to the police station. Nearly every demonstrator ... had blood flowing from some sort of injury; some were doubled up in pain. Women and men were crying."[8]

And a man was killed by one "immense blow to the head."[9] The dead man was Blair Peach, a schoolteacher from New Zealand then working in England.

The day after the funeral of Blair Peach, in 1979, an admission was voiced by the Commissioner of the Metropolitan Police at a press conference that is quite shocking. He told a black man, a newspaper reporter, that he understood "the concern of your people. But if you keep off the streets of London and behave yourselves you won't have the SPG [Special Patrol Group] to worry about."[10]

Commissioner McNee might have been expected to be back walking the beat by the following day. His statement is a confession that black people are identified as a target by the Metropolitan Police authority. Not only are "you people" targeted by elite units such as the Special Patrol Group, but I—a Commissioner of the Police—am not in a position to stop them.

Sir David McNee was advising the public that he was not in command of the elite unit who killed Blair Peach. This was an elite unit working inside his own command but who was not subject to it. If he was not in command who was? If the person on the topmost rung of the ladder cannot stop them then who can? Is the elite unit "out of control"? Or is there another ladder? Is the chain of command of the police authority contained within an even higher ladder? Perhaps in the newer military-style policing that occurred in Southall there was a greater point of command than the police authority.

The black communities of the United Kingdom had been warned yet again, this time in person by the Commissioner of the Metropolitan Police: Stay home or go home. An additional warning had been issued to anyone from the white communities with a similar impulse to freedom, truth and justice as had Blair Peach: resist empathy, avoid public expressions of solidarity. Racists had free rein. So too had fascists.

Keep off the street and out of sight. Don't be here. If you are not here you won't be killed. Only you, the potential victim, can stop them. You do this through your absence. As long as you are absent from the streets of London you have nothing to fear. As long as you are absent from the premises when the special unit dealing with immigrants appear you will not face accidental death, death by misadventure, or being killed unlawfully. If violence and horrors are perpetrated upon you and your people you should not expect protection under the law or that the criminal perpetrators will be brought to account. Yes, indeed, "we" have a democracy but "you" belong to "them" and are excluded.

In discussing the press conference statement by Sir David McNee a most significant factor appears to have been ignored by most everybody: Blair Peach was white, not black.

When the Commissioner of the Metropolitan Police referred to a far more "dangerous enemy" than "black people," he was outlining the basic position of the British State. This enemy embraced black people, Asian people, any minority people, and moved even more widely than that. The enemy are those who defy the State. People who commit to the sanctity of humanity, of all human beings, regardless of so-called difference, are the enemy.

Forty years later and there are people in Southall who have never forgotten the schoolteacher from New Zealand who happened to be working in England, and came in solidarity with the struggle against racism, and lost his life in the process.

The death provoked a massive wave of public sympathy, *much from within the community itself*. Just days after the death, ten thousand people marched silently past the spot where Blair had been struck down; in June, eight thousand people mourned his passing as his body lay in state at the Dominion Theatre; thousands were later to attend his funeral in East London. And June 1979 also saw a 2,000-strong first Black people's march against state harassment through central London.[11]

But what response followed the "massive wave of public sympathy"? Outside of the minority communities did change occur? In what way did the State's ruthless attacks on minorities affect the mainstream left?

The General Election had taken place the month before, where the National Front "contested the largest number of seats of any insurgent party since Labour in 1918. Nevertheless [although they] 'flopped dismally'" the NF membership didn't go away and undergo a miraculous conversion to the cause of humanity: they helped vote in the Tory Party, content to go along with the new leader, Margaret Thatcher.[12] All sorts of racists, neo-fascists and extreme right factions seemed to have found a home, controlled by who knows, and open to who knows.

(2020)

A Notorious Case

Stephen Lawrence was murdered in April 1993. Once again the racism at the heart of the British State was revealed. The family campaign for justice demonstrated beyond reasonable doubt that racism is institutionalised within the United Kingdom and permeates through every department of the British State. Prejudicial attitudes and behaviour towards people of other races and ethnicities begins from notions of "them" and "us" and are woven into the fabric of bureaucratic policy and strategy.

This case has become notorious. Its notoriety derives not by the brutality and cowardice of the murderous attack on Stephen but by the practices of the British State. There is no doubt that the police and legal authorities set out to deny justice to the family of the dead youth.

Stephen had been standing at a bus stop with his pal. Five youths around the same age group as himself were passing by. His pal managed to escape but they attacked and murdered Stephen. "Within the first twenty four hours" four of the five killers were named and identified as "very dangerous knife users" in a list passed to the police. The name of the fifth came later. Additional information implicated the five in many other racist assaults, marked by aggravated violence and further stabbings.[1] A later video of the five showed the extent of the youths' knowledge of how to stab a human being to cause the maximum damage.

When the investigation began the police spent much of their time checking out the Lawrence family and their friends, and anyone else who visited. The police investigation would have revealed that members of the five were linked to at least one other killing. Four days passed from the time of the murder before the police visited any of them. If they had followed up the trails when they received the information it is probable that they would have found relevant evidence. The murderers had time to destroy any evidence they thought appropriate.

This need not have occurred by intention. There are a number of factors that might be examined here other than supreme inefficiency. These include the workings of individual police officers known to have had links to the wider families of the five, at least two of whom were gangsters and dangerous people. The police might all have been racist. There are other possibilities and a few more could be dredged up as required. One answer is not an answer but worth stating anyway, that there was no one cause. Various factors were at work.

The one fact established clearly by the existence of the Lawrence family campaign in the early years, 1993–96, was its necessity. Without this there was nothing. Without the will to pursue justice there was nothing. Without the commitment to that there was nothing.

Without the family there was no campaign. One of the few things left to a bereaved family in the circumstances is the idea of justice: small consolation but something. Those who committed the crime should be brought to trial and made to account for it. The horror should be revealed to the public. People are encouraged in the belief that justice will occur in the course of events, that the authorities will see to it, that they will recognise the wrong, then correct it.

A few weeks after the murder Stephen's parents were photographed in the company of Nelson Mandela. People were surprised. Why had Mandela taken the trouble? What had a killing on a London street got to do with a fascist regime in

South Africa? It was an expression of solidarity. Mandela was expressing solidarity with the parents of Stephen Lawrence.

In the United Kingdom solidarity is not encouraged. Among workers the authorities have dealt with solidarity as they would a contagious disease. The essence of solidarity is empathy. Human beings stand together in the face of tragedy and gain succour and support from one another. A man from South Africa could express this. Within the UK such could not be taken for granted. Already there were rumours that all was not as it seemed with the police investigation.

The image of Mandela with Stephen's parents confirmed that justice does not occur of its own accord. If justice is to be served then prepare for a struggle, and prepare for the worst. This is your struggle: take care where you place your trust.

Mandela was making a statement about being black in a white racist society. There was more to it. His fight was against other forms of tyranny. This was about being human: having people close to you violated, attacked and killed, and having to come to terms that the only justice you will receive is when those in power are left with no option.

Mandela could not have been more clear than he was back in 1964, when he delivered his "speech from the dock": his fight was against both white and black domination. Race was not the issue, it was justice, it was humanity: the rights of people, of human beings. He and his comrades had fought against fascism and for the liberation of their country. This was why they had been imprisoned, twenty-five years earlier. People across the globe could quote sections of his "speech from the dock":

> I have fought against white domination, and I have fought against black domination. I have cherished the ideal of a democratic and free society in which all persons live together in harmony and with equal opportunities. It is an ideal which I hope to live for and to achieve. But if needs be, it is an ideal for which I am prepared to die.[2]

Justice is a concession. The State never concedes, not without a fight, not until the bitter end. Everything about that image would have induced hostility from sections of the British State. Twenty-five years in prison? They would have let him rot, and his comrades too. The British State produced its own heroes. Margaret Thatcher recently had retired. The UK public were encouraged to picture "Maggie" with fond affection, as a sort of stern auntie who had no time for sloppy tradesmen and always got the work done. Thatcher was the popular image of a ruthless authoritarian State and marked its progress from the mid-1970s, when she became leader of the Tory Party. She labelled Mandela a terrorist.

A few weeks after Nelson Mandela's meeting with the parents of the dead youth the five white suspects were arrested and two of them charged. A couple of weeks later the charges were dropped and all five were released "through lack of evidence."[3] This was July 1993. The Metropolitan Police "refused to comment ... but said 'the murder hunt will continue.'"[4]

What is the meaning of "murder hunt" in these circumstances? There were no other suspects. What might the police do now that they hadn't done in the first place? (And why hadn't they done it in the first place?)

No matter, the family were left to get on with it all. Their son had been stabbed to death by a gang of five notorious racists who didn't bother to conceal their contempt for the legal process and later were filmed laughing together. Their contempt was proving justified. Following their release their criminal activities continued, including serious criminal harassment of black and Asian people.

The family had received support from people and from left-wing groups but much of this proved a hindrance. Some were attached to political parties who believe that the essence of the struggle for justice by one family is securing justice for all families. The immediate trouble with this is how it leaves the family behind while marching ever onward. The family discovers eventually that by the time justice exists they will have long gone. The death of their son is no longer the primary factor and their pursuit of justice has been transformed into the means to an end. The Lawrence family had been abandoned by the State authorities but political support of that sort can be worse than useless—it damages the campaign.

In the autumn of 1993 came an offer of support from the Monitoring Group of Southall. The Monitoring Group was not based or aligned with any political party. It had been "established in the early 1980s by community campaigners and lawyers who wished to challenge the growth of racism in the locality."[5] There were no worries on motivation or the idea that the family came second to the struggle. Without the family there was no campaign.

From the earliest days the police had begun seeking ways to discredit the family and their supporters. The timing is important. This was *before* their involvement with the Monitoring Group. If the hostility to the family had begun afterwards it would have been predictable. Only five years earlier the Metropolitan Police had branded the Monitoring Group "a pernicious organisation spewing out lies and propaganda in pursuance of their own ideological aims."[6]

The Monitoring Group has been one of the leading anti-racist, human rights groups in England at least since the early 1980s. Their work begins from the individuals and families who have suffered the pains and consequences of racially motivated crime and have had "to go public" not only to obtain justice but protection. The work of the police includes protecting the public. Or does it?

Some see the existence of such human rights agencies as a criticism of the police and legal authorities. And that is what they are. Most every campaign is a criticism. If justice existed of its own accord there would be no need to fight for it. Some of that may explain the hostility of the Metropolitan Police but not all, and why in such lurid terms? This is the language of the authoritarian right. It is the kind of stuff we expect to see quoted in leaflets put out by neo-fascists and nazis, white supremacists.

When the five white murderers of their son had just been released and all charges against them had been dropped the inference was that if the Lawrence family didn't like it, why didn't they go home. Except, of course, this is where they were: London was their home. The British State had waved farewell but the family were still there. No doubt behind closed doors other questions had been raised. Where was their place of origin anyway? Were they entitled to be here? And what about Stephen, was he the argumentative type? He looked like a strong boy, did he go looking for a fight? What exactly was his attitude? And what about that so-called friend of his who was supposed to have witnessed the attack at first hand, what was his background ... and so on and so forth.

The inquest on Stephen's death had been fixed by the Crown Prosecution Service (CPS) for December 1993. By this time Mike Mansfield QC was part of the family's legal team, all working pro bono. They asked that the inquest be postponed on the grounds that new evidence had been discovered. The request was granted. In April 1994 they presented the CPS authority with new evidence to consider for a prosecution of the five murderers but the CPS rejected it.

The campaign group continued building the case amid discussions with the family and legal team. Eventually they thought their evidence strong enough to bring three of the five murderers to trial.

In September 1994 they launched a private prosecution for murder. They set out to do what the British State had failed to do: prosecute the guilty. "Unlike the CPS ... their legal team [would] mount an 'enlightened prosecution,' respecting the rules of evidence and the right to be considered innocent until proven guilty."[7]

This was an immediate challenge. It meant that in the opinion of the family the CPS, the State legal authority, had failed to mount an "enlightened prosecution." And if it was "unenlightened" then it was not fit for purpose. So why was it happening? Did the CPS not know what they were doing? That was not possible. They knew what to do but were not doing it. It did not matter the reason, not at this stage. There was the other part of the statement by the Lawrence family, that the State legal authority did not "respect the rules of evidence." They could not be clearer. The CPS had disregarded "the rules of evidence." Again, it did not matter the reason, not at this stage.

The basic fact shines through: the bereaved family was on one side and the British State was on the other. Why would the British State seek to deny a family justice for the murder of their son?

The next stage in the campaign was the Committal Proceedings, scheduled for August 1995, inside Belmarsh Prison, the top-level security prison in England.[8] It was the job of the family legal team to show the authorities that the evidence they had gathered was enough to convict the three men. This was not the trial. Their job was to show that a conviction could happen, all things being equal, that the evidence gathered was sufficient to make the case against the three men.

The authorities accepted that all of the evidence gathered and presented by the legal team was sufficient to bring the three murderers to trial. The date was fixed for April 1996, and to be heard at the Old Bailey.

But at the Old Bailey the family's case "collapsed after identification [and other crucial] evidence [were] ruled inadmissible." Some of what was now being called "inadmissible" had already been presented and accepted at the earlier Committal Proceedings. Other evidence provided damning evidence of the physical lengths of violence the five were prepared to go in expression of racism. This was kept from the jury. When the jury appeared the judge advised them that they "had a duty" to find the three "not guilty." And so they did. The double-jeopardy ruling was then in operation. It meant the three of the five could never again be tried for the crime.

Information on this and related areas are available online and through the writings of the people closest to it, namely the Lawrence family and their legal team.[9]

The defence casework, decisions and findings of the State's legal authority now made sense of all the police time spent sorting through the family and friends of the family. Their primary intention was to discredit potential witnesses, avoid the discovery of incriminating evidence and ignore utterly the criminal forms of racial harassment previously carried out by the gang.

Now four years after the murder of Stephen Lawrence the five white murderers were still walking free, although everybody knew who they were. The inquest took place in February 1997. The jury found that he "was unlawfully killed in a completely unprovoked racist attack by five white youths."

From this point the family campaign altered substantially. The morning after the inquest ended a right-wing populist newspaper led with a front-page spread, complete with photographs of the five youths, calling them "murderers" and with a challenge: "If we are wrong [then] sue us."[10]

The newspaper was the *Daily Mail*, whose typical position on campaigns for justice was to ignore, dismiss, marginalise, undermine or smear them. Their anti-racist stance in this instance was close to unique. It was revealed that the newspaper's involvement had come through the personal intervention of the editor. He had had some building work carried out in his home by Neville Lawrence. This acquaintance led to his personal interest in the case.

There were important turning points in the family campaign and the *Daily Mail*'s intervention had a singular effect. Overnight it became politically safe. In effect the campaign had been highjacked. Prior to this the central issue had been the failure of the authorities to deal with the targeting of black people. Neville Lawrence had stated the position unequivocally: there could be no rest until "the killers and the hidden perpetrators of all racial attacks and murders are brought to justice, and for the whole truth to be known." The *Daily Mail*'s intervention transformed the case into a mainstream mix of morality and law and order.

This focus suited the police and legal authorities. They could agree to everything and do nothing. Of course they would buck up their ideas. Of course killing people is wrong and they would be the first to admit it. Of course crucial evidence should never go missing. Of course time is always of the essence. Of course it is their job to protect the public and in future they would see to it that this would happen. Of course they would like nothing more than to perform at full throttle: unfortunately in times of austerity the police and legal authorities, like all authorities everywhere, are unable to perform miracles.

The very day after the newspaper had published its "challenge" to the racist murderers, the Tory Prime Minister and a number of Tory Party MPs heeded the call for justice. That made it safe for one and all. The establishment could support the family campaign for justice now that it fitted the staple mainstream issues on the merits of "our" police and legal authorities, at the same time managing to occupy the moral high ground.

It is worth noting that a General Election was scheduled several weeks from then. In the event the Tory Party was kicked out anyway. The Labour Party was elected HM Government. It was the party's first time in power since the "landslide victory" which had brought Margaret Thatcher to power eighteen years earlier. The new Home Secretary was Labour MP Jack Straw.[11] One of his earliest actions was to instigate an official inquiry into the killing of Stephen Lawrence.[12] The man selected to lead the team was Sir William Macpherson.[13] The Inquiry became known as the Macpherson Inquiry.[14]

It is of value to note that the Home Secretary was spurred into action not by any personal or party commitment to justice but by the campaigning stance of the *Daily Mail*, with whose editor he was acquainted. Two years after the inquest the report of the Macpherson Inquiry was produced. This was six years after the murder, and with the gang of white racists still walking free.

Any critique of this Inquiry should begin from the beginning. What was it? What was its purpose? The Macpherson Inquiry was a "judicial inquiry into the killing and subsequent investigation—to identify lessons for police in dealing with racially motivated crimes."[15]

These terms of reference presume that black people are at the receiving end of racially motivated crimes, but not that they are being targeted. The purpose of the inquiry is to help the police deal with all racially motivated crime, whether against black people or anyone else. It excludes the fact that some of the very worst racist crimes are committed by police officers. It presumes that police officers are not themselves black. It excludes the fact that black police officers are also victims of racially motivated crime. In later years members of the five white murderers released from police custody to roam the streets battered a black police officer.

Within the terms of reference the primary truth is denied, that the targets of racially motivated crime are black people and minority communities typically defined as black, to include communities from the Middle East, the Indian Subcontinent and also Asia.[16]

According to its terms of reference the Macpherson Inquiry could have succeeded and made no serious impact on the foundational racism of the British State.

Institutional racism and foundational racism are not the same. Foundational racism refers to every State institution, whereas to say that "institutional racism" exists allows other institutions to escape the charge. Institutional racism is a tighter use of the bad-apple, rotten-egg argument but it amounts to little more than that.

Individuals within the police and legal authorities were said to have failed to do their job properly. But what was their job? Perhaps their "job description" was not the same as "doing their duty."

The findings of the Inquiry might or might not help individual police officers "learn from their mistakes." But these same findings would allow upper managerial figures to maximise efficiency within "our" police and "our" CPS authorities. What major lessons can "we" learn? Nothing is essentially wrong with "our" law-and-order programme but more training in race relations would certainly not go amiss. "We" just need to get things right. The tragic death of this young black man is a lesson to "all of us."

The State authorities have become the victims. They need proper resources to provide a proper policing service, more officers recruited, more patrol beats introduced, more squad cars, more training resources to deal with multiculturalism and more multicultural groups recruited into the service.

In the event the Macpherson Inquiry went further than some would have anticipated and the hostile reaction from the right wing indicates this.[17] In 1999 the Home Secretary received the report and was able to advise the Westminster Parliament that

> The conclusions to be drawn from all the evidence in connection with the investigation of Stephen Lawrence's racist murder are clear. There is no doubt that there were fundamental errors. The investigation was marred by a combination of professional incompetence, institutional racism and a failure of leadership by senior officers. A flawed Metropolitan Police review failed to expose these inadequacies. The second investigation could not salvage the faults of the first investigation.[18]

For the various Departments of State it was a case of as you were, but take greater pains in future, and with more discretion. This had been inevitable following the *Daily Mail's* hijack of the campaign. It was not intentional. But if it was, so what. It is pointless to blame the right wing for acting the part.

The Macpherson Inquiry did not "fail" because it did not address the issue, as made clear by its terms of reference. The declaration that one particular State institution, the Metropolitan Police, was racist was certainly of value. People knew this anyway but hearing the political authorities concede the point was worthwhile, even as so-called news.

One direct effect of the Inquiry was the ending of the "double-jeopardy" ruling.[19] This would allow criminals who have escaped a judicial finding of guilt to be retried. In this particular case it pointed the way to a prosecution of the "five white murderers," three of whom were at that time "beyond the law." They were the three brought to trial by the family's private prosecution. When the case broke down through the "inadmissible evidence" ruling the three were not only released from captivity, they could not be re-tried for the same crime. Now that the double-jeopardy ruling had ended, the situation had altered. The Macpherson Inquiry team consolidated this when they described all five of the gang as "white murderers": "We refer to [the gang] as [five white] murderers because that is exactly what they were; young men bent on violence of this sort rarely act on their own. They are cowards and need the support of at least a small group in order to bolster their actions. There is little doubt that all [five] would have been held to be responsible for the murder had they been in court together with viable evidence against them."[20]

They stated the case unconditionally. These five men are murderers: why are they free? From now on there is no double-jeopardy ruling. So prosecute and convict them, they are guilty, lock them up.

It seemed straightforward that within the United Kingdom the Macpherson Inquiry was a major step forwards. If so, and how significant a step, are questions for racial, ethnic and other minorities. But if it was straightforward why did it take thirteen more years to convict anyone of the murder? Even then, only two of the "five white murderers" were prosecuted. For many people that sums it up.

The report of the Macpherson Inquiry was produced in 1999 and the Home Secretary was able to deliver to the British State what its authorities wanted to hear: further action may be called upon, on the other hand it may not.

For black people there never was any "double-jeopardy" ruling in the first place. Every time they stepped outside the house they were on trial. Everywhere they went they had to prove their right not to be punished, to justify their presence, to demonstrate their innocence. What was the crime? Difference was the crime. People were guilty of being black. "Black" signified race. Their crime was racial difference. The so-called sus law was an aspect of this. The law here was manipulated by police officers to target whoever they wanted. But that was only an aspect; the British State had tougher stuff than that already in place, it just wasn't examined. The concept "institutional racism" let them off the hook.

In 2012, nineteen years after the murder of Stephen Lawrence, the forces of law and order finally convicted two of the "five white murderers." This was fifteen years after the inquest, when the "full might" of the establishment entered a campaign for justice now led by a right-wing daily newspaper. This "full might" embraced a Tory Prime Minister backed by all kinds of mainstream politicians and just about all of the mainstream media. It included the report of a team of investigators pushed into action by a Labour Party Home Secretary, on behalf of HM Government and led by an actual hereditary peer. Macpherson was a genuine aristocrat: the twenty-seventh Chief of Clan Macpherson. Major pressure was being brought to bear on established authority. Even so, the British State avoided doing anything for another fifteen years. Then the *Daily Mail*, as right-wing and reactionary as ever, was able to headline the fallacy "Stephen Lawrence's Killers Finally Brought to Justice."[21]

They basked in the glory, its editor a mainstream hero. And so came the statement that "the two murderers" had been imprisoned, ignoring the fact that there were five of them, and all achieved through the "sheer bloody perseverance and brilliant detective work" of the Metropolitan Police: "British policing at its best is still something to be proud of. It's a glorious day for British justice, which shows that, while mistakes can be made, our judicial system does provide redress for every member of British society, whatever their racial background."[22]

(2021)

Murder in the Line of Duty

The value of campaigning lies in the spread of knowledge and making information available. It is the campaign itself that makes the news. Not the tragedy. There are countless tragedies. The world is full of tragedy. Avoiding tragedy is a daily event for millions of people. This is one good reason why demonstrations, days of protest, benefit events and other shows of solidarity are so important.

The Lawrence family campaign had launched the private prosecution in 1994 and a year later, inside Belmarsh Prison, the Committal Proceedings took place.[1] It was raining heavily on the first day and only three campaign members were allowed into the court at a time. The campaign group erected a marquee tent in the parking area, where they could meet with folk who came along in support. Among them were family and friends of Joy Gardner, who was killed in an act of racist barbarity. The horrific death she suffered was not due to an act of barbarism on a London street; she was killed by the Metropolitan Police in the privacy of her own home, in the presence of her five-year-old son. "At about 7 a.m. on July 28, 1993 [they] broke in to Joy's Topsfield Avenue home, and used force to restrain her."[2] While her five-year-old son Graeme looked on, "she was restrained with handcuffs and leather straps and gagged with a 13-foot length of adhesive tape wrapped around her head. Unable to breathe, she collapsed and suffered brain-damage due to asphyxia. She was placed on life support but died following a cardiac arrest four days later."[3]

Those who knew of the case were revolted. The idea that such bestial treatment might be meted out to another human being is beyond anything most of us can comprehend. Other cases too had come to light. The media was focusing on the murder of Stephen Lawrence but information on others filtered through, in particular the deaths of black people in prisons or in police custody. These were being monitored. In the ten-year period prior to the murder of Joy Gardner there were fifty-two cases where State authorities were directly responsible: fifty-two killings, fifty-two families left bereft, all searching for answers.[4]

Black people were known targets on the street but these killings were the work of State employees. This is what police and prison officers are. British taxpayers pay their wages. The men who killed Joy Gardner were employed within an elite unit known as the Alien Deportation Group. She "died as a result of the restraint methods employed by three officers from [this] secretive police unit that specialised in forcible deportations. Its activities were controlled and authorised by the Home Office and the Home Secretary" who at that time was Michael Howard.[5]

"They say she was 'illegal,'" said Joy's mother, Myra, "but she wasn't illegal. She came here legally, she paid her fare, but she overstayed her time." Later it "emerged that letters warning Joy Gardner of her impending deportation were 'deliberately' delayed so that she had no warning of her removal."[6]

Eventually "three of the police officers involved stood trial for … manslaughter, but were acquitted."[7] The charge of murder would have been more appropriate. These men trussed Joy Gardner like an animal and they did this within the "safety" of her own home. They did it in front of her five-year-old son. This little boy was witnessing his mother being put to death by the British police. What effect has this had on her son? These men who killed her had no evidence to suggest that a woman in early middle age whose underlying medical condition was completely unknown to them might endure and survive such bestial treatment. What sort of constitution would have been necessary to survive it? Joy Gardner endured the treatment but she did not survive it. This was murder. All five men were guilty, those who committed the actions and those who "omitted to act" to stop it from happening.

The atrocity took place in May 1993, which was the same month the charges against the murderers of Stephen Lawrence had been dropped and his "five white murderers" released back into the community.

The British mainstream hero, Margaret Thatcher, had just retired and John Major was the new Tory Prime Minister. The Home Secretary was Michael Howard, a senior politician. Immigration matters were the work of his department. He was there when the Kurdish politician Kani Yılmaz was arrested in 1994, outside the House of Commons, where he had come to speak to Members of Parliament at the express invitation of a Member of Parliament.[8]

The strength of the political bond between the British and Turkish states was revealed when "the London Metropolitan Police announced they were setting up a special team to tackle crime and terrorism in the Kurdish and Turkish communities." Earlier the "head of MI5" had said the Kurds were the "only potential source of 'terrorism' in Britain besides the IRA." Soon after this the authorities used their powers to stop Kani Yılmaz from addressing the MPs and set out to have him extradited. Kurdish folk and their supporters were outraged at the dishonesty and cowardice of HM Government, allowing the Turkish State to dictate the content of meetings inside the Westminster Parliament. When Yılmaz "appeared at Bow Street Magistrates Court" to have the case heard, a protest meeting gathered

> outside the court [and] police in riot gear told protestors
> to take down a banner with a picture of the PKK leader

Abdullah Ocalan. When Kurdish people refused to do so, they were attacked by police using their new long truncheons and dogs. Two Kurds were hospitalised and five arrested and charged with assaulting the police.[9]

These were the "new long truncheons" that the elite units within the Metropolitan Police had been looking for since their murder of Blair Peach. The Special Patrol Group had complained that the truncheons they were issued with officially weren't powerful enough to batter people properly. This was why they had been forced to supply weapons of their own manufacture. Now they had the proper tools for the job, brought in from the USA, where a far more powerful armoury existed to control the population.

At the end of December in the same year a death in police custody took place at the north London police station in Stoke Newington, which was notorious, with an appalling record "of corruption, racism and brutality [which had] seen officers jailed for involvement in drug dealing and even stealing property from corpses." The killing of Shiji Lapite[10] shocked and horrified those who had come to know of it. He had been strangled or asphyxiated following "his arrest by two plain-clothes policemen":

> At the inquest officers admitted kicking Mr Lapite in the head, biting him and placing him in a neckhold. Pathologists' evidence and post-mortem reports revealed bruising and abrasions to his body, that he had suffered 36 to 45 separate injuries and that his larynx and neck were bruised and a cartilage in his voice-box fractured. Police officers could not explain the disparity in injuries received by Mr Lapite and themselves.... The inquest jury [said] Mr Lapite had been unlawfully killed, demonstrating that they did not believe the police version of events.[11]

The Crown Prosecution Service (CPS) declared that "criminal charges are not to be brought against police officers."[12]

A picket of the police station was organised by Shiji's family, friends and supporters. Members from the Hackney Community Defence Campaign were going to attend the picket in solidarity with the family. This campaigning group had "carried out extensive investigations into corruption at Stoke Newington police station" on previous occasions. The night before they were to join the picket, their own premises in Hackney were broken into and "burgled [and] members suspect that the Special Branch [or MI5] was responsible."[13]

Supporters of campaigns such as these are the enemy. Following the CPS decision that no police officers would be charged or brought to account for the killing of Shiji Lapite the Committee for the Prevention of Torture made its presence known. This committee is

> the European watchdog on torture and degrading treatment which highlights failures in prosecuting and disciplining police officers and others for death or mistreatment of persons across the European Union.... Prompted by three cases, including that of Lapite, in which inquest juries had returned verdicts of unlawful killing but the Crown Prosecution Service (CPS) had decided not to prosecute, [members of the European committee] visited Britain in September 1997. The committee [found that] "it is extremely rare for police officers [in Britain] to be convicted of a criminal offence as a result of an investigation arising out of a complaint. For example, during the year 1996–97, only one Metropolitan Police officer was convicted of a criminal offence as a result of an investigation arising out of a complaint. This should be viewed against an annual number of complaints against that force of between five and six thousand, of which, in recent years, over

two thousand per year have involved allegations of assault."[14]

During this early period in the Lawrence family campaign for justice came another horrific killing of a young black man. This one too was committed by the Metropolitan Police authority. He was battered to death by one of the new truncheons the British State had purchased from US suppliers. He was Brian Douglas. The Metropolitan Police officers gave him a savage beating. After it they left him in a cell for fifteen hours (despite him vomiting and being visited by four doctors). He was taken to hospital, slipped into a coma and died five days later.

> It later emerged he had a fractured skull and damage to his brain stem.... At the inquest [PC] Tuffy said his baton had accidentally slipped when he hit Douglas on the shoulder. Evidence at the inquest said the force of the blow was equivalent to being dropped from 11 times his own height onto his head.[15]

A lie of this nature is particularly significant. This one, that the officer's "baton accidentally slipped," takes the form of a joke. It is inconceivable that such a thing could have happened. He is ironic, taking part in a process he knows not to take seriously. There is an extreme example of this in the video film of the five white murderers of Stephen Lawrence that the court judged to be "inadmissible" in the eventual trial of 1996.[16] It is horrific. The five outdo one another to show the depth of their hatred of Pakistanis and various black people. They know they are being filmed. They know they are escaping justice. There is an irony at play, in a similar vein to PC Tuffy, the police officer and member of another elite unit. Here he is cracking a joke about a situation in which he and his fellows are smashing a man to death.

Of course it indicates the contempt held for the public as well as the legal process. But this reveals more than that. This is a debased and warped human being. The absence of empathy, of any sense of basic humanity, suggests psychopathy, whose "symptoms include shallow affect; lack of empathy, guilt and remorse; irresponsibility; impulsivity; and poor planning and decision-making."[17]

Those who commit, aid and abet these outrages are spurred by a form of reasoning that dehumanises not only the targeted individuals but their sadistic tormentors and killers. These "elite police units" designed to terrorise the public should have a Special Reactive Hospital unit of their own, designed to deal with sadistic psychosis and post-psychotic trauma.

A "consultative meeting" was arranged in Brixton so that matters might be aired between the authorities and the family of Brian Douglas. After the meeting the police were caught making "a clumsy attempt to covertly film" the family as they left the building.

Once again the State authorities decided there was "insufficient evidence to prosecute the officers involved [and] refused consent to disclosure of statements taken by the investigating officers."[18]

Before the end of the year another young black man had died. He was Wayne Douglas (no relation to Brian). Eyewitness reports indicate he was armed with a knife. He was surrounded by fifteen policemen who were screaming at him to "put it down, put it down." Douglas threw the knife to the ground and was then attacked by a number of officers, in an assault described as "beyond belief" by one of several people who witnessed the incident. According to a Police Complaints Authority press release "he was found not breathing" in his cell an hour later. Although the post-mortem revealed that he had died of heart failure, the "inquest into his death showed that he had been held face-down with his hands cuffed behind his back on four separate occasions."[19]

This case sparked off what became known as the Brixton Riots: "Violence was triggered by a standoff between the police and about 100 demonstrators. Witnesses have reported hearing groups of black youths shouting 'Killers, killers' at the police."[20]

The inquest into the death of Stephen Lawrence took place in February 1997. A couple of months before this another black family had been left bereaved by yet another brutal killing. The dead man was Ibrahima Sey, from Gambia, a father of two. He was

> set upon by six to eight officers, one of whom grabbed him in a bear hug from behind while others grabbed his arms and legs so that he was brought down to the ground, and he was then rolled onto his stomach for his hands to be cuffed behind his back … face down on the ground where he seemed to go limp on each occasion while officers continued to hold him down.
>
> On the third attempt to raise him, he was still on his knees, with his hands still cuffed behind his back.… [One] of the officers sprayed him with CS which hit him in a stream around his nose and mouth, and he was seen to lick off the solvent as it dripped down his nose.
>
> Once he was on his feet, his head was pushed down towards his knees so that he was doubled over, with his hands still cuffed behind his back, and in that posture he was walked backwards into the police station until he collapsed in a corridor.[21]

An example of the degradation of the Metropolitan Police authority appeared at the inquest into the death of Ibrahima Sey. A police officer explained how he had swapped the handcuffs he placed on Ibrahima with those of a colleague because he did not want to do the overtime involved in accompanying the prisoner to hospital.

The inquest jury heard how Mr Sey

> was then carried face down and feet first for the rest of the distance into the custody suite where he was placed

face down on the floor with his hands still cuffed behind his back. Some four to six officers continued to hold him down by his head, arms and legs—including two officers with their feet on his legs—for the next 15 minutes or more. It was while he was still restrained in this position that he suddenly became relaxed and, after being checked, was found not to be breathing.

[The] ambulance crew have described their surprise and shock to find Mr Sey still on the floor of the custody area with his hands still cuffed behind his back when he was showing no signs of life whatsoever. They took him to hospital where he was pronounced dead.[22]

The guidelines for using CS gas to poison human beings as a form of restraint are given to the police officers by the Association of Chief Police Officers who draw them up themselves. These guidelines "are not generally available to the public." The public is advised that CS spray is used "primarily for self-defence." There again, it may also be used "to provide officers with a tactical advantage in a violent encounter," as deemed "violent" or appropriate by themselves. They have license to do what it takes, whatever is necessary. Those who have nothing to fear have nothing to fear. Anyone else is in trouble.

The post-mortem "was carried out at 5 pm on the same day in the presence of three pathologists" who were there on behalf of the Coroner, the Police Federation and the Metropolitan Police. The family could have had their own pathologist present to monitor and record the condition of the dead man but the authorities did not advise them of "their right."

The inquest jury into the death of Ibrahima Sey "decided that the nature and the extent of the force used in the restraint was so unreasonable and unnecessary in the circumstances so as to render the death an Unlawful Killing."[23]

I think it was murder. Here is my reasoning: Unless it can be shown that a potential victim who is a human being is not "suffering from asthma, or using other drugs, or subject to restraining techniques which restrict the breathing passages, there is a risk of death."[24] Surely this is another instance where manslaughter is not appropriate? Somebody could escape a charge of manslaughter, but not murder, not in these circumstances.

It wouldn't have mattered anyway: "On 1st October 1998 the Crown Prosecution Service announced that no officers would be charged over the death of Ibrahima Sey, despite the unanimous verdict returned (to a standard of criminal proof) by the inquest jury."[25]

In the 1990s Home Secretary Michael Howard (nowadays Baron Howard of Lympne), who was in charge during the expansion of the British State security system, by means of civilian conscription, forced thousands of State employees to premiss their work on racial difference. They are forced to become racist. They must distinguish one human being from another by virtue of race and skin colouring. That is their job. People of colour are suspect. The burden of proof is on them. They must prove their "innocence," that they are legally entitled to exist in the country. He claimed that "lawful residents in Britain (had) nothing to fear" and in this exhibits a callous disregard for people of "difference."[26] He had to know people would die. He could not have *not known*. Anyone who looks like "them" rather than "us" had become the primary target in matters connected to immigration and the search for asylum. "Difference" being criminalised. Further deaths were now guaranteed, whether on the street or away from the public gaze.

Following the murder of Joy Gardner about the only policy adjustment to have occurred within related matters of State was one that increased the probability that such so-called accidents would occur more frequently. Henceforth the Department of Immigration would not have to call in one of the Metropolitan Police special units to violate, attack and kill human beings; they could do this aspect of their work by themselves.

A range of public-sector workers, including health workers, school teachers, job-centre clerks and ambulance drivers, were "trained to identify illegal immigrants." Trained racist became part of their job description. The British State would pay them to be racist as others are paid to drive buses. Tens of thousands of State employees were expected to stop being a racist at the end of the working day. People were to return to humanity on their way home from work.

The use of stereotyping transforms physical attributes and difference into grounds for suspicion. This prepares the way for the loss of civil rights. Once people can be shown to differ in certain fundamental ways then these rights are in danger. People end up having none. If violence and horrors are perpetrated upon them they have no right to expect protection under the law or that the criminal perpetrators will be brought to account for their actions. This ends in the criminalisation of minorities.

In the identification of illegal immigrants racial origin is the primary piece of evidence as far as State employees are concerned. This most basic point is illustrated at an acute level by the testimony of one State employee in the case of yet another death of yet another black man.[27]

This time the man who was killed was not under any "wanted for questioning" list at all. He had nothing to do with anything except being in the wrong place at the wrong time. The police and immigration officers had gone to a third-storey flat to question somebody else altogether. During the operation this man who had nothing to do with anything fell to his death from the balcony. His name was Joseph Crentsil. This horror might have been predicted when the police officer began his testimony: "he saw 'a black male appear from the toilet.'"

That was all he had to say. Nothing more was necessary. The police officer detained him immediately. Nothing else about this man was required to signal potential crime, other than skin colouring, a physical characteristic so loosely superficial that it cannot be taken seriously, and never would if it had to do with painting the walls of our living room or how we describe a pair of shoes. He would now pass this "black male" over to the immigration authorities to prove that he is not guilty. The policeman had marked the difference: "I saw a black male [and asked] him to wait." The burden of proof is on the person challenged. The "black male" is immediately suspect and guilty until proven otherwise.

Some of the grounds for this appalling state of affairs are laid down by the British State:

> Chapter 46 of the Immigration Services' Operation Enforcement Manual allows officers to question people living in a communal residence other than a named offender to "eliminate them from their enquiries." ... This rule basically allows immigration officers to go on "fishing raids" if they have what they consider to be "reasonable grounds"—to suspect that a person is an immigration offender.
>
> At the time of Joseph [Crentsil's] death, police officers attended all private-address immigration visits because immigration officers did not have powers of arrest. But they do now. Over 80 per cent of immigration officers in London are now arrest-trained.[28]

The Home Office made sure of that. An "arrest-trained" Immigration Officer was now at liberty to collude in future acts of barbarism. They could stop "a black male or female" and ask them to account for their presence in "our" country, to turn out their pockets, to provide ID, to hand over their cellphone, bankers' cards and anything else they liked. Don't worry, says the State: "Lawful residents in Britain will not be affected and have nothing to fear."

This is hypocritical humbug. What of the extreme fear that afflicted Kwanele Siziba to such an extent that she fell to her death while attempting to escape a "summons" intended for her brother-in-law? Here was one woman who was lawfully resident. According to the State she had nothing to fear. But she did fear. It cannot be doubted that this woman did fear. How do we know this? By the very fact that she made this desperate dash to escape the situation. This was *an expression* of fear. There is no other conceivable explanation. On this one case alone the British State stands guilty.

Kwanele Siziba feared. There had to have been something that induced the fear. She was scared, she was scared of something.

It does not matter if that particular "something" merited fear in the eyes of the person who set the lie down on paper, whether a clerk at the Home Office or the Home Secretary himself, Michael Howard. This woman was terrified and she died in her flight to escape.

It is a psychological nonsense to give guidelines on what one person is to fear rather than another. Of course Michael Howard had nothing to fear from the Department of Immigration. How could he have? He was the Home Secretary, he was party to the creation and incorporation of these rules in the first place. He "held Cabinet positions under the governments of Margaret Thatcher and John Major" and is now Lord Howard, "appointed to the Order of Companion of Honour in 2011."[29] More to the point, he was a QC. He should have been prosecuted on a charge of terrorism. Through the work of that one piece of legislation hundreds of thousands of people throughout the United Kingdom have walked in fear, terrified of being in the wrong place at the wrong time, and some have died as a direct effect of this HM Government policy.

Almost all of this information was available to the British Labour Party when they were successful at the 1997 General Election. The only thing they heeded was the front page of a right-wing newspaper. Anthony Blair was the new Prime Minister. He appointed Jack Straw to the Home Office. Both Blair and Straw occupied positions to the right of the right of the right of the centre right of the UK centre mainstream. After serving his time as a parliamentarian it was thought Jack Straw would achieve a move upwards to the House of Lords. This wasn't to be. He remained with the plebs. His time in politics ended in ignominy.[30]

Nevertheless he will be remembered for one intervention from his first year in office. He instigated the Macpherson Inquiry into the killing of Stephen Lawrence and the surrounding events.

A few months later, in 2013, Doreen Lawrence spoke publicly about the corruption within the Metropolitan Police. She "said [how] she was always baffled about why family liaison officers were recording the identities of everyone entering and leaving their household [and] always suspected police had been gathering evidence about her visitors to discredit the family." Her suspicions were borne out by a police officer who admitted his involvement in covert operations against the family. The undercover officer described how he "had come under 'huge and constant pressure' from superiors to 'hunt for disinformation' that might be used to undermine those arguing for a better investigation into the murder [and] revealed how he participated in an operation to spy [and] find 'dirt' [on the family] that could be used against [them]."[31]

The use the legal authorities made of their covert activities was clear when the ruling of "inadmissible evidence" had destroyed the prosecution. The police had targeted Stephen's pal, the youth who had been there alongside him when the five white murderers attacked to such horrific effect. They set out to subvert his credibility, to discredit him as a human being, to undermine and, essentially, destroy his testimony. Instead of pursuing justice the police and CPS pursued every direction they could in order to deny it. They did not fail; they succeeded.

In 2018 Doreen Lawrence called on the authorities to admit that the other three white racists had escaped justice, twenty-eight years after her son was murdered.[32]

The rottenness at the core of the British State remains as before. Racism is more than endemic, it is a method of control, the very foundation of immigration and other social controls, exercised as a weapon twenty-four hours out of every day. A finding of "institutional racism" suited the State. The authorities were left to bring the human resources people into the discussion, make stuff a matter of policy rather than law, and find further methods to manipulate human rights legislation so that "we" gain some more of the ground lost to human rights justice seekers since the end of World War Two, the general humanitarian effects of the Nuremberg Trials.

A significant finding surfaced recently, enough to make a horse laugh, that British State authorities had concealed crucial evidence from the Inquiry team led by Sir William Macpherson. And they concealed it without advising poor old Jack Straw, the Home Secretary, the very man who initiated the Inquiry! It would have been fine to engage in a cover-up, but to do it behind his back! That made him "furious."

The true nature of the British State was now exposed. The explosive piece of "news" was not that the State authorities had concealed crucial evidence[33] but that Jack Straw should have been so angry when he discovered the truth.[34] HM Government is temporary; the British State is permanent. It is difficult to imagine a parliamentarian of his experience being guilty of such naivety. Can there be such a thing as a permanent State authority that will not withhold information from a temporary administration?

Any form of external meddling in the more serious affairs of State is inadvisable in general, and HM Government counts as "external." Even worse when the Labour Party is the Party of Government. The permanent State continues to regard the Labour Party as left-wing, and some go more deeply, that it represents "the enemy within."

(2021)

Arise Ye Torturers-to-the-Crown

What ground exists between the police and the military? Who fills the gap? In particular domestic situations the British State identifies a need for stronger powers than the police. A year after the murder of Blair Peach a siege occurred at the Iranian Embassy. "When the first hostage was shot" Police Commissioner McNee "immediately handed control of the operation to the British Army who deployed the Special Air Service."[1]

The year after that a horror occurred in South London 1981 when around sixty black teenagers attended a girl's sixteenth birthday party. There was a fire and thirteen died. During investigation by the Metropolitan Police, the "line of inquiry into a [racist attack by firebomb] was quickly dropped in favour of a theory that a fight had broken out and that the unruly black youth had caused their own deaths."[2] Soon after this the police were found to be "'forcing statements' out of black youths without lawyers or parents being present."[3] The New Cross Massacre Action Committee was formed as a result. They "declared March 2 [1981], the 'Black People's Day of Action' to demonstrate against the Met's mishandling of the teenagers' deaths."[4]

More than twenty thousand people marched through the city of London that day. It was massive. "Newspapers were hostile [and ran] with headlines such as 'Rampage of a Mob' [*Daily Express*], and 'The Day the Blacks Ran Riot in London' [*The*

Sun]."[5] A second inquest was held in 2004 at which HM Coroner "accepted the fire was started deliberately, but rejected that it was a racist attack [and returned] an open verdict."[6]

At this time of writing, 2021 and forty years later, "[no] one has ever been charged ... and the case remains unsolved." There is good work available online in regard to the tragedy and its aftermath, way beyond the scope of this essay.

John La Rose was Chairperson of the New Cross Massacre Action Committee and many years later he spoke of the day:

> It was something that had not happened since the Chartists, back in the 1830s. People had not marched across London into the City. We had to negotiate with the Police, I would chair the meetings. And that decision came from within the meetings of the Black People's Assembly. People would be saying: "Man we have got to do something about this thing. The Police can not get away with this thing!" That kind of talk went on. And they said, "Yes we'll go on a march." "Where are the guns!" That kind of talk. "We want some guns!" And I said, "Have you heard of a man called Brigadier Kitson, *Low Intensity Operations?*" If you haven't read his book then you should read it. Because if you are talking about going to Parliament with guns you have to take on Kitson." He had been the Commander in Northern Ireland, he was G.O.C. in Britain. I said, "Let's talk seriously, you are starting at the end, let's start at the beginning."[7]

La Rose was familiar with the strategy and methods that Kitson would have brought to any conflict. There would have been no negotiation. The job of the army was the imposition of order, and that was that. The Brigadier Kitson he referred to was

> an archetypical scion of the upper military caste of the British élite. The eldest son of a rear-admiral, he

attended one of England's leading public schools, Stowe, in the mid-1940s, and was head boy of his house. Stowe was an experiment by a leading educationalist, J.F. Roxburgh, to produce a ruling imperial cadre "with the cobwebs brushed off" that was capable of meeting the mounting challenges to the British Empire. Stowe was the second choice for the British ruling class, after Eton.[8]

This was tradition of which Kitson was a part. All of his schooling and university education, his training, his experience and all that he was through his upper class family background, his position within the chain of command, prepared him to exercise anything and everything that he might bring to the role designed for him. Essentially he managed the deployment of assassins. His one and only allegiance was to the role he occupied as a functionary of the Crown.

In 1979 the insight of the *Punjabi Times* reporter could not have expressed the matter more aptly, in the wake of the police occupation of Southall. In that military-style action he had recognised another form of domestic policing, a colonial policing. The reporter had paralleled "the police behaviour with the Jallian-Wala Bagh holocaust … when hundreds of men, women and children attending a peaceful protest meeting were gunned down by the British Army."[9]

These policing methods may have been new to the wider UK public but not to black and Asian communities, those with experience of colonial occupation.

> General Sir Frank Kitson, as he eventually became …
> was a counter insurgency expert and theorist who had
> seen service against the Mau Mau in Kenya, against
> Eoka in Cyprus, against Communist guerrillas in
> Malaya and on behalf of the local Sultan in Oman.[10]

La Rose knew of what the Brigadier was capable, not only through reading his books but his own work on the Committee for the Release of Political Prisoners in Kenya, of which he was a founder member, alongside Ngũgĩ wa Thiong'o. La Rose knew of the barbarism, the devastation and the suffering Kitson and the men under his command had wreaked in the colonies.

In his early career, while a young officer in the British Army, Kitson worked in Kenya alongside the high-ranking Colonial Police Officer Ian Henderson, a notorious torturer. The primary purpose of colonial policing was to break the indigenous population into submission. This would allow the British State to steal whatever they liked in the presence of the local population. In this case the British ruling elite wanted everything, land included. The indigenous people had an alternative: service the invaders or die. Some resisted; they struggled and they fought and they tried to resist the might of the British imperial forces. It was a war to the death. It was freedom or death. This struggle for liberation was described by the British State as "the Mau Mau uprising."

The Colonial Police assisted the Armed Forces in their search for the slightest show of resistance. At least "80,000 of the Kikuyu ethnic group were held in detention camps without trial."[11] Other reports suggest that "hundreds of thousands of people were spread across labour camps and concentration camps."[12] They were humiliated and beaten at the point of entry, stripped, "heads shorn, hit with fists and/or slapped with the open hand." At the first sign of "defiance [or] obstinacy" they were punched and kicked "about the head, stomach, sides and back."

> Witnesses came forward to recount tortures and murders committed throughout the eight-year emergency involving ... white officials and local soldiers under British command. One man says he was castrated and blinded for defying his captors. A woman recalls how her two-year-old child was whipped to death by a white police officer. Women claim that thousands of

civilians—mainly women and children—died of beatings, starvation and disease.[13]

The bestial treatment meted out to the people of Kenya makes difficult reading. This was the place and these the conditions where Frank Kitson gained his earliest and practical experience of destroying the will and resistance of a people so that their country could be stolen in the interests of the British ruling elite. In spite of all there were Kenyan people fighting to defend against the invading forces. The Colonial Police worked with the army to find and destroy them. Under the command of the sadist Ian Henderson, known by the Kikuyu as Torturer-in-Chief, the Colonial Police had developed their own "interrogation tricks [which] included slicing off ears and boring holes in eardrums; pouring paraffin over suspects who were then set alight; flogging suspects until they died; and the burning of eardrums with lighted cigarettes."[14]

Henderson was commanding authority of the Colonial Police when Dedan Kimathi Waciuri was captured. He was a legendary figure, a great hero of the liberation struggle, holding the rank of Field Marshal. He was captured by a policeman called Ndirangu, "a member of the colonial homeguards, considered a traitor working for the colonial Government as a tribal police officer."[15]

Ndirangu told how he chased and shot a man who would not stop when ordered. The man fell. When Ndirangu reached him he saw it was the great hero of his own people. The mark of the man was evident when he asked Ndirangu, "Are you the one who shot me?" When Ndirangu confessed that he was, Dedan Kimathi replied, "Ni wega" (It's okay).

The British State paid Ndirangu a "share of £500" for his capture of the Field Marshal. But for the rest of his life he was treated "like Judas" and his "children [were] outcasts."[16]

The Torturer-in-Chief was nowhere around when Dedan Kimathi was captured. He was in Nairobi having a meal with

Princess Margaret and her white hunters, safari experts, her staff, servants, ladies-in-waiting and her team of faithful retainers; in particular the Colonial Police and a British Army battalion who surrounded the restaurant to ensure their peaceful lunch.[17] One of Kenya's functions was as an adventure playground. "Robust policing" was demanded to safeguard the supremely rich of the British ruling class while they enjoyed the local facilities and resources of colonial life.

In 1952 Princess Elizabeth was en route to the Crown possession of Australia with her husband and stopped off for a break in Kenya when receiving word that her father died—King George VI. They heard the news while "relaxing at a game-viewing lodge, taking cine films of elephants at a nearby watering hole before retiring to their cabin high up in the trees," while watched over by a peace-keeping security force.[18]

Immediately she returned to London with her husband, her servants, staff and faithful retainers. Days later she stepped forward and "formally proclaimed herself Queen and Head of the Commonwealth and Defender of the (Anglican) Faith: 'By the sudden death of my dear father I am called to assume the duties and responsibilities of sovereignty. My heart is too full for me to say more to you today than I shall always work, as my father did throughout his reign, to advance the happiness and prosperity of my peoples, spread as they are all the world over.'" Had her speechwriters resisted using the plural, "peoples," this humbug might have been avoided. They should have referred to the "happiness and prosperity" of her own particular people, the upper reaches of the British ruling class. If so "pernicious" old lefty ideologues like myself would have resisted "spewing out" the truth. But as it was they gave the new Queen a lie of staggering proportions, and she voiced it at her enthronement, within the radioed hearing of millions of people "all the world over."

Queen Elizabeth is a figurehead but she was not attached to the prow of a sailing ship, she was a human being, twenty-five years of age. She and her husband were of adult intelligence and with full use of their sensory powers. It was impossible not to know something of the horrors endured by the people of Kenya. This barbarism, this extreme cruelty, was practised against them in the name of the Crown. Now that she occupied the throne she was the top rung of the Crown. Only God was above her, and the Crown held the copyright to His Word, courtesy of the King James-led translation of the Protestant bible five hundred years earlier.

The British State called Dedan Kimathi "a terrorist [which] allowed the authorities to describe their cowardly murder of the man as an execution."[19] Meanwhile they continued a programme of terror, led by their military wing, under the command of Kitson and his superiors. Whatever was necessary, and more besides. This was a colonizing process of the vilest bestiality and wholesale slaughter such that "the dark shadows of racist-based genocide were becoming ever more obvious."[20]

It was so bad that a General of the occupying army, recently arrived from the UK, was "horrified at [the] indiscriminate shooting" of black people by army units and Colonial Police, some of whom were keeping scores: "recording kills" in competition with one another. Meanwhile "in the bars of Nairobi hotels [men were] swanking about how many Kukes they have 'potted.'"[21]

One "company sergeant-major" admitted that he had been advised by the captain of his battalion that "he could shoot anybody he liked as long as they were black."

This definition of the colonial enemy gets to the nub of it.

Who is the enemy?

Anyone who is "this" is the enemy. It is irrelevant whether "this" is that, that, that or that.

Black = this. It is irrelevant whether "black" is man, woman, babe-in-arms, child, elderly lady in a sickbed, elderly man on crutches.

Black = enemy. It is irrelevant whether this black is an insurgent, a shopkeeper, a farmworker, a student, a terrorist, a schoolteacher or schoolchild. "The practices included a £5 reward for the first sub-unit to kill an insurgent. Mr Frank Kitson, a member of staff, artlessly commented: 'Soon after, three Africans appeared walking down the track towards us: a perfect target. Unfortunately they were policemen.'"[22]

Otherwise Kitson and his "sub-unit" would have murdered the three men. The sole attribute to disqualify a target was their identification as sub-members of the occupying army. "Unfortunately" we should not murder people who wear the uniform of our local Colonial Police and carry out whatever orders we care to give them. These three men were "tribal police officers … colonial homeguards … working for the colonial Government."

Note that Kitson is seen as "artless" by the new commanding officer. He is a young upper-class officer "learning the ropes." He later developed the use of "sub-units" to police the lower-order population of the United Kingdom, beginning with "Northern Ireland."

Rumours of the horrors taking place in Kenya were escaping the net, the State default position of silence, of nothing at all, where by one thing or another no news reaches beyond State control. Eventually, these rumours were so persistent that they surfaced in Her Majesty's Palace of Westminster.

A cross-party delegation of British MPs arrived from the House of Commons. They made the voyage to Her Majesty's colony under the protection of Her Majesty's Armed Forces to discover the truth. Some Labour MPs were among the delegation. Those who voiced concerns or criticism were labelled Communists.[23]

In the later speeches and discussion that took place in Parliament a basic question was raised by one Labour MP as to why were "we" in Kenya in the first place?[24] He relayed the answer himself:

The justification of our presence in [Kenya], as in any other Colony, is that the Kikuyu are irresponsible; that they are people incapable of governing themselves; that they require protection and guidance. It is never for the protector and guide to place the blame for what goes wrong upon the colonial people, any more than it is right that a parent or a schoolmaster should place upon his children the blame for mischief which he ought to have controlled.[25]

This extraordinary statement was made by a member of the Parliamentary Labour Party.

In this instance the Labour MP was an Eton-educated QC: Reginald Thomas Guy Des Voeux Paget, Baron Paget of Northampton, who also "served as junior opposition spokesman for the Royal Navy and the Army."[26] This is not to question the man's integrity. People are not imprisoned by their background. Reginald Paget had broken with family tradition in becoming a member of the Labour Party. Quite a few Labour MPs have had an upper-class background and, like Reginald Paget, many have become QCs. But at that elemental level the one presupposition is the right of the British State to be wherever it lies in its interests to be. This is class interest. The interests of the British State are always those of the ruling elite. They cannot be other than that. This factor binds together Paget and Frank Kitson. Both were from a similar upper-class background, born into parallel levels of the ruling elite; the family background of each touched on aristocracy, particularly in the case of Kitson. He and Reginald Paget moved within the higher circles of the ruling elite. Kitson was a member of the military wing of the British State, Paget of the judiciary. It is the management of "our Colonies" that is the issue, not the right to be there. This was clarified by Paget's earlier statement, which is classical racism, where any race that is not ours is subordinate, is inferior, and that by definition. Paget's vision would have been shared by the vast majority of the Westminster Parliament, including both Houses.

In his role as Queen's Counsel, Reginald Paget defended the German military commander Fritz Erich Georg Eduard von Manstein, a Prussian aristocrat and war criminal. When he gave his speech in the Commons he prefaced his comments on the childlike nature of the Kikuyu by referring to a "wise German commander" who told how "Hitler was always saying to us 'You must make the inhabitants more frightened of you than of the guerillas.'"[27] It was an exemplary comment. This was precisely the end of the practices carried out by the British Armed Forces. These strategies were not learned from Adolf Hitler. It is likely that Hitler learned from the annals of British imperialism.

Paget's client, the aristocratic war criminal, was of the belief "that in order to stop the spread of communism it was necessary to remove the Jews from European society."[28] Eventually he was revealed to have "agreed with Hitler's idea that the war against the Soviet Union was a war to exterminate Judeo-Bolshevism."[29]

The anti-Communist element is crucial. The real threat is always Communism. It is this which draws together the ruling elites, no matter the political or religious opinions professed, nor their country nor culture of origin. In defence of the man who had advocated the "extermination of Judeo-Bolshevism" the Labour MP Reginald Paget described the Soviets as "savages" but "Manstein showed restraint as a 'decent German soldier' in upholding the laws of war."[30]

By the early 1960s the Kenyan people had struggled through the horrors of British State colonial occupation to a form of independence.

Ian Henderson was deported immediately. For his services to the Crown, Queen Elizabeth II honoured him with "the George Medal (1954), the highest award for bravery to non-military personnel, and later the Bar to the George Medal, for suppressing" every attempt the Kenyan people made to resist the atrocities perpetrated against them.[31] He was soon back in business, "installed by the UK government as head of security in Bahrain in 1968 [or 1966] when the country was a British protectorate."[32]

Bahrain became independent in 1971 but the al-Kalifa regime had such a regard for methods employed by Henderson that they kept him in charge for thirty years. He was known for his barbarism. They called him the Butcher of Bahrain. He taught the local security forces the Brit-style methods of torture for use on subversive elements, justice seekers, political dissidents, trade unionists, lefty activists, campaigners and all kinds of potential terrorists. Survivors have described how they were "electrocuted on the genitals, while others were raped by the guards with glass bottles ... hung by the hands and feet 'like animals' and beaten with hard rubber hoses."[33]

For his commitment to the security of his paymasters he was "honoured by the Government of Bahrain with The Order of Bahrain (*Wisam al-Bahrein*) 1st Class (1983) and The Medal of Military Merit (*Wissam al-Khidmat al-Askari*) 1st Class (1982)."[34] In 1984, Her Majesty, the Queen of the United Kingdom, gave him another award: "the OBE."

In the year 2000 Amnesty International advised the British State that "the UK Government, under international law, [had] an obligation to conduct an inquiry into Major-General Henderson's role in the use of torture in Bahrain [which was] a crime against humanity when committed on [such] a widespread or systematic basis."[35] The British State authorities did as recommended; they conducted an inquiry. They then decided that "Britain's Klaus Barbie"[36] should have "no charges filed against him."[37]

In 2002 His Royal Highness the King of Bahrain stepped in to ensure his Butcher should enjoy a peaceful retirement. He granted "amnesty to human rights abuses committed by any

Government officials prior to 2001."[38] That settled any human rights nonsense.

In Bahrain the King controls everything, except his territorial waters presumably, which are ideal for "operational effectiveness in a volatile region." He is a "generous host" to the British Navy and RAF. His "territorial waters" provide a base for another of his overseas friends and protectors: the Fifth Fleet of the US Navy. Meanwhile the Foreign Office, in 2015, confirmed that "The UK is working closely with the Government of Bahrain to provide reform assistance focused on strengthening human rights and the rule of law."[39]

Brigadier Kitson had returned to the United Kingdom following Kenyan independence. He was no longer "artless," he was an expert in his particular field. Her Royal Highness the Queen of the United Kingdom awarded him an additional bar to the MBE he already had, "for exceptional skill and leadership as a Company Commander during jungle operations. By his devotion to duty he attained the virtual elimination of two communist party branches in a difficult area."[40]

His reputation extended elsewhere: "In 1963 he was one of a group of counter-insurgency experts invited to Washington by the Rand Corporation to give advice on how the US should wage the war in Vietnam, then being expanded by President John F Kennedy."[41] The authoritarian right was on the march. Indigenous populations were defending themselves throughout the world. State authorities targeted whoever they could.

One strategy involved definitions: if sections of the populace could be defined along the lines of an enemy of the State, then stuff like rules of law and the rights of civilians and one thing or another might be bypassed and superseded. If that were achieved the State was free to act accordingly.

In 1968 the leader of the UK Tory Party was Edward Heath. He stated the position of the British State: "The primary goal [is] to bring terrorism to an end at the earliest moment, without regard for the inconvenience to the civilian population."[42]

The interesting point here is that when Edward Heath made the declaration he was not the Prime Minister. He did not make his declaration within the House of Commons. He was talking at a closed meeting of upper-level figures: stalwarts of the British State.

In these circles the higher authorities were free to discuss how to assassinate individuals deemed irksome or dangerous. In the British colonies it was straightforward. Killing people was easy. Soldiers looked out the window and shot passersby. At home more care had to be taken. Doors were to be kept closed, where possible, and the legal squad kept on standby.

Discussions of this nature were impossible within the Westminster Parliament. Closed meetings allowed the "practicalities." Individuals who attended those meetings included "key military personnel [and] senior members of the British Cabinet." They shared the view "that it was perfectly legal for the army to shoot somebody whether or not they thought they were being shot at because anyone who obstructed or got in the way of the armed forces was by that very act, the enemy."[43]

Edward Heath did not become Prime Minister until 1970. This followed a protracted period of the destabilisation of HM Government which for the past couple of years had been managed by the Labour Party. The main thrust of the destabilisation process was personal, directed against Prime Minister Harold Wilson by State intelligence operatives, aided by the mainstream media.[44]

Towards the end of the 1960s Brigadier Kitson was seconded to the University of Oxford on a visiting fellowship. The plan was that he pursued his studies and developed his theories on containing, breaking and pacifying the local population. He wrote a book that has become seminal and thanked the "many officers of the British and United States Armies who helped [him] during [his] visits to their various schools, colleges, units and establishments."[45]

He was put to work "testing his theories" on how to deal with domestic populations in quasi-colonial settings, beginning in "Northern Ireland. The duty of an Army is to impose order, not law and order. Whatever was necessary was necessary. The imposition of law and order is the job of the political, police and judicial arms of State." Whatever the theories and whatever the means the end was control: "to contain the republican-nationalist threat" which would be achieved regardless, whether by "terror, manipulation of the rule of law [or by] infiltration and subversion. [This was] core to the Kitson military doctrine endorsed by the British army and the British government at the time."[46]

When the British State settled on its military wing to impose order on "Northern Ireland" the various authorities had to allow them to do their job. It was no good calling in the Armed Forces and tying them up in red tape. The politicians and judiciary had to clear the path. The Armed Forces were ready to resolve the problem but required the appropriate freedom. The military top brass expected their path to be cleared, no repercussions and all advantages to remain intact. Fighting a battle meant killing people. If the political and legal authorities could take care of "the paperwork" then they would do their job. Kitson expressed the opinion that they would have it finished in five years.[47] Brigadier Kitson reminded the authorities of the historical project across the Irish Sea: "Suppression of the Irish [and] the Defence of the Protestant Religion."[48]

West Belfast is where Kitson's theories were first tested on countering the threat of the civilian population: his boys were sent in to the heart of the community, where they murdered and "wounded a large number of [defenceless people] in Ballymurphy in August 1971."[49] That was the immediate effect of Operation Demetrius, the imposition of a strategy designed to capture and imprison the civilian population at will. The massacre was carried out in a clandestine operation. The only witnesses to their atrocities were the military forces and their victims, their families, their community. The army burst in and raided their homes at 0400 hours one morning and "during a 3 day period young and old were shot and beaten as they were dragged from their homes without reason. During this 11 people were brutally murdered" and very many injured.[50]

Months later in December it was followed by another massacre, also in Belfast, this one of fifteen people, in McGurk's Bar, including two children. This was "the greatest loss of civilian life in a single bombing in Ireland since the Nazi Blitz of Belfast, 16 other civilians were injured."[51] The fabrications of the British State suggested that loyalists could not have been involved in the bombing, that it was the work of the IRA or probably the Provisional IRA who had blown up all these Catholics and nationalists by mistake. Then the campaign for justice organised and run by the bereaved families uncovered evidence implicating Brigadier Kitson directly in the cover-up.

By then the Ulster Volunteer Force had been found culpable. Then it was discovered that the Ulster Volunteers, a murder squad, were being issued orders by a special unit created by Kitson. This was the Military Reaction Force (MRF). The MRF were giving the UVF their orders. They controlled the murder squad. The MRF "organised the bombing [of McGurk's Bar] and helped the 'murder-squad' get in and out of the area."[52]

Six months after the bombing of McGurk's Bar, "Kitson's Private Army" continued "testing their theories," this time in Derry City. They murdered fifteen people and injured very many more. Fifteen thousand witnesses had gathered to take part in a civil rights demonstration against the imposition of internment. The massacre took place there and then.

The British State answered their critics concerning the massacre. Their Secretary for "Northern Ireland, Karen Bradley and defence secretary Gavin Williamson [said] that British soldiers in Northern Ireland were 'fulfilling their duties in a dignified and appropriate way,' and should be above the law."[53] This astonishing statement is entirely consistent with the committees referred to earlier, where Edward Heath had looked for ways of killing people without having to worry about any civic consequences. This was confirmed by

> the British Army Chief of the General Staff, Lord Michael Carver [who] admitted he had been urged by the Heath government to allow the British Army to shoot people in the North of Ireland regardless of whether they were armed or not. Heath had been assured by the highest judicial authority, the Lord Chancellor, that such action was totally legal.[54]

Lord Michael Havers wrote the foreword to Kitson's *Low Intensity Operations*. He was Kitson's superior in colonial Africa, as he had been in "Northern Ireland." He was used to killing indigenous people as and when appropriate. These three massacres in the space of a few months were each very different. It was a show of the most extreme barbarism, delivered as a short, sharp lesson to the people of "Northern Ireland." Do as you are told. Keep out of sight. Don't be visible. You are the enemy. If we see you we see the enemy.

Brutality of this nature is a useful tool of the authoritarian right. People from other cultures might have questioned Kitson's sanity but if they had they would have discovered that his superiors were marching to the beat of the same fyfes and drums.

The media were present throughout the massacre on Bloody Sunday. The potential confrontation had been advertised. The British Armed Forces were teaching them all a lesson. Everybody. This was how an army operated. If the State employs an army then this is what happens. The leading figures in the barbarism that took place in the Crown colonies were now at the heart of military affairs in the United Kingdom. Their connections to colonial Africa remined strong. Their friends and former colleagues in the white supremacist, fascist regime of South Africa had come to their aid and "backed loyalist paramilitaries during the 1970s."[55] These links continued into the 1980s and 1990s. When these people saw Mandela standing with the parents of Stephen Lawrence they were seeing the enemy.

The situation in "Northern Ireland" had been open to manipulation in various ways. From the early 1960s "operatives" from there had come and gone "to South Africa and Rhodesia [in] links fostered between shadowy loyalist group Tara and ultra right-wing groups."[56] High-ranking army officers were well aware of this and personally acquainted with the higher echelons of the white supremacist regimes. What else was colonial Kenya? Such links and personal connections were crucial in the work carried out by intelligence agencies.

In the 1960s the serial sex offender William McGrath was allowed to hold the position of "house master at [Kincora], the notorious east Belfast hostel."[57] In Kincora and other care homes of the period child sex offenders were in direct control of young people and children, some as young as ten years of age. McGrath was prominent within the far right: in Loyalist, Orange Lodge and fundamentalist Christian groups. He was also MI5, as were other child sex offenders of the period. This is why it took so long to have him imprisoned—not until 1981.[58]

In 1985 "a senior UDA intelligence officer" was in South Africa "to arrange a huge arms shipment bound for Ulster." He was Brian Nelson, who was "controlled by the British Army's Force Research Unit (FRU), a secret section of the Intelligence Corps."[59] Four years later Brian Nelson led the murder gang who shot dead the civil rights lawyer Pat Finucane in his own home, in front of his wife and three children.

The FRU may have been secret but it was the successor to the "Military Reaction Force, the prototype intelligence group established by the British Army's counter insurgency guru, General Sir Frank Kitson" before he was brought back to

London.[60] "Its track record of direct and indirect involvement in murder, the endless lies and cover up's, the deceptions and dirty tricks all culminating in FRU veterans hacking computers for Rupert Murdoch must be one of the most sordid tales in the history of British intelligence."[61]

In these operations the military and intelligence wings of the British State got away with murder. The atrocities were not carried out by "rogue personnel." It was their job. They were employees of the Crown and were being paid a wage to murder people in the line of duty.

In the aftermath of the massacre in Derry City Frank Kitson returned to the British mainland, ready for the next stage in countering urban terrorism. He was given "a CBE" for the three massacres by the Head of the British State and given control of "the Infantry School at Warminster ... to train and indoctrinate a new generation of British soldiers in his counterinsurgency framework."[62]

The British State had drawn harsh lessons from Edward Heath's period as Prime Minister; the class warfare included a miners' strike. "The 'national war plan' was redrawn with greater emphasis on meeting an 'internal enemy'—i.e. the left and the unions." Kitson gave his own assessment of the situation:

> The whole period of the [1972] miners' strike made us realise that the present size of the police force is too small. It is based on the fundamental philosophy that we are a law-abiding country, but things have now got to the state where there are not enough resources to deal with the increasing numbers of those who are not prepared to respect the law.[63]

In the months following the military-police occupation of Southall and the murder of Blair Peach it was discovered that the operation had been undertaken by an elite unit operating within the Metropolitan Police, who appeared to operate autonomously. The police Commander admitted that he had no authority over the Special Patrol Group in the press release immediately following the murder.[64] A few months later the BBC hosted a four-part documentary detailing the necessary tactics "of modern war and how to combat urban terrorism." This was programmed a few months prior to the New Cross Massacre. Here is the BBC's profile on the central figure:

> General Frank Kitson—the army's leading expert on guerrilla warfare, who calls himself "a military radical"—is Commandant of the Staff College. Under him, the officers—the young elite of the army—learn about modern war and how to combat urban terrorism. Tonight they discover, through a tough 24-hour battle exercise, what it would be like to mount a counter-revolutionary campaign—in mainland Britain.[65]

This is a significant example of how to normalise the abnormal. (How to humanise the inhuman comes later.) We are in a police state. This is how it is. The man in charge is General Sir Frank, a fellow we can trust to do the job. He will teach the young cadre of our ruling elite to assume authority of our military wing. The State's terrorist-in-chief had been transformed into a form of anti-hero for society as a whole, but a full-blown hero for the young males of his class. Kitson would train them in how to dehumanise ourselves; to subsume empathy, become inured to depravity and engage in bestiality; and how to organise murder as a means to an end. He would teach them how the Armed Forces identify an enemy; how not to distinguish one human being from another. The "young elite" were to learn absolute respect for the chain of command and follow orders no matter what. A couple of years later, following the Falklands War came the confrontation with the urban terrorists of the mining community. Consider the powers the British State called upon in 1984–85 to destroy a trade union and put the fear of death into the remnants of the labour movement: "MI5, police Special Branch, GCHQ and the NSA [who] were mobilised not only to spy on the [miners] but to employ agents provocateurs at the highest levels of the union, dirty tricks, slush funds, false allegations, forgeries, phoney cash deposits and multiple secretly sponsored legal actions to break the defence of the mining communities."[66]

The might of the establishment, now let loose on the mining community and their supporters, took people by surprise, people who should have known better. It was the sheer ruthlessness of the British State that surprised the labour movement, illustrated by the powers they were willing to unleash.

These people were prepared for anything. They would have called in the army if necessary, but that was not necessary. The army were already there. British Army units were assisting and supporting the State authorities when, where and as directed. Nurses, miners and the LGBT standing together: Kitson's elite units would take care of them. His soldiers were "jolly good" servants to the Crown and would combat solidarity and put the fear of death into the lot of them, all these justice seekers. Anything smacking of left-wing politics was the enemy. The British State was out to destroy "the enemy within"[67] and the Armed Forces were the primary tool. No negotiation. The imposition of order.

Her Royal Majesty, the Head of the British State, awarded General Sir Frank "a commander's badge for gallantry [and] the grand cross in 1984 when colonel commandant of the Royal Green Jackets."[68] Further awards followed. Kitson was promoted as Aide-de-Camp General to the Head of the British State. Then she made him a Knight Grand Cross of the Order of the British Empire and in 1989 her Deputy Lieutenant of Devon.[69] This was the same year one of his murder gangs shot dead Pat Finucane in the presence of his wife and children.

There were repeated calls for a public inquiry into the murder of the civil rights lawyer. A few months later the bereaved family and the public were advised that there would be none, at least not in public. Word arrived that there would be an inquiry after all. This would be conducted by the local police. This was reminiscent of the investigation into the murder of Blair Peach.

"Amnesty International UK called it shameful …" It was more than shameful. It was a blatant show of contempt for the UK and Irish public. "This decision will add fuel to the fire of suspicion," said Amnesty International, "that there is and continues to be a sinister cover-up of the full extent of official involvement in this murder."[70]

There is no question about the "official involvement." Of course there was a "cover-up" but to describe it as "sinister" does the British State a service. It suggests a conspiracy which would be naive nonsense. Suppressing information is straight-forward. Disguising reality for the better control of the public is the day-to-day business of State and those who collude in it. Leave conspiracies to the classroom. There was no need for any "cover-up."

Some forty years later, the lawyer acting for the Finucane family campaign describes this period as "a dark moment in the country's history." What other moments have there been?

He found it "difficult to imagine a more serious allega-tion against a liberal democracy founded in the rule of law." A "liberal democracy"? What is that? What exactly is "the rule of law"? Imagine discussing such concepts in side rooms along the shadowier passages of Westminster or the mess rooms of HM Armed Forces and their RUC colleagues, or those of the intelligence agencies, wherever in the world they happen to be. The Finucane family lawyer ended by saying, "What am I missing?"[71]

The history of the British State, was the answer. One of Frank Kitson's superiors in "Northern Ireland" was Henry Tuzo, Major General and Director of Royal Artillery, later the Chair of the Royal United Services Institute.[72] This is one of the more powerful right-wing think tanks in the world. Its members move to safeguard the rights of regimes, dictator-ships and tyrannies who practice torture and terrorism as a routine.

People associated with the authoritarian right and far-right think-tank network move on the theory that the so-called liberal democracies have become a soft touch, they "lack a cohesive identity which [makes] it vulnerable to enemies within and without."

Those engaged in exonerating State authority abroad want the same freedoms at home. Vice Admiral Sir Jeremy Blackham KCB BA has "suggested ... the partial removal of defence policy from democratic control [and complains] of a 'lack of leadership from the majority which in misplaced deference to "multiculturalism" [has] failed to lay down the line to immigrant communities.'"[73]

It is the "fragmentation" of "our" society and "our" culture that is to blame. The liberal democracies are "soft" and vulnerable to anyone with a mind to interfere with "our" way of life. Compare this, for example, to the "Islamist terrorist enemy, within and without" who know exactly what they are, who they are, where they come from—and where they are heading. How can "we" responsible people fight the "extremists" if "we" are being held back by all these justice-terrorists, truth-subver-sives, namby-pampy do-gooders and empathy-proponents who seek to transform "our" soldiers and "our" security officers into actual people who are answerable to the public not in their roles as State functionaries but as actual human beings!

In private meetings and discussion groups here we should expect to find higher-end Commanders of one authority or another, often retired; senior members of the Westminster Parliament, both Lords and elected members; ex-MI5, ex-MI6, ex-army, ex-navy, ex-RAF, aristocracy, academics, retired law enforcement authorities and very wealthy benefactors.[74] Most of this is the usual right-wing guff. The trouble is that the people who hold these views are in control of the British State.

"On the 14th July 2008, thirty six and a half years after the McGurk's Bar Massacre, the British government was forced to apologize for their black (*sic*) propaganda that perverted the course of justice and abased the human rights of innocent civilians."[75] But they did not admit that it was on their own behalf and on a command directed by their own military unit that the massacre had ever taken place, that the fifteen people had been murdered. In 2019, almost fifty years after the Ballymurphy Massacre, the British State allowed an inquest to take place. In their reports on the proceedings the BBC called in their man with the specialist knowledge, their idea of a reliable witness. He was Lieutenant Colonel Derek Wilford of the First Battalion, the Parachute Regiment, primary member of "Kitson's Private Army." Here we are back on familiar territory, and the "two sides to every story" argument. Forget the murderous assault on a defenceless community in West Belfast and the declared object of the exercise, the "Suppression of the Irish [and] the Defence of the Protestant Religion."[76] Ignore all of that and focus on the humanity of the murderers. The BBC report focused on Wilford's normality, his sensibility, his humanity, his work as an artist: "tough, outspoken and charismatic, adored by his men whom he adored in turn."[77] Wilford was directly involved in the Ballymurphy atrocity. Months later the "humane artist" was on command in Derry City where he managed to shelve his humanity in the line of duty, and in the absence of Frank Kitson who is said to have been someplace else on the day. Wilford "commanded Parachute Regiment soldiers on Bloody Sunday [and] was awarded the OBE in the new year honours" by the Crowned head of Great Britain for his part in the slaughter of so-called British citizens.[78]

The first inquiry into the massacre in Derry was headed by Lord Widgery, appointed by Edward Heath, the Prime Minister. His appointment as impartial expert would have occasioned many a guffaw in the messrooms of HM Armed

Forces, not to mention Masonic Lodges and Orange Halls. Widgery was "an extremely enthusiastic Freemason of grand rank, holding office as Past Junior Grand Warden and Past Senior Grand Warden."[79] His "contemptible first report"[80]

> blamed civil rights protesters, blamed the IRA and, most despicably, blamed the victims, those shot and killed by British paratroopers.... [He] colluded in the branding of those shot dead as "gunmen and bombers" and in doing so declared their deaths at the hands of British paratroopers to be legitimate.[81]

At the second inquiry into the Bloody Sunday massacre Frank Kitson, tactical genius of the authoritarian right, responsible for countless atrocities, massacres, rapes and murders, was called upon to give evidence at the Saville Inquiry in 2002. Kitson said,

> "The Paras were just jolly good and there was no conceivable way you could overlook the fact that they got there very quickly, they were ready to go at the drop of a hat and they were experienced." ... Standing a few feet from the families of the dead and wounded, Kitson claimed that the soldiers responsible for the killing of fourteen men were in fact caring professionals, dedicated to saving lives, who had shown great "compassion" for the dying and wounded.[82]

In 2010 the report of the Saville Inquiry on the Derry Massacre carried out by Kitson's Private Army appeared. The Tory Prime Minister of the day admitted that

> It was impossible to defend the indefensible.... Men of the support company of the 1st Battalion ["Kitson's private army"], the Parachute Regiment, had shot without justification. Victims had been shot in the back, or while they were crawling away. Soldiers had

lied under oath. The episode would never be forgotten, could never be forgotten.[83]

Perhaps not forgotten but never acted upon. Forty-five years later the "Police Service of Northern Ireland (PSNI) began a murder investigation ... and by 2016 had submitted their files to the Public Prosecution Service." In September of 2020 "the decision not to prosecute 15 former soldiers in connection over the Bloody Sunday shootings [was] upheld [by] Northern Ireland's Public Prosecution Service (PPS)."[84]

In 2015 Frank Kitson was served papers for negligence and misfeasance by the widow of Eugene "Paddy" Heenan who was killed in 1973 by members of the Ulster Defence Association.[85]

Almost fifty years after the massacre in Derry, only one soldier, identified as "Soldier F," was awaiting trial. Until in July 2021, "the PPS said it would not be proceeding with prosecution ... that evidence relied upon in the prosecution of two former soldiers for the killing of Official IRA member Joe McCann in Belfast in 1972, was inadmissible [and] has now concluded that there was no longer a reasonable prospect of key evidence in proceedings against Soldier F being ruled admissible at his trial."[86]

The political wing of the British State orchestrated the conditions that made the massacre of these citizens of the United Kingdom possible. The military wing conducted the massacre. The legal wing have ensured that the murderers have walked free. At this time of writing, a legal challenge has been launched by the bereaved family which takes us into 2022, the fiftieth anniversary.

The inquest on the Ballymurphy Massacre of August 1971 began in 2018 and ended March 2020. In May 2021 "a fresh inquest found that the ten people murdered by the British Army's notorious Parachute Regiment ... were 'entirely innocent,' and their killings 'unjustifiable.'" It was further disclosed by the Coroner's Office "that tissue samples and an organ ... of five of the deceased [had been] retained for the past 50 years."[87]

In these circles, "murder" must be kept in quotations: it is a legal term. Beings who are not human are not murdered, except metaphorically. As a general rule the indigenous folk, the natives, are not regarded as real people. Terms such as "murder" apply when the argument switches to legalities. The targeted people have no rights in law and should have no expectations in regard to protection. The natives, the Irish, the blacks are subhuman. So too were the miners, the socialists, the communists and the anarchists and whoever else the far right seek to identify. These are the enemy within. Whoever they are. This is how it is.

The soldier-invaders are not killing actual people, they are killing subhumans, which is the logical extension of imperialism. Let us turn it around. Those who suffer at the hands of the soldier-invaders are the human beings. Those who commit these barbaric and bestial atrocities are the subhumans.

Onward marched the gallant Brits in the war for plenty, drums a-patter, blood a-splatter, pipes a-blowing; another battle, another triumph, glory, God and the State.

(2021)

Home Truths

Scotland is my country. Not Britain and not the United Kingdom and it can be difficult to explain this to people from other places. If I insist I am faced with different reactions: a shrug of the shoulders, polite curiosity, occasional irritation. People tend to identify the United Kingdom and the British State as the same thing, a right-wing political formation. They may distinguish between England, Wales, Northern Ireland and Scotland but are blinkered by their hostility. They forget that a state is not the embodiment of a people. It may act to represent a people but that is not the same. In the late 1970s PKK were interested in Scotland, as they were in any struggle grounded in issues around the validity and survival of indigenous languages and culture; issues around self-determination, "home rule" or independence. Forty years later and Scotland is no further ahead. The perception is of a people whose divisions are the product of cultural ignorance, political infantilism and a lack of nerve. All and more of that can be said of most peoples of most countries, and it may be true, but is beside the point. When the people of a country are blamed for the actions of the State the only winner is the State itself.

At the core of State propaganda are notions around unity and democracy, making use of the fallacy that everybody has a voice and every voice counts, that the State wouldn't exist unless the people put it there. But it doesn't bear scrutiny. It even begins from a confusion as between State and government. Citizens don't vote a state into power, they vote for a party to form a government. The State forms itself.

What role do the Turkish people have in the Turkish State? Can the non-Kurds be held responsible for the practices of the Turkish State?

Millions throughout the world hate the USA and all that it represents, but what does it represent? The people there would give answers so widely apart that they will seem to be talking about a different country. Anyway, what American people are we talking about? Asian Americans, African Americans, Middle Eastern Americans, Indian Subcontinental Americans, Hispanic Americans, European Americans, Native Americans? And are we referring to Asian American atheists, Middle Eastern American Jews, Indian Subcontinental American Christians, African American right-wing Buddhists? How do we define the non-Hispanic South American American Muslim ex-marine who is gay, works for the CIA and reveres his Asian American grandfather who died on a picket line following a blow to the head delivered by a Native American cop wielding a long-handled baton?

Critics of a right-wing state such as Turkey, UK or USA who blame the domestic population must be blaming them for failing to overthrow the State.

In everyday parlance, when the talk is of "unity" of decision-making, it doesn't mean everybody arrives at the same conclusion no matter the point of origin. The idea is that everybody has had the chance to voice an opinion. Unity assumes consensus. A sort of a vote seems to have taken place. Some say yay, some nay, and the rest stayed silent, which is treated as a vote for the status quo.

Where the State has established the fallacy that its authority is vouchsafed by the home population the blame for its activities and practices is attached to "the country," as though the country, the people and the government are the same thing, and that unity reigns.

In the United Kingdom only a Monarch reigns and how power operates baffles those who have none, which amounts to the vast majority of the population. Firstly there is the Crown: everything not owned by any one individual, group or other plurality is the property of the Crown. This extends via land, rivers, seas, mountains, lochs and sky; and from there stretching a number of miles upwards, downwards and sideways east, west, north and south. The number of miles depends on necessity and will be resolved by the financial and political interests of the ruling elite and those who work on their behalf.

Anything likely or conceivably to be found or discovered within these areas belongs to the Crown. The rights of property extend through any matter organic or inorganic: all living animals, insects, fish, birds and sea life; all plant life, mineral deposits, buried treasures and booty ancient or in worlds and times to come; all pre-Neolithic relics, non-human remains from the beginning of time; all alien life stranded or captured within UK bounds and not otherwise owned by legal right as defined by International Law if not the Law of England and Wales. Everything that has ever existed and may exist to the ends of eternity are the property of the Crown.

And what is "the Crown"? No one is quite sure but all Members of Parliament across the mainstream political spectrum "are required by law to take an oath of allegiance to [it]." The matter is placed more clearly in front of those who seek to become UK citizens:

> "I, [name], swear by Almighty God that, on becoming a British citizen, I will be faithful and bear true allegiance to Her Majesty Queen Elizabeth the Second, Her Heirs and Successors according to law." Pledge: "I will give my loyalty to the United Kingdom and respect its rights

and freedoms. I will uphold its democratic values. I will observe its laws faithfully and fulfil my duties and obligations as a British citizen."

Members of the Westminster Parliament "cannot take their seat, speak in debates, vote or receive a salary until [then]. They could also be fined £500 and have their seat declared vacant 'as if they were dead' if they attempted to do so."[1] Thus in mainstream UK the Crown appears beyond politics. All those who enter Parliament abide by its rules, by its policies, its practices, procedures and most everything else it does.

The Westminster Parliament consists of every politician from each of the two "Houses": the House of Lords and the House of Commons. Thus when we talk about the Westminster Parliament the reference is to *both* Houses. Taken as a whole, the function of the Westminster Parliament is to check, balance and monitor the work of the actual government.

The House of Lords has a membership of more than 800 human beings. Among their ranks are hereditary members of the aristocracy; semi-retired judges and semi-retired police Commissioners; semi-retired Commanders of the army, navy and Royal Air Force; semi-retired Commanders of the Intelligence Services; full-time Commanders of the Church, Commanders of Commerce, Commoners of Privilege and others too, plenty others.[2] The 800 human beings who make up the numbers of the House of Lords are not elected. They are there because of who they are; their family heritage, the office they hold, or because they have been chosen by higher-order members of State. The myth is perpetuated by the establishment that these 800 human beings represent every shade of opinion within UK society. This is such hogwash that nobody takes it seriously. But its power is beyond question.

The House of Commons is the other section of the Westminster Parliament. This has a membership of 650 human beings. The population of the UK is more than 67 million. The

establishment maintains that these 650 human beings represent the interests of these 67 million people.

The 650 are divided into political parties. The two
largest parties are the Conservative (Tory) Party and the
British Labour Party. From these 650 members of the House
of Commons an election takes place every five years or less.
The party with the greatest majority of votes will form Her
Majesty's (HM) Government. The present Party of Government
is the Conservative Party.

All parties who lose at the General Election have the collective name of HM Loyal Opposition. HM Loyal Opposition
includes all the mainstream "left-wing" and "nationalist"
parties who are elected MPs. They swear allegiance to the
Crown at the very point of entry. This includes the Scottish
National Party and Plaid Cymru, the Welsh national party.
This must be kept in brackets in any such discussion. The
British Labour Party is the traditional home of the mainstream
labour and socialist movement. Every trade union affiliated to
the Trades Union Congress operates within the mainstream
political system and has a tacit allegiance to the Crown, so too
a handful of parties of a more radical position, who believe it
better to fight within the system.

This has implications in wider areas of struggle and has
a real impact on solidarity, both internationally and domesti-
cally. Any campaign for justice seeks solidarity. Every political
exile and exiled liberation group must survive in spite of the
society they find themselves within. Invisibility is the goal but
solidarity the key. These bring major pressures. There is no
room for local issues. Political exiles must not draw attention
to themselves. If they do they should prepare for reprisals.
The default position is to consign local politics to the margins.
Exiles may justify this with a Leninist-style argument that
local campaigns and struggles do not carry the weight of *the*
wider struggle. Thus they find ways to avoid solidarity, arguments not to act, to keep their head below the parapet.

Survival in exile for many requires covering the eyes, sealing the ears and avoiding the traps that come about through empathy. In any right-wing society, the less contact the better. The trouble is they live among people in desperate situations, engaged in their own struggle against the racism, the repression—the policies and practices conducted by State authority. It is from this area of society that some of the worst violations will occur, and from where campaigns for justice enter life, typically on the back of death.

A life-or-death situation is exactly that. There is little more a human being can do than volunteer their life to a struggle, unless the lives of those closest to them.

In either case human beings commit themselves as the means to an end. The end is a complex: solidarity, justice, empathy, and perhaps more than that.

Martyrdom does not enter into it. Those who introduce the concept see a different end, often defined as "the Cause." It is applied in connection to so-called greater goods. "Greater goods" include religious difference, patriotic ideals, notional class identity and some others.

A few with radical political views adopt a similar position. "The Cause" is primary. This could be a named party or an ideal such as freedom and justice for all regardless of race, creed, sexual preference, gender, class or caste. No matter how "the Cause" is defined the final goal—freedom and justice for all—cannot be achieved until the radical group, faction or party has managed to gain entry into a position to bring about the change.

Each generation of political activists produces ideological warriors who seek to transform the United Kingdom, revolutionise Great Britain and Northern Ireland and make "our nation" a place where justice is primary, where equality reigns, where respect for life is uppermost.

They go along to public protests, attend meetings and organise petitions and connect with folk of similar views. They become members of parties and attempt to realise their ideas and dreams within it. They work very hard to do this, forming allegiances and friendships, attending meetings and joining committees, changing and turning all kinds of things upside down.

Some are chosen by their party to stand for election to the House of Commons, so that they can upset the applecart. Some are returned MPs following a General Election. They work very hard, forming other allegiances, connecting with other practical people and changing things as best they can, turning them inside out as well as upside down. They attend planning meetings. One such meeting calls on those present to support a global petition to the board of directors of a global corporation who are not only "destroying the plant life of the world" in the pursuit of personal gain, but the plant life of the world to come and all or any such plant life in any other world that may exist in this universe or an adjacent one according to the diktats of international law as it pertains to the global corporation, as represented by its company lawyers.

Platform speakers call upon the lawyers to call upon the board of directors of the global corporation to consider the genocidal consequences of their pursuit of profit. Representatives of the suffering indigenous communities talk of the death of wildlife, fauna, forests, plants and the destruction of all sorts of resources and commodities. A respected teacher of biology from a local high school advises the meeting that "our planet" cannot recover for an estimated 2.7 million years. He sits down to a huge roar of applause from the students who are present for the occasion.

The meeting calls for one of the newly elected MPs, a man, to raise this issue in the House of Commons. Several months on from then the newly returned MP is given a spot on the timetable to put a question to the leader of Her Majesty's Party of Government.

The leader agrees with every aspect of the question and congratulates the newly elected Member on his ethical stance but begs to remind the Honourable Member that ethical systems and economic systems are separate fields of endeavour and recommends to the newly elected Honourable Member that a sub-clause or amendment be inserted, calling for shareholders to reconsider whether such investment is wise in these problematic times where issues concerning the future of the world are uppermost, notwithstanding the perfectly legal existence of the relevant financial scheme.

A huge roar of approval greets this from the benches of Her Majesty's Government, amid jeers and catcalls from the benches of Her Majesty's Loyal Opposition.

The House then moves to consider the next question from another newly elected Member, a woman. She calls upon "this House" to agree with her that murderous fascists continue to act as murderous fascists and it is surely high time that every last member of "this House," regardless of party loyalty, should append their name to a recent petition that is to be presented to the president of aforementioned Fascist State that he should renounce murderous fascism altogether or resign from public office forthwith.

The interests of the British State are the interests of the ruling elite. The ruling elite *includes* the ruling class, spreading the net far wider than that—as wide as necessary. Among those are found top-level layers of political control, of legal and military command (navy, air force, army); internal and external security formations (MI5, MI6 and the secretive sections formed and removed when appropriate); Commissioners of Police and Lord Chief Justices; Supreme Court Judges, Lord High Stewards and Lord Chancellors; sundry billionaires and landowners; bankers, stockdealers, financiers, major industrialists and plenty others too. It will be noted that the majority of those who make up the numbers within the House of Lords share many of the interests of the ruling elite.

It is the case that certain matters are discussed by State authorities which do not involve the public and are no concern of the public. Some take place inside the Palace of Westminster and some take place outside.

The public should not expect to gain entry into these discussions. There is no conspiracy to exclude them. Particular matters of State are none of their business; they are the business of the ruling elite and those who act on their behalf.

There are no conspiracies. Conspiracy theories suit the State. These are sustained by misunderstandings on the nature of class interest.[3] The owners of the mainstream and populist media, for example, do not need to hold secret meetings with their editors to commit feature writers to undermine, discredit or marginalise undesirables. Attacks on these individuals and groups will occur as a matter of course.

"Undesirables" may be defined as any individual or group perceived as offering a challenge. This will range through "extremists," "terrorists," "radicals," "leftists," "justice seekers," "users-of-bad-language," "liberals," "bereaved families," "do-gooders." Negative and hostile news features are always in place. These reflect the interests of the establishment. Those who work for the owners of the mainstream and populist media are not employed to criticise, damage, discredit or destroy them. The case of the British State Broadcasting Corporation (BBC) is beyond the scope of this essay.

The primary task of Her Majesty's Government is to implement the policies and measures that have been designed, created and invented to protect, sustain and enhance the interests of the ruling elite. The end is twofold: ultimate control of all wealth, property, land and resources; and the freedom to exploit these as to suit themselves. A wise government will introduce awkward measures by subterfuge: quietly, peacefully and respectfully, without panicking the citizens.

State authority begins from the same mind and the right mind. Parallel policies and lines of action are guaranteed. There is nothing else. There are innumerable areas of interest but the end is shared, and the end is survival.

Public reminders of the physicality and armoury of the police and armed forces will be displayed. People will learn that the Law is the Law and beyond the reach of human tampering. Those may act as a deterrent but periodically a heavy hand is required. A robust government will land that blow. A moderate government will negotiate, where possible, then breathe a heavy sigh and ask that the appropriate authorities get on with doing their job but that they do it with grace, sympathy and respect for the targeted groups and communities who are to suffer the consequences.

In the United Kingdom, as in any representative democracy, the people pass along, taking what they can, surviving as they can, presenting petitions and calling upon their elected representatives to ask questions on their behalf.

Beyond here only bad news can exist.

The primary allegiance of the British State is to the Crown. The Crown is represented by the reigning Monarch. The reigning Monarch is the Head of the British State of which the Crown is the embodiment. The primary allegiance of the British State is to the embodiment of itself. But these are murky waters and require unbiased logicians to create a value-free equation powerful enough to clarify the matter for the present writer.

(2022)

A Brief History

Racial and sectarian prejudice remains strong in Scotland, occasionally vicious, occasionally murderous; and without it the continued existence of Northern Ireland is hardly conceivable. The depth of the prejudice is beyond class and may be traced back several hundred years, much further than the Protestant Reformation, and its roots are seen in the struggles between the Celtic people and those who went to war with them, whether Romans, Anglo-Saxons or Vikings.

In 1603 there was a union of the crowns of England and Scotland. King James VI of Scotland became the first King James of England. In England the ruling elite were not particularly interested in a British empire. They were building their own, stealing from one and another and the English people as a whole. Decades earlier America had been named and claimed by agents acting on behalf of the Spanish elite and, at a further remove, the Vatican. This and other areas of the world were being divvied up by their European counterparts. Rich pickings indeed. The English ruling class had coveted Ireland for a long time and were in the process of stealing it too, and anything else that occupied space.

The Scottish elites envied them and sought to improve their own opportunities "by fastening onto [their] coat-tails." England was England but what if the wider physical entity of Britain were to be established as a political reality? Elizabeth I would become Empress of Britain as well as Queen of England. If so English empire builders might become British empire builders and the Scottish ruling elite, having become North Britons, would acquire diverse "entitlements" in the process, including legitimate access to the spoils of empire.

And so it came to pass that by the end of the sixteenth century the ruling elites of the three kingdoms of England, Wales and Scotland were united under King James VI of Scotland, henceforth designated James I, King of England, France and Ireland, Defender of the Protestant Faith. According to a BBC spokesperson, given that the working class and the peasantry had no say in the matter, they were reconciled to passivity anyway and were always quick to unravel the carpets for crumbs fallen from the banquet tables.

Barely a year on from the union of the ruling elites "the worst bondage began." The law of the land was changed to ensure that those landowners whose properties included raw sources open to mining had access to the best kind of labour: slaves. It wouldn't matter how these people strived, not even the grandchildren of their grandchildren. They were born slaves and they died slaves. By 1606 the Crown had enslaved its entire mining community: the men, the women and the children of the three kingdoms, England, Wales and Scotland. The Crown had united the lot under his control. Henceforth they were the material property of the owners of the mining industry and so it stayed for two hundred years, right the way through the years of the Enlightenment until the end of the eighteenth century.

By 1610 the Crown had awarded a charter to the owners of the Northern Virginia Company on the other side of the Atlantic Ocean which also "granted [to them] the whole island" of Newfoundland. The Crown then planted a people in the north of Ireland and attempted the same in the western islands of Scotland, in the continuing war to wrest control from the Celts who remained a threat from what was left of the Lordship.

The assimilation process had begun. James I of Great Britain and Ireland had studied under George Buchanan, poet, historian and educator, and had learned about wise "conquerors [who] tend not to drive out or exterminate the conquered race, but to form a landed aristocracy, with more or less servile occupiers of the land under them."[1]

This way of establishing imperial authority was used by the Romans. All empire builders take their lead from them. Across the world dictatorships impose control, oust local authorities, send in governors of their own, introduce toadying lickspittles from the indigenous community to do their bidding. Generally, the toadying lickspittles are members of the local nobility and upper classes. The English imperialists used these methods in Scotland and Ireland, seeking out, or creating, a domestic "landed aristocracy" with the "servile occupiers of the land under them." This way of manoeuvring is fundamental to imperial expansion. It is what the British State did in the Indian Subcontinent, in Africa, in Southeast Asia and right into the twentieth century following the breakup of the Ottoman Empire, securing land and material resources where possible, establishing ruling elites from the subservient locals.

Unlike Emperor Hadrian and his Roman troops, the British ruling elite found stealing the land from its inhabitants straightforward. They arrived and took what they wanted. If that didn't work they sent in the army, then the diplomats and religious authorities, and their legal team set the rules of acquisition that allowed them to retain their stolen goods with minimum fuss. They exploited the people who were living there, killed them or expelled them, whichever was most convenient to themselves, their associates and minions. Now into the twenty-first century they continue to pass it backward and forward among themselves, using their preferred systems of exchange, under their own interpretation of laws established by themselves on behalf of themselves, all these multi-billionaires, trillionaires, financiers and royalty, helpers to monarchy, sheiks, emirs, kings and sundry religious authorities.

The Hebridean island of Lewis was home to my own grandmother's family for centuries. I had no knowledge of my great-grandparents but my granny and her siblings all left the island. Did they have a choice? I don't know. A roof over their head would have been a help. Gàidhlig was my grandmother's first language. She gave birth to six children, of whom four boys survived. My father was the youngest. He and his brothers were reared in English, taught in English and learned to know their mother's language as an inferior irrelevance.

In later years she spoke to me in Gàidhlig but it was not something shared. Gàidhlig was hers, it was never ours. Where I went wrong as a boy lay in thinking we were excluded. It was my granny who was excluded. The rest of us were welcome, assimilated members of the lower orders, with no language but that of the Brits, no culture, no tradition, no history. The Brits were boss, we learned to negotiate. She never could, and never did.

There are few beings more civil than a deer unless, perhaps, a sheep. Both creatures were planted in Lewis at the expense of the natives: the deer by the earlier rulers of Clan Mackenzie and the sheep by their descendants. The chief of the clan was given the island by King James I of Britland on condition he and his ilk quell the natives and pay allegiance to the Crown. In the years to follow the families from these townships were cleared to make way for a great hunting forest. The successor Clan Chiefs stocked the area with red deer.

Once the land was acquired the authorities granted the old ruling class the right to continue living there, subject to the new authority. King James and his Court were following empire builders since the time of the Romans. Whether the local elite assimilated to Brit culture was up to them but given this was the culture of authority, of those who had allowed them the property, it would have been foolish if not dangerous to do otherwise. The clansmen were now in thrall to the Clan Chief, as they were in thrall to the Crown, a sort of blanket term that covers the ruling elite of the new British State. This was reinforced from the 1707 Union of Parliaments. Four hundred years later the Crown maintains its control; land properties are bought, sold, rented or exchanged as the ruling elite sees fit.

Assimilation to standard Britishness is taught by State authority and rewarded by State authority. But for that primary division in Scottish society the pro-independence vote would have had an overwhelming majority in each of the two referendums that have taken place in my lifetime. The burden of proof is always on the self-determination or nationalist position. Being a Brit is to accept unity, accept unionism and a core anti-republicanism. "Republicanism" is viewed as anti-British, as Irish, and Irishness is pro-IRA. The Irish Republican Army has been outlawed as a terrorist organisation by the British State and the USA.

The State promotes the existence of monarchy, and how fundamental hierarchy is to a healthy and morally upright society. Along the way people are advised that hierarchy is a necessary feature of a fair and just democracy. Protestants far outnumber Catholics. One of the more essential titles held by the Monarch is Defender of the Faith. "Faith" refers not to the Christian religion but to Protestantism. The British Monarch is regarded as a bulwark against the Pope and Roman Catholicism. This is a core position of the Free Church of Scotland whose

> Ministers and Elders ... humbly offer Your Majesty the expression of our continued loyalty to Your Majesty's Person and Throne and to the Constitutional Monarchy of which you are the honoured Head and Representative. [It] is our duty and privilege, regularly to uphold Your Majesty's person, family and governments, before the throne of grace. We commit ourselves and our

congregations to do so in obedience to the exhortation of the Word of God, "that supplications, prayers, intercessions and giving of thanks be made for all men, for kings and all who are in authority, that we may lead a quiet and peaceable life in all godliness and reverence."[2]

People are encouraged to believe that the British monarchy is the envy of the world. Some children think that if they don't behave properly the Queen might take her Royal Family and go away and live someplace else. They do have a choice. They could go to live in any one of the following countries and feel at home: Canada, Jamaica, Antigua and Barbuda; New Zealand, Papua New Guinea, St Kitts and Nevis; St Lucia, Grenada, Belize, St Vincent and the Grenadines; the Solomon Islands, Barbados, Australia, Tuvalu and the Bahamas. Each of these countries also has a monarchy: whoever happens to reign in Great Britain and Northern Ireland. Queen Elizabeth is their ruling Monarch too.

In most countries of the former British Empire the language of the British ruling class remains the language of law, the language of the court, the language of government, the language of power, and it suits the ruling elites of these countries of the former Empire to retain the language of power as the primary aid to the control of their own population.

People of the lower orders learn that the language used by themselves is not really a language at all but a hotchpotch gaggle of utterances which makes sense to those who use it but not beyond. They are grateful to the British State authority for allowing them to use the term "dialect" and to think that their "dialect" somehow or other relates to the Queen's English. English literature is an expression of that. Writers who wish to create their stories and poetry from non-standard cultures and communities must fight or assimilate. Standard English Literary form exists as the means of expression. Use it, or beware the consequences.

The issue is always unity. Non-standard literary works are treated as an attack on that. Standard English Literary form is the Voice of the Imperialist and the colonizer, the voice of the British ruling class and those who adhere and assimilate to that.

The principle of etiquette is inculcated. There is a right way and a wrong way to conduct oneself. The manners and behaviour of the British ruling elite provide the key. They are to be aped as a method of social advancement. Watch how our rulers conduct themselves! See! Their conduct is beyond reproach. If we can conduct ourselves in similar fashion then we too can succeed, we too can fight our way out of the mud. This is drummed into children by parents and community leaders. The person who speaks "properly" during a job interview has a major start over somebody who doesn't.

The etiquette of the ruling elite is generally confused with a sort of "moral law." It seems to exist outside of human experience. The manners, behaviour and general deportment of the ruling elite are thought to have an intrinsic value. It is no longer seen as a particular behaviour cultivated by a particular community, that class of being known as "the ruling elite." It is now seen as the way all human beings should behave, no matter their ethnic, racial or cultural background. The fact that the ruling class conduct themselves according to their own rules and procedures becomes evidence of their *inherent* superiority.

Between English literature and British society the effects of imperialism and colonization are inescapable. People of other races and classes are an easy target, and they are targeted. The most basic forms of racism and elitism are practiced. Sometimes we see it and often we don't, sometimes we fight and sometimes we don't. I worked as a bus conductor then driver on several occasions, alongside Pakistani Muslims and Punjabi Sikhs, a few of whom were trained schoolteachers and health workers. Most had additional jobs in restaurants, take-away diners and small grocery stores.

In the Manchester factory where I worked in the manufacture of asbestos boards, my fellow workers were East Europeans and Jamaican. On building sites in London, my fellow workers were Irish, Jamaican and Trinidadian. On one site the job was unionised and our union was the one known nowadays as Unite, formerly the TGWU (Transport and General Workers' Union). Our branch was strong. It was strong because the workforce was strong and politicized. Strength and politicization go together. Branch members knew what they were about and learned from one another. Their political awareness had derived from being at the receiving end of imperialism, the overseas legal and military wings of the British Empire. There were no illusions here on fair play, truth and justice.

That experience contributed greatly to my own understanding. On the domestic front notions of racial identity and the unity of (Anglo-Saxon) Britishness were delusions only treated seriously by sections of the white working class. And it was entirely consistent that a few of those always discover the most appropriate display of racial solidarity with the British ruling class to be the insignia of nazism and fascism.

People from other cultures knew the reality of anti-imperialist struggle and they knew the workings of the British State. The more working-class people experienced the power of the State the less likely they were to confuse their own communities with that of the ruling class.

The resistance to racism, sectarianism and other forms of discrimination is where the struggle remains. In the 1970s the British State and other right-wing factions developed one basic project, which was to dismantle if not destroy the labour movement.

In retrospect it can be seen that preparations had been in place at least since the 1960s. How far could they go in order to claw back the gains made by the labour, the socialist and the democratic movement in general that had taken place from the 1960s? Could the British State, for example, find ways to murder dangerous dissidents or other members of the public without being held accountable in law? These issues were under discussion. A soldier or policeman on overseas duty couldn't just open the window of a lounge bar and shoot to kill a passerby.

Or could they? Well, yes. It depends on the country under occupation. On a balance of probability the passerby is a local. If the local population resented the invading army they might be defined enemy. If a dead person can be defined as more likely than not to belong to the enemy camp, then the soldier or policeman on overseas duty will rarely be held accountable.

These issues were easier to resolve when the locals belonged to a non-Caucasian race. Members of the imperialist military often killed civilians in Africa, India or China "without cause." It was up to the legal authorities of the occupying force to deal with issues of culpability.

But where the British military were occupying areas of Britain itself then a different set of rules, principles and procedures had to operate. The British State sought ways to define sections of its own population as the enemy. In resolving such matters the experience of the military and legal wings of the British Empire were especially crucial.

Throughout the 1970s the British Army and the British police targeted its own population in the north of Ireland, on the mainland the black and Asian communities. These were fundamental areas of experience for the legal and military authorities. The British State saw a need to widen the target area, to include its radicals and dissidents and those sections of the general public who did not accept the authority of the ruling elite.

Many political exiles and exiled groups fail to recognise the political reality of the United Kingdom. They don't see Wales, Northern Ireland, England and Scotland; they see one country which is Great Britain and act as though this is an authentic democracy and that the labour movement, led by the Labour Party and the trade unions, is the authentic voice of opposition. Members of the wider left should bury their differences and come to the aid of the exiles. Anti-parliamentarians, anarchists, libertarian and revolutionary socialists should march as one with the Labour Party. Unity is the cry! Let us bury our differences and move onwards, yelling boo to the goose then retiring to one of Her Majesty's Westminster lounges for a nice cup of tea.

The experience of those who know the workings of empire is there to be taken, explored, adapted and used. This surely begins with the war on racism, of taking courage from those who are forced to deal with it in every area of society, offering support and solidarity, and learning the depth of the struggle, and the need to develop methods of defence appropriate to that.

Vedat Türkali, a Kurdish novelist, once said in reference to his work that he was "hard to please, but I know that being fond of perfection is a dead-end street." He was making the point about a novel he had written, that the finished result might not have been as good as he hoped, but he had to jump in and write it, then stop and move on. A beautiful truth.

Revision is eternal, if we allow it. As in art, so too in learning, we make stuff. We learn and we make. The resources available through the internet reach the point of saturation. We need to stop prior to that. Otherwise we do nothing. Gathering information becomes an end in itself. We can all be students. But we must stop the study to write the essay. Learning leads to making, and this includes making sense. We use what we have and push ahead. And while pushing ahead we make even more sense. This is radical history. We have to make it ourselves.

(2022)

The 1997 Gathering in Istanbul for Freedom of Expression

The inaugural event of the Gathering in Istanbul for Freedom of Expression took place on March 10–12, 1997. Here is a facsimile of the pamphlet published for the occasion. It was produced in photostat form to replicate the original but with the addition of the named foreign writers as "co-editors." Under existing Turkish Law, all writers whose names appeared as co-editors were in breach of the Law.

GATHERING
IN ISTANBUL
for Freedom of Expression
March 10-12th, 1997

DÜŞÜNCE SUÇU!?NA KARŞI GİRİŞİM
Initiative "FREEDOM for FREEDOM of EXPRESSION"
Nacak Sok. 21/8 TR-81200 İSTANBUL
Tel.: 0090216/3432761
Fax : 0090216/4920504

GATHERING IN ISTANBUL
for Freedom of Expression
10–12 March 1997

"GATHERING IN ISTANBUL for Freedom of Expression" has
been realized between 10–12 March 1997 with participation of 20
guests (3 of them observers) from 12 countries:

Ms. Louise Gareau Des-Bois (Quebec PEN-Canada), Mr. Kalevi
Haikara (Finnish PEN), Mr. Rajwinder Singh (German-East
PEN), Ms. Maria Van Daalen (Holland PEN), Mr. Milo van der
Burgt (a.i. Holland), Mr. Rob Brouwer (a.i. Holland), Mr.
Avraham Heffner (writer-Israel), Mr. Jehuda Atlas (writer-
Israel), Ms. Maja Bejerano (writer-Israel), Mr. Ronen
Zeidel (a.i. Israel), Ms. Puah Shalev-Toren (Israeli PEN),
Ms. Shulamit Kuriansky (Israeli PEN), Ms. Soledad Santiago
(San Miguel PEN-Mexico), Ms. Hanan Awwad (Palestinian PEN),
Mr. Alexander Tkachenko (Russian PEN), Mr. Lars Erik
Blomqvist (Swedish Writers' Union), Mr. Ola Sunesson
(Swedish PEN), Mr. M. Moris Farhi (PEN Int.-UK), Mr. James
Kelman (writer-UK), Ms. Joanne Leedom-Ackerman (PEN Int.-
USA).

On 10.03.1997, at 09:30, a voluntary group went to the
State Security Court for the "Declaration of Crime!?". At
12:30, after the press conference where the guests were
introduced to media, two groups departed to visit Prisoners
of Conscience, Dr. İsmail Beşikçi and his publisher Ünsal
Öztürk in Bursa, and journalist Işık Yurtçu in Adapazarı
prisons. But the Ministry of Justice did not give the
necessary permission.

On 11.03.1997, they witnessed the hearing of KAFKA trial,
in which actor Mahir Günşiray was tried because he had read
a paragraph from Franz Kafka during his questioning at the
State Security Court. Later on, they were invited to
a forum at Istanbul University by the students and the
teachers together. But the police did not let them into the
University with the excuse that they did not have
a permission!? from the rector.

On 12.03.1997, although the Prosecutor of the State Security Court did not take their "Declaration of Crime!?" into consideration, they went to the Court for being questioned voluntarily. The State Prosecutor -hard to believe- refused even taking the application officially. This is an open violation of the Constitution!

In the afternoon, they joined the meeting "Writers and the Freedom of Expression" of writers and artists, and a farewell dinner on a ship sailing through the Bosphorus.

The Gathering had a positive response by the media, especially TVs.

Events during the "Gathering in Istanbul" were organized by Initiative "Freedom for Freedom of Expression", Pen Writers Association of Turkey, Writers' Union of Turkey, Literarists' Association, Editors' Unification of Turkey, and Istanbul Bar Association.

Brief description of the background to the events:
On 23 January 1995, Yaşar Kemal was tried in İstanbul's No. 5 State Security Court regarding one of his articles which was published in Der Spiegel magazine. On the same day, intellectuals who gathered outside the court in support of Yaşar Kemal decided to collude in the 'crime' by jointly appending their names to the articles and speeches which had been alleged to be 'criminal'. The initiative "Freedom for Freedom of Expression" was born. A petition was started. Within
intellectuals from various fields had been collected. On 8 March 1995, these signatories, mostly Turkish writers and intellectuals, co-published a volume of articles entitled "Freedom of Expression". Most of the authors of the articles in the book had already been tried and imprisoned. (1)
===
(1) Turkish Penal Code article 162; re-publishing an article which is defined as a crime constitutes a new crime. The publisher is to be sentenced equally with the writer. The writers of the illegal articles in the book include: Yaşar Kemal, Dr. İsmail Beşikçi, Leyla Zana and others

This event, unprecedented in world publishing history was followed on 10 March 1995 by the "publishers" voluntarily presenting themselves before the State Security Court Prosecutor to face charges of 'seditious criminal activity'. To expedite the legal process and cut short the prosecutor's cross-examinations, all the accused signed and photo-copied an agreed formal statement which read: "I knowingly and willingly assume responsibility as a publisher of this book. I have nothing further to say".

On 24 August 1995, at the completion of questioning in the preliminary hearing of the first 99 people, the prosecutor demanded the accused be tried under Article 8 of the Anti-Terror Law and Article 312 of the Turkish Penal Code ("disseminating separatist propaganda"). He also demanded that infamous Article 8 be examined by the Constitutional Court and be rescinded on the grounds that it violated the Constitution. This request was refused by the court. After six months, 185 people have been on trial. Unfortunately we have lost the prominent writer, the late Aziz Nesin. Now we are 184.

What is arguably the most grotesque farce in Turkish legal history now threatens to become a protracted business likely to result in 20 months prison sentences for the accused and a vast increase in Turkey's shamefully large prison population.

The Turkish government will then be left with the old dilemma: either democratise the law and the constitution or face the opposition of Turkish and world democratic opinion and the stench of another major scandal.

The professions of the "accused":

The professions of the accused include 34 journalists, 7 television programme makers, 12 cinema actors or directors, 7 theatre actors, 20 writers, 8 politicians, 8 painters and cartoonists, 8 musicians, 8 trade unionists, 10 academics, 12 lawyers, 2 architects and 43 from various other professions. Let us examine the possible consequences if the accused are imprisonment:

* A minimum of 10 very popular television programmes will have to be cancelled because their stars or directors, will be in jail.

* 5 series will have to find new stars and change their story-lines. The media will lose over 30 well-known journalists; 15 popular columns will be left blank.

* 8 professorial chairs will be left vacant, and universities will require new teaching staff.

* Theatre stages and film sets will require many artists, directors, musicians, etc.

* 20 new books about prison life will be added to our literature if every author writes one.

International Solidarity and "the Mini Freedom of Expression" Booklet:

It was not long before these events began to attract international attention. Through the efforts of the PEN International, Writers in Prison Committee, PEN organisations in various countries moved into action. Within a short time, signatures of 141 well-known writers from 20 countries had been collected. A booklet was produced entitled "Mini Freedom of Expression" containing a paragraph from each of the articles published in the book "Freedom of Expression", together with Ahmet Altan's "Atakurd" article, which had led to the author receiving a 20-months prison sentence and these 141 names were included. For the second booklet, the same procedure was followed, but this time the State Prosecutor dropped the charges against the foreign authors on the grounds that he would not be able to bring them to İstanbul for trial.

However, the Turkish intellectuals participating in the preparation and distribution of this booklet will be tried.

We want to assure those whose names are included among the list of "publishers" that they will not find themselves in any legal difficulty for the following reasons:

1. If the State Prosecutor cannot locate an accused person and bring a case against him or her within six months, then there is nothing further that he can do. For example, of the 1,080 'publishers' of the main book "Freedom of Expression" only a total of 185 people were questioned and had cases brought against them. Nothing further can be done regarding the remaining 895 people.

2. The State Protector told us that he is unable to request the extradition of "offenders" from the USA or UK because such an "offence" does not exist in US or English law.

3. Thus the volunteers can only be questioned if they come to Turkey and this is exactly what we hope will happen.

4. There is no danger of being detained or taken into custody. Even we ourselves are not in custody.

5. This is only the pre-trial phase. At the end of this, the prosecutor may, or may not, bring a case. Even if he does bring a case, he will not be able to force anyone to come to Turkey to be tried.

DGM yabancı yazarlara soğuk

"Düşünceye Özgürlükçük-Ek: 1" kitapçığının yayıncısı olan 12 ülkeden 19 yabancı yazar, İstanbul DGM'ye kendileri hakkında suç duyurusunda bulundu. Bu konuyla ilgili ilk suç duyurusu dilekçesinin 4 martta İstanbul DGM Başsavcılığı'na verildiğini belirten Şanar Yurdatapan, ancak başsavcının dilekçeyi kabul etmediğini söyledi. Yabancı yazarların Türkiye'ye gelerek ikinci kez kendi haklarında suç duyurusunda bulunduklarını ve ifade vermek istediklerini bildiren Yurdatapan, "Başsavcı ikinci kez dilekçemizi 'Burayı şov meydanına çevirmeyin. Kasıtlı olarak yapay soğuk oluşturulmaya çalışılıyor. Böyle uyduruk şeyleri kabul etmem' diyerek geri çevirdi" dedi. Daha sonra Gazeteciler Cemiyeti'nde toplantı düzenleyen yabancı yazarlar adına konuşan Joanne Leedom-Ackerman ise PEN'in yılda iki kez hazırladığı rapora göre yazarları en fazla öldürülen ya da hapsedilen ülkelerin başında Türkiye'nin geldiğini söyledi. Yabancı yazarlardan Kanadalı Louise Gareau ile PEN Yazarlar Birliği İkinci Başkanı Feyza Hepçilingirler, Türkiye Yazarlar Derneği Temsilcisi Necati Mert ve Tomris Özden, Sakarya Cezaevi'ne giderek gazeteci Işık Yurtçu'yu ziyaret etti. PEN 2. Başkanı Leedom Ackerman ile Finlandiyalı Kalevi Haikara da Bursa Cezaevi'nde bulunan İsmail Beşikçi'yi ziyarete gittiler. (KAAN SAĞANAK)

CUMHURİYET, 11.03.1997

STATE SECURITY COURT BEHAVED COLDLY TO GUEST WRITERS
Photo:(Left to right) Tkachenko, Haikara, Sunesson, Yurdatapan, Van Daalen, Leedom-Ackerman, Kelman, Singh, Farhi.

Günşiray: Çok yaşa Kafka, iyi ki varsın

'Kafka' davasına yabancı yazar desteği

İSTANBUL - "Düşünce Özgürlüğü ve Türkiye" adlı kitaba yayıncı olarak imza atan ve savunmasında Kafka'nın romanından alıntı yapan tiyatro sanatçısı Mahir Günşiray hakkında "mahkeme heyetine hakaret" iddiasıyla açılan davaya devam edildi. Duruşma, 12 ülkeden 19 yabancı yazar tarafından da izlendi.

Günşiray hakkında, İstanbul 3 No'lu DGM'de daha önce yaptığı savunmada Franz Kafka'nın "Dava" romanından uyarlanmış "Duruşma" adlı tiyatro oyunundan bir bölüm okuyarak "mahkeme heyetine hakaret" ettiği iddiasıyla açılan davaya, dün İstanbul 10. Asliye Ceza Mahkemesi'nde devam edildi. Duruşmada söz alan Mahir Günşiray, "Çok yaşa Kafka, iyi ki halen varsın ve ben mahkeme salonunda değil, tiyatro salonlarında halen 'tiyatroyu' gerçekleştirebiliyorum" dedi.

Duruşmada, Günşiray'ın avukatının bir önceki celsedeki talebi üzerine, DGM'de Günşiray'la aynı şekilde savunma yapan 45 kişi hakkında da dava açılıp açılmadığının sorulduğu İstanbul DGM Cumhuriyet Başsavcılığı'ndan gelen cevabi yazı okundu.

Gelen yazının soruya yanıt niteliği taşımadığını belirten hakim, aynı konunun tekrar sorulması amacıyla İstanbul DGM Başsavcılığı'na yeniden yazı yazılmasını kararlaştırarak, duruşmayı 9 Nisan gününe erteledi.

Müzisyen Şanar Yurdatapan'ın yanı sıra "Düşünce Özgürlüğü İçin İstanbul Buluşması" toplantılarına katılmak için Britanya, Almanya, ABD, Filistin, Finlandiya, Hollanda, İsrail, İsveç, Kanada, Meksika ve Rusya'dan gelen yazarlar da, Günşiray'a destek vermek amacıyla duruşmayı izlediler.

DEMOKRASİ, 12.03.1997

INTERNATIONAL SUPPORT TO "KAFKA CASE"
Photo:(Left to right) Blomqvist, Van Daalen, Singh.

'İnsanlarınız cana yakın ama bu ülke çok soğuk' diyen yazarların ortak görüşü:

'Ülkenize güneş doğmamış'

Meslektaşlarına destek vermek amacıyla Türkiye'ye gelen yabancı yazarlar, demokratik hakları umduklarından daha kötü bulduklarını ve gergin ortamdan çok ürktüklerini belirttiler.

Esin Delay

Yabancı yazarlar öğrencilerle birlikte Beyazıt meydanında.

İstanbul- "İstanbul olağanüstü güzel bir şehir ama burada yaşadıklarım çok dramatik. Kalabalıkların içinde yaşadıklarımdan korktum. Özellikle de İstanbul Üniversitesi'nin önündeki öğrenci ve polis kalabalığından... Ben uçmaktan da korkarım. Yarın İstanbul'dan ayrılmak için uçmak zorundayım ve bu beni ilk kez mutlu ediyor..."

Bu sözler, "Düşünce Suçuna Karşı Girişim Gurubu'nun İstanbul Buluşması'na katılan yabancı yazarlardan İsrail'li Avraham Heffner'e ait. Yalnızca Heffner böyle düşünüyor. Meslektaşlarına destek vermek için gelen 21 yazar, Türkiye'de gördüklerin-

den korkuya kapılmış.

"Düşünce Suçuna Karşı Girişim Grubu'nun davetlisi olarak İstanbul'a gelen yabancı yazarlar, buradan ayrılmadan önce bir Boğaz gezisi yaptı. Gezide, yabancı yazarların yanı sıra PEN Yazarlar Derneği, Türkiye Yazarlar Sendikası, Edebiyatçılar Derneği ve Düşünce Suçuna Karşı Girişim Grubu üyeleri de katıldı.

Kanada'dan gelen Louise Gareau Des-Bois İstanbul Üniversitesi'nin önündeki binlerce öğrenciyle ilgili izlenimlerini aktarırken, "Gençler özgür olabilmek için savaşmak zorunda kalmamalı, bu beni çok etkiledi..." diyor.

Bu buluşmaya Almanya'dan katılan PEN temsilcisi yazar ve gazeteci Rajvinder Singh,

yaşadıklarını özetliyor; "İstanbul, güzel kadınlar ve güzel yemekler diyarı. İnsanlar çok cana yakın ve kırmızı şarap mükemmel. Ama demokrasi konusunda gördüklerim beni çok ürküttü. Keşke bizim buraya gelmemize hiç gerek kal-

masaydı..."

İngiltere'nin ödüllü İskoç yazarı James Kelman ile Türkiye'deki demokratik hak ve özgürlükler konusuna oldukça politik yaklaşıyor; "İstanbul çok güzel ve çok tipik bir şehir. Tekneden ve denizden

bahsedersem herşey olağanüstü... Gerisini hatırlamak istemiyorum."

İsrailli şair ve yazar Maja Bejerano "Şok geçirdim" diyor; "Herşey o kadar karışık ve dehşet verici ki, olayların politik yoğunluğu ve İstanbul'un tarihi güzelliği içiçe geçince ne yapacağımı bilemedim. İnsanlar çok cana yakın ama bu ülke çok soğuk, insanı üşütüyor. Sanırım güneş hiç görmedinizin için!"

Uluslararası Af Örgütü'nün gözlemcisi olarak İstanbul Buluşması'na katılan Robert Brouver ve Milo Van Der Burgt, Türkiye'deki demokratik ortamı duyduklarından daha kötü bulduklarını söylüyorlar; "Özellikle üniversite öğrencilerinden duyduklarımız dehşet verici. Türk hükümeti düşünce özgürlüğü konusunda gerçekçi ve samimi adımlar atmazsa her zaman Avrupa Birliği'nin dışında kalacaktır."

YENİ YÜZYIL, 14.03.1997

SUN DID NOT RISE IN YOUR LAND YET
Photo:(Left to right) Blomqvist, Van Daalen, Singh.

Beyazıt'taki gösteride polis sıkı önlemler aldı. Eylemde Şanar Yurdatapan, PEN 2. Başkanı ABD'li Joanne Ackermann ile Rus Alexander Tckachenko da birer konuşma yaptı. Ali Özlüer. (SHA)

Öğrencilere PEN desteği

Ankara ve Manisa'da öğrencilere hapis cezaları verilmesi, İstanbul Üniversitesi'nde protesto edildi. Gösteriye 12 ülkeden gelen 21 PEN üyesi de destek verdi.

Üniversitenin Beyazıt'taki Merkez Binası'nda toplanan öğrenciler, saat 14.00 sıralarında ellerinde pankartlarla sloganlar atarak, merkez kapısına yürüdü. Dışarda bekleyen Çevik Kuvvet ve özel hareket ekipleri, içeri girip gru-

bun önünü kesti ve dış kapıyı kapattı. Fen-Edebiyat Fakültesi'nden çıkan bir grup da Beyazıt Meydanı'na geldi. İşi, grubun önünü kesti ve içeriye girişini önledi. Foruma destek amacıyla gelen Düşünce Suçuna Karşı Girişim Grubu Sözcüsü Şanar Yurdatapan ile Uluslararası Yazarlar Birliği'nin (PEN) 21 üyesi üniversiteye alınmadı.

Eyleme müdahalede bulunmayan polis, içerideki öğrencilerin dışarı çık-

masına izin verdi. Gruplar, bazı demokratik kitle örgütlerinin de katılımıyla Beyazıt Meydanı'ndaki üniversite ana giriş kapısı önünde toplandı.

Burada yapılan açıklamada, Ankara'da 8 öğrencinin toplam 96 yıl, Manisa'da 12 kişinin 76, yine Ankara'da 22 üniversitelinin 235 yıl ağır hapis cezasına çarptırılmalarını protesto edildi. Açıklamada, "Arkadaşlarımızın işlediği suça, biz bu suçu her gün bin kez işle-

yeceğiz" denildi. Şanar Yurdatapan, Rektör Bülent Berkarda'nın, PEN yazarları için "Onlar kim? Onları tanımıyorum" dediğini öne sürdü.

PEN 2. Başkanı Amerikalı Joanne Ackermann ile Rusya PEN Başkanı Alexander Tckachenko da birer konuşma yaptı.

Basın açıklamasının ardından, gösteriye katılanlar sessizce dağıldılar. Cemal Köyük-Cem Eser-Nejdet Çokan.

SABAH, 12.03.1997

PEN SUPPORT TO STUDENTS
Photo:(Left to right) Tkachenko, Yurdatapan

'Yasaların yazara saygısı yok'

YAZAR ve DÜŞÜNCE ÖZGÜRLÜ...
PEN YAZAR...
...EDEB...
DER...

GATHERING IN ISTANBUL FOR
MARCH 10-12 TH 1997
DÜŞÜNCE ÖZGÜRLÜĞÜ İÇİN İS...

(Fotoğraf: KADER TUĞLA)

Meslektaşlarına destek olmak için gelen yabancı yazarlar uygulamalardan şaşkınlık duydular

'Düşünce özgürlüğü doğal bir haktır'

DUYGU DURGUN

ABD Uluslararası PEN 2. Başkanı Joanne Leedom-Ackerman, Türkiye'nin yükümlülüklerini yerine getirmek zorunda olduğunu vurgulayarak, herkesin doğal hakkı olan özgürlüğün yazarlara da tanınması gerektiğini belirtiyor. Rusya PEN Başkanı Alexander Tkachenko ise Rusya'da da yargının tamamıyla bürokrasinin elinde olduğunu ifade ederek, "Rusya'da da durum üç aşağı beş yukarı Türkiye'ye benzer" diyor. *(Fotoğraflar: KAAN SAĞANAK)*

LAWS HAVE NO RESPECT TO WRITERS
Photo: Representatives of Turkish Writers' Organizations.

FREEDOM OF EXPRESSION IS A NATURAL RIGHT
Photos: Leedom-Ackerman, Tkachenko.

41 kitabından 29'u 'mahkûm'

DENİZ GÖKÇE

İSTANBUL - Yayıncı Ünsal Öztürk, Yayıncılar Birliği'nin öncülüğünde başlatılan "Ünsal Öztürk'e özgürlük" kampanyasıyla toplanan para ile özgürlüğüne kavuştu. Öztürk, hapis cezasının sona erdiği aralık ayında yaptığı açıklamada, "1 milyar 110 milyon lira para cezasını ödemeyi kabul etmiyorum" diyerek tahliye olmamıştı.

Öztürk, 1987 yılında kurulan Yurt Yayınları'nın sahibi. Yayınevinin bugüne kadar yayımladığı 41 kitap hakkında dava açıldı. Bunların 36'sı ya-

saklandı. Yasaklanan kitapların 29'u ise İsmail Beşikçi'ye ait.

Beşikçi'yle tanışma

İsmail Beşikçi'yle tanışmalarının ardından gelişen dostluklarının kendisine çok şey kazandırdığını düşünüyor. "Beşikçi'yle bizim tanışmamız 1991'de DGM kapılarında oldu. Tanışmamızın ardından kitaplarını yayınlamaya başladım" diyor Öztürk.

İlk yayımladıkları kitapla birlikte, yayınevi defalarca basılmış, gözaltına alınmışlar. 1 Ağustos 1991 günü yani kitap yayımlandıktan birkaç hafta sonra Beşikçi tutuklan-

muş. Öztürk'ün günleri de mahkemelerde geçmiş. Öztürk yayımladığı kitapların 29'unun mahkûm edildiğini, yayınevinin çıkardığı 41 kitap hakkında da dava açıldığını belirtiyor.

1994'te Öztürk de tutuklandı. Yayıncıyla, yazar Metris Kapalı Cezaevi'ni paylaştı. Öztürk 8'inci maddede yapılan değişiklikle bir sene sonra tahliye edildi. Süren davaların sonuçlanmasıyla 26 Eylül 1996'da tekrar cezaevine girdi. Bu kez Bursa Cezaevi'nde birlikte yattılar 19 Aralık günü hapis cezasının bitmesine karşın para cezasını ödemeyerek, ken-

di isteğiyle tahliye olmadı Öztürk.

Protestoya düşünce özgürlüğü üzerindeki çifte standarda dikkat çekmek için başlamış. Öztürk "Bazıları düşüncelerini söylediğinde neden cezaevine girmiyor da ben söylediğimde giriyorum. Bunun tartışılmasını istedim. Yayıncıların ceza almasını içeren bir kanun maddesi yokken bizler sorumlu yazıişleri müdürü muamelesi

yapılarak yargılanıyoruz. Yasalarda bir fiil bir kez cezalandırılırken biz aynı kitaptan neden birkaç kez ceza alıyoruz. Bunlara dikkat çekmek için para cezasını ödemedim" diyor.

RADİKAL, 15.03.1997

29 OF HIS 41 BOOKS BANNED

Ünsal Öztürk, publisher of Dr. İsmail Beşikçi's books. He was in prison because he was not able -and also refused- to pay the fine of 1.100.000.000 TL. (Around10.000 US Dollars) But with the help of Turkish Publishers' Union and also with contributions from guest writers and their organizations, he was set free and participated at the Gathering in İstanbul on the last day, 12.03.

Yazarlar 'mutsuz' ayrıldı

İstanbul'da yaşadıklarını çok dramatik bulan İsrailli yazar Avraham Heffner şöyle diyordu: "Uçmaktan herkesten çok daha fazla korkuyorum. Ama yarın İstanbul'dan ayrılmak için uçmak zorundayım ve bu beni mutlu ediyor"

CELAL BAŞLANGIÇ

Kabataş'tan denize açılan 'Semiramis 1' yatı Beşiktaş kıyısına gelince 'Düşünce Özgürlüğü İçin İstanbul Buluşması'na katılan yabancı yazarlar birbirlerine bakıp gülümsediler.

Üç günlük 'İstanbul Buluşması'nda Beşiktaş'taki DGM binasına iki kez gelip kendilerini ihbar etmek istemişler, ancak bir türlü içeri girememişlerdi. Karayoluyla giremedikleri DGM binasını karşılarında görünce 'Bu kez de denizden de-

Yabancı yazarlar, Türkiye'den ayrılmadan önce İstanbul Gazeteciler Cemiyeti'nde gözlemlerini anlattı.

durumunu tüm açıklığıy-   ney" diye niteliyordu: - İstanbul'da yaşadıkla-   rı dürüst bir yer bulama-   biydiler. Sık sık "Siz nasıl

RADİKAL, 15.03.1997

WRITERS LEFT UNHAPPY
Photos: Leedom-Ackerman, Tkachenko.

The Mini FREEDOM OF EXPRESSION

Ahmet Altan, Günay Aslan, Fikret Başkaya, İsmail Beşikçi, Münir Ceylan, Oral Çalışlar, Haluk Gerger, Doğu Perinçek, Kemal Yalçın, DEP MPs, Human Rights Association representatives

This book was compiled from articles and speeches authored by the above who were prepared to face charges for the work as "crimes of thought" in order to draw attention to the absence of freedom of expression in Turkey.

Translated by: Sheri Laizer

FOREWORD AND POSTSCRIPT

We, named below, 93 writers from 23 countries, knowingly and willingly consent to the publication of the book entitled "The Mini Freedom of Expression Book".

AUSTRALIA

Beverley Farmer

AUSTRIA

Utta Roy-Seifert

CANADA

Louise Gareau-Des Bois
Isobal Harry

CROATIA

Mirko Mirkovic

CZECH REPUBLIC

Jana Cervenkova

DENMARK

Solvej Balle
Niels Barfoed (Pres. of Danish PEN)
Jens Lohmann

FINLAND

Kalevi Haikara

FRANCE

Tahar Benjelloun
Pierre Bourdieu
Helen Cixous
Max Gallo
Eduardo Manet
Philippe Minyana
Edgar Morin
Serge Rezvani
Antoine Spire

GERMANY

Brigitte Burmeister
Karl Otto Conrady
Eva Demski
Uwe Friesel
Inge Jens
Walter Jens
Wend Kaessens
Gisela Kraft
Siegfried Lenz
Erich Loest
Beate Morgenstern
Dieter Schlenstedt
Johannes Mario Simmel
Rajvinder Singh
Klaus Staeck
Carola Stern
Johano Strasser
B. K. Tragelehn
Günther Wallraff
Herbert Wiesner
K. D. Wolff
Elsbeth Wolffheim

GREAT BRITAIN

Margaret Drabble
Moris Farhi
James Kelman
Harold Pinter
Lucy Popescu

HOLLAND

Maria Van Daalen

JAPAN

Mitsukazo Shiboh

KENYA

Sam Mbure

MALAWI

Edison Mpina

MEXICO

M. G. Garcia Barragan
Anthony Cohen
Lucina Kathman
Charles Kuschinski
Micholas Patricca
Soledad Santiago
David Wright

NEPAL

Archana Singh Karki

NORWAY

Hans Butenschon
Helen Eie
Sindre Guldvog
Annila Heger
Anders Heger
Elisabet W. Middelthor
Ase Ryverclen
Eric Sauar
Sigmund Strömm

PALESTINE

Hanan Awwad

POLAND

Anna Treciakowska

RUSSIA

Andrei Bitov
Zoya Boguslavskaya
Anatoly Kim
Anatoly Makazev
Vyacheslav Pyetsukh
Lev Timofeev
Alexander Tkachenko
Arkady Vaksberg
Andrei Voznesensky

SWEDEN

Lars Erik Blomqvist
Inger Johannson
Eugene Schoulgin
Ola Sunesson
Thomas von Vegesack

SWITZERLAND

Freddy Alleman
Fawzia Assaad
Beat Breehbühl
Serge Ehrensperger
Barbara Traber
Verena Wyss

USA

Joanne Leedom-Ackerman
Anthony Cohan
Siobhan Dowd
Hannah Pakula

'ATAKURD'
Ahmet Altan

What if Mustafa Kemal had not been born in Salonika, but
had been born an Ottoman pasha in Mosul; what if, after the
Turks and Kurds had together won the War of Liberation, he
had taken the first step of founding a new Republic and had
named it the 'Republic of Kurdistan', and had with the
consent of the Assembly adopted the name of 'Atakurd'...

...What if at school we learned of the 'seven thousand
years' of the Kurds in history, that the original owners of
Anatolia were the Kurds, and that their forefathers were
the Mongols, Huns and Etruscans, and we read in our classes
of the heroism of the Kurdish pashas of Ottoman times.

...There are both Turkish and Kurdish citizens in this
country. However, history has been mapped out in Turkish.
Had it been the other way around and today we were not
accepted as 'Turkish' -even though this is what we want the
Kurds to accept- this groundless demand has finally
erupted. Behind the country's 'terrorism' lies a civil war.

...Those who claim that it is just not worth it are the
same ones who want 'democracy'.

> In addition to being sacked from Milliyet
> newspaper after the publication of this article,
> Ahmet Altan was sentenced to 20 months
> imprisonment in İstanbul No. 4 State Security
> Court on 18.10.1995. The sentence was suspended
> for a five-year period.

HISTORY IN MOURNING
Günay Aslan

...Turkey's 'Kurdish policy' is a most expressive term. To be a Kurd in Turkey's Republic is the same as to have been a Jew in Hitler's Germany, a Black in Botha's Africa, or a Palestinian in the Israeli-occupied territories. The most accurate expression of Turkey's Kurdish policy can be understood from such examples as Dersim, Zilan, Xratel, Sefo, Şırnak, Guruza, Deve Geçidi and most recently, Kasaplar Deresi...

The year is 1943. There is neither any uprising, nor any resistance. The Kurds are well-behaved and quiet. However, in the county of Saray, within the space of only two months, two massacres are commited. In Xratel, twenty poor Kurdish villagers are murdered, and in Sefo Deresi, another thirty-three are slaughtered.

Having been guilty of no crime other than being Kurdish, the No. 3 Commander General of the Army, Mustafa Muğlalı Pasha, was tried in the Turkish army's highest military court for having given the order 'Kill', for the villagers to be shot. He was sentenced to death in the General Staff Military Court...

In our own time when the expressions "to become democratised" and "to become civilised" are mostly bandied about, when the orders 'arrest and kill' are photocopied and distributed, and hundreds of innocent people are murdered under these orders, why is it that no case has been brought against the Commander of the Tunceli Brigade, Osman Citim, and that conversely, in August 1989, he was promoted at a meeting of the Military Council?...

On account of the extracts above from Günay Aslan's book, "33 Bullets", Aslan was sentenced to prison and fined under Article 8 of the Anti-Terror Law. He is at present living abroad as a political refugee.

THE NATIONAL LIBERATION STRUGGLE'S 'NATIONAL' ISSUE
Fikret Başkaya

...For so long as the Kurdish issue is not evaluated as
part of the whole, the evolution of Turkish social analysis
is doomed to remain incomplete. It is not possible to
evaluate the whole when neglecting a part of which the
whole is composed. The analysis itself loses its scientific
authority, whether one likes it or not, if one of the
constructive elements of a given social period is excluded.
Turkish intellectuals 'protesting' against racist-fascist
repression in remote parts of Africa, Asia and
Latin-America remain unblinking over the tragedy of another
nation being played out right beneath their noses, each one
equally bigoted and chauvinistic when confronted with the
Kurdish problem these are opposed to the dictators, yet
behave like dictators in their own right displaying their
double-standards. Doubtless, in order to debate these
issues amongst themselves, these same Turkish intellectuals
need to abolish those restrictions in their minds which
determine their very thoughts.

> Dr. Fikret Başkaya was sentenced to heavy
> imprisonment and fined under Article 8 of the
> Anti-Terror Law on account of his book "The
> Bankruptcy of Paradigms", from which the above
> article derives.

A LETTER TO UNESCO
İsmail Beşikçi

...The Imperialist endeavour to divide Kurdistan took
place between 1915-1925. Undoubtedly, this had its roots in
the 19th century or even in earlier periods. But, it is
particularly necessary to examine those years; especially,
the period between 1919-1923. The western imperialists like
Great Britain and France collaborated on this front with
the Kemalists. As is understood, prior to the First World
War, Arab lands such as Iraq, Syria, Arabia, Yemen,
Lebanon, Palestine, Egypt, Tunisia, and Algeria lay within
the borders of the Ottoman Empire. Balkan territories such
as Albania, Bulgaria, Greece, Bosnia-Herzegovina, and
Yugoslavia also lay within the boundaries of the Ottoman
Empire. After the First World War, the Kemalists laid no
claim to these territories. They did not claim that 'these
lands belong to our forefathers', 'the horse of our
forefathers rode across these lands', 'these lands were
watered by the blood of our forefathers' and so on. They
did not compose literature claiming 'down the ages, we
lived with these peoples in brotherhood, our brother in the
Faith'... As far as the Arab lands were concerned they
·reached a ready agreement with the western Imperialists
like Great Britain and France...

Associate professor, Dr. İsmail Beşikçi was
sentenced to heavy imprisonment and fined under
Article 8 of the Anti-Terror Law for his book
entitled "A Letter to UNESCO" from which the above
extract derives. İsmail Beşikçi is still serving
his sentence in Ankara prison. İsmail Beşikçi was
also tried and sentenced on account of his books.

DEBT...
Haluk Gerger

...When I was sentenced to one year and eight months imprisonment and a 208 million Turkish lira fine under the Anti-Terror Law in the Ankara State Security Court, I said that "I accepted that I was paying off an installment of my debt to the working class, labour and the Kurdish people". The other day I received a letter from a reader friend. This reader wrote saying "I understood what you meant by your debt to the working class and to labour, but I would like you to explain a little what you meant by your debt to the Kurdish people. Considering that there could also be others who were similarly curious about this, I thought about writing my response to this request in Özgür Ülke newspaper and decided to send this article to the appropriate colleagues.

My first intention concerning 'my debt to the Kurdish people' was this: within the perimeters of my own thinking I had been late in grasping the justness of the Kurdish people's struggle and being of assistance...by virtue of which I also have a debt to pay to the Kurdish people...

> Associate professor, Dr. Haluk Gerger was sentenced
> to heavy imprisonment and a fine under Article 8
> of the Anti-Terror Law for having sent a message
> on the occasion of a concert commemorating Deniz
> Gezmiş. He completed his term of imprisonment
> and was subsequently released! However, he
> was again charged under the same Article of
> the same law for the article above; the case
> is being heard in the Supreme Court of Appeal.

THE KURDISH PROBLEM CAN BE RESOLVED THROUGH FRATERNITY
Doğu Perinçek

...The State is now in the situation where it has become the biggest terrorist of all. The State has become illegal. The State forces quarry a man in the mountains... Vedat Aydın... later they come and he is shot dead by the roadside. The President of Hilal City Council, Yakup Kara is taken down from the back (of a vehicle) with five friends and shot one hundred meters along the other side by the State forces. Our member for Cizre, İbrahim Sarıca is taken from his home and shot right in front of the entire village. The Kurdish provinces have become death markets. It has been turned into a death trade. We need to recognise this.

Look at the documents I am holding. There are orders which say "Arrest and kill them". These date from 1986. The originals exist as well. They brought this fax from Istanbul. I have the originals. I passed copies to Adnan Kahveci, (a member) in your government. They state openly "Arrest and kill them". They have been signed. They say in critical places, "Don't bother to guard the Kurds"...

> Doğu Perinçek was sentenced to heavy imprisonment and fined for infringing Article 8 of the Anti-Terror Law during a speech he made quoted from above, shown on TRT during the elections of October 1991 on an open platform of leaders.

I CAN'T TELL YOU THAT YOU HAVE DIED
Kemal Yalçın

...

I can't tell the Great Mesopotamian Plane Tree,
or the 3000 year old Aegean olive tree:
"You have died".

I can't tell the bud of Kurdistan
shining in the heart of the laurel leaves,
"You have died".

This year in Kurdistan t
here is a different Newroz enlightenment,
The Kurdish villager has overcome his fear,
rises to his feet,
Turns to face the mountains
and gazes at the rising sun.

> A case was brought against poet, Kemal Yalçın
> under Article 8 of the Anti-Terror Law on
> account of his book "The Roses of Deportation",
> from which the above extract derives. The book
> won first prize for poetry in the 1991 competition
> sponsored by Petrol-İş. The Court of Appeal
> overturned the court's acquittal. The judgement
> of the poet has recommenced.

TOMORROW WILL BE TOO LATE!
Münir Ceylan

...Those who examine the Anti-Terror Law carefully will
readily observe that it is not a law which is simply
directed at the Kurdish people, but which is also targeting
the labour, freedom and democracy struggle of the masses,
the working class and labour force.

Because of these laws and today's "State Terror", our
labour force as a whole should oppose them, not just the
Kurdish people. The correct response on the part of trade
unions to this problem is absolutely vital and of greater
import than passing it over lightly by simply putting up a
few fliers.

> Münir Ceylan was sentenced to heavy imprisonment
> under Turkish Penal Code No. 312 for the publication
> of this article in "Yeni Ülke" newspaper on
> 21 July 1991. He served the full sentence and was
> released.

THE KURDISH QUESTION ACCORDING TO ÖCALAN AND BURKAY
Oral Çalışlar

Çalışlar: There is as yet no legal route open to a Kurdish party.

Burkay: Certainly. There is not such thing, none at all in any case. The government is also determined not to open up the way. In my view, had the government been able to face this, the terror, the violance would have stopped; it would have stopped bi-laterally. The government does not countenance the prospect of the legalisation of the Kurdish movement. They do not countenance the establishment of legal Kurdish parties with their own programmes. They do not want to go down this route. In my view, the key to the problem lies here.

Çalışlar: But to some extent, with motivation and effort, it will happen...

Burkay: ...I value the legal struggle going on in the country at present. That within the framework of the HEP, right now with the DEP, and outside that. Of course, this is important. If I had had some control over conditions, I would have considered returning to Turkey and carrying on the struggle in this way, I would have faced the risks. But as I said a moment ago, I do not possess the rights to citizenship at all. The second point, the party I head is guilty under Turkish law. In other words, they could impose a sentence of 15 years imprisonment minimum on me.

Oral Çalışlar was sentenced to heavy imprisonment and under Article 8 of the Anti-Terror Law for his books entitled "The Kurdish Question according to Öcalan and Burkay". The sentence was later postponed under the pretext of a change to Article 8.

APPLICATION OF PETITION TO THE CSCE
Sırrı Sakık, Hatip Dicle, Ahmet Türk, Leyla Zana, Orhan Doğan, Mahmut Alınak

...Today in Turkey no one may remain quiet or disinterested while living in the present deeply-troubling times. Foremostly, against the background of violence which derives from the rebuttal of the Kurdish people's identity and national rights, with every passing day the possibility of reaching an internal accord, attaining democracy and winning respect for human rights is increasingly in jeopardy... An average of 30 people each day lose their lives in clashes. In just the past two months, in close on 30 provinces and counties in the East and South-east, on the pretext that the State security forces have encountered some disturbance, these same security forces open fire on all the homes and businesses in settled areas deploying both light and heavy arms, resulting in a loss of life and destruction to property which, one can justly claim, amounts to trillions of Turkish lira. As the analysis goes, it may concluded that the tendency is for this to have become a general policy in the region. Bearing in mind the practice of treating our people as guilty by suspicion, they are hostages to fortune, powerless under the fire of the State forces...

> The 'Declaration' and 'Petition' from which the above extract derives was considered to be one of the elements constituting an offence which opened the way to the trial being brought against the DEP MP's in the Ankara State Security Court's testimony.

The Mini FREEDOM OF EXPRESSION

In this booklet you will find one paragraph
from each article existing in the book named
"Freedom of Expression", which was published
by 1080 intellectuals. This is one of the the
most popular acts of civil disobediance in
Turkey and 184 of the "Publishers!" are being
tried by the State Security Court of.Istanbul.

The first -and complete- article "Atakürt"
by Ahmet Altan, which caused him to be
sentenced to 18 months of imprisonment, is
added to the booklet to make sure to violate
the article 162 of Turkish Penal Code which
says "Republishing an article defined as a
crime, is a new crime. The publisher is to
be sentenced equally as the author."

The 144 authors from 20 different countries,
whose names are listed at the first edition of
this booklet -except the ones who will visit
İstanbul on 12.03.1997 for questioning at the
State Security Court- are not repeated here.
The names you will find in the first pages, are
the authors who sent their signatures later.

İstanbul, 28.02.1997

Notes

Introduction

1   Gerard Seenan, "He Fled from Hell in a Turkish Prison, Only to Die a Bloody Death in Glasgow," *Guardian*, August 6, 2001, https://www.theguardian.com/uk/2001/aug/07/politics.immigration.

2   David Leask, "Anti-terror Police Probe Turkish Kurds Terror Group Operations in Edinburgh," *Herald*, January 6, 2017, https://www.heraldscotland.com/news/15008363.anti-terror-police-probe-turkish-kurds-terror-group-operations-edinburgh.

3   David Leask is the named journalist of the 2017 feature.

4   Alistair Bell, whose January 4, 1994, *Herald* article "Europe Clamps Down on PKK Guerrillas" is available at https://www.heraldscotland.com/news/12702786.europe-clamps-down-on-pkk-guerrillas.

5   Leask, "Anti-terror Police Probe Turkish Kurds Terror Group Operations in Edinburgh."

6   See the essay "Murder in the Line of Duty" later in this book for fuller information on this.

7   Joseph Maggs, "Fighting Sus! Then and Now," *Institute of Race Relations*, April 4, 2019, https://irr.org.uk/article/fighting-sus-then-and-now.

8   See the following essay, "Oppression and Solidarity."

9   In a press release by the Freedom of Thought initiative, referring to the pamphlet *Gathering in Istanbul for Freedom of Expression: March 10–12, 1997*.

10   See the campaign literature for Öcalan's fight for freedom, an "international appeal" to writers and artists, February 1999. See more on this in Abdullah Öcalan, *The Political Thought of Abdullah Öcalan: Kurdistan, Woman's Revolution and Democratic Confederalism* (London: Pluto Books, 2017), https://files.libcom.org/files/Ocalan,%20Abdullah%20-%20The%20Political%20Thought%20of%20Abdullah%20Ocalan.pdf.

11   Mehmed Uzun, "The Kurdish Resistance in Exile," *Autodafe: The Journal of the International Parliament of Writers*, Spring 2001.

12   For a full account of this, see William Clark, "Byzantine Politics: The Abduction and Trial of Abdullah Öcalan," *Variant* 8 (Summer 1999), published as a *Variant* magazine supplement.

13   Ibid., citing the *New York Times*, February 20, 1999.

14   *The Kurdish Observer*, November 28, 1999. See also Abdullah Öcalan, "Statement by Abdullah Ocalan (PKK) on His Abduction from Kenya," translated by Arm the Spirit from their mailing list archives, November 26, 1999, http://www.hartford-hwp.com/archives/51/162.html.

15   He had studied under George Buchanan, historian, poet and educator.

16   See the *Basilikon Doron*, by James VI of Scotland (first published 1599) and cited by John Miller in his *Early Modern Britain, 1450–1750* (Cambridge: Cambridge University Press, 2017). James VI became James I in 1603, first king of the newly formed United Kingdom.

17   See Frank Kitson, *Low Intensity Operations: Subversion, Insurgency & Peacekeeping* (London: Faber & Faber, 1971), 24, where Brigadier Kitson refers to the historical project: "Suppression of the Irish [and] the Defence of the Protestant Religion."

18   "Catholic Emancipation," *Encyclopaedia Britannica*, April 24, 2019, https://www.britannica.com/event/Catholic-Emancipation.

19   In Ballymurphy and in Derry six months later.

20   "Didim," Wikipedia: The Free Encyclopedia, last modified January 14, 2023, https://en.wikipedia.org/wiki/Didim.

21   LuddendenTurk, "Re: Is It Safe to Holiday in Kusadasi?," Tripadvisor, 2015, https://www.tripadvisor.co.uk/ShowTopic-g297972-i1664-k8274811-Is_it_safe_to_holiday_in_kusadasi-Kusadasi_Turkish_Aegean_Coast.html.

22   "Doğuş Group," Wikipedia: The Free Encyclopedia, last modified August 14, 2022, https://en.wikipedia.org/wiki/Do%C4%9Fu%C5%9F_Group.

23   "Banco Bilbao Vizcaya Argentaria," Wikipedia: The Free Encyclopedia, last modified February 28, 2023, https://en.wikipedia.org/wiki/Banco_Bilbao_Vizcaya_Argentaria.

24   Lockheed Martin, "All Systems Are Go: Lockheed Martin Welcomes Approval from Shetland Islands Council for SaxaVord Spaceport Construction," news release, February 28, 2022, https://lockheedmartinuk.mediaroom.com/index.php?s=2429&item=122569.

25   Dheirin Bechai, "Lockheed Martin Wins Development Contract against Threats from Iran and North Korea," *Seeking Alpha*, April 7, 2021, https://seekingalpha.com/article/4417895-lockheed-martin-wins-against-threats-from-iran-and-north-korea.

Oppression and Solidarity

1 Gerard Chaliand, ed., *A People without a Country: The Kurds and Kurdistan* (London: Zed Press, 1980), 87.

2 The *Glasgow Keelie* was a radical newssheet created and distributed by the group known as Workers City that operated in the late 1980s and early 1990s.

The Freedom for Freedom of Expression Rally, Istanbul 1997

1 İsmail Beşikçi, *Selected Writings: Kurdistan & Turkish Colonialism* (London: Kurdistan Solidarity Committee, 1991).

2 With France and Iran (Persia), the USA stayed somewhat in the background.

3 Ismet Sheriff Vanly, "Kurdistan in Iraq," collected in *A People without a Country: The Kurds and Kurdistan*, ed. Gerard Chaliand (London: Zed Press, 1980).

4 *Evening Times* (Glasgow newspaper), April 21, 1997, encouraging its readership to "fly to Turkey this autumn."

5 Amnesty International, "Children at Risk of Torture, Death in Custody and Disappearance," news release no. EUR 44/144/96, November 1, 1996, https://www.refworld.org/docid/3ae6a9842c.html.

6 Sertac Bucak and Johannes Düchting, *The Kurds and Kurdistan: Thinking Is a Crime* (Bonn, Germany: International Association for Human Rights in Kurdistan, 1996), a report on freedom of expression in Turkey; additional information from Voice of Kurdistan.

7 At Edinburgh University.

8 Had prepared for an audience I assumed would consist almost exclusively of Scottish people, but roughly half were Kurdish exiles.

9 My earlier "Oppression and Solidarity," originally published in the collection *Some Recent Attacks* (Edinburgh: AK Press, 1992).

10 Except where stated, and with apologies to Kendal. The book was reprinted a year later after the fall of the Shah of Iran, with an extra section: *A People without a Country: The Kurds and Kurdistan*, edited by Gerard Chaliand; Kendal's essay is entitled "Kurdistan in Turkey."

11 Among the literary works I presume proscribed in Turkey is my 1949 Penguin edition of Xenophon's *The Persian Expedition*. In his translation Rex Warner not only refers to "Kurdistan," he refuses to censor or suppress Xenophon's account of his encounters in 400 BC with the "Kardouçi" (which is spelled "Carduchi").

12 See Mustafa Nazdar, "The Kurds in Syria," in Chaliand, *A People without a Country*.

13 For evidence of this, read almost any issue of *Statewatch* journal (support and access back issues here: https://www.statewatch.org). A public meeting was held in 1997 in London on the issue of "the Criminalisation of the Kurds in the UK and Europe."

14 Information from *Statewatch* 6, no. 6 (November–December 1996).

15 Later dropped the hyphenated part, now known as John Austin.

16 For a discussion of a South African/Turkish connection in the murder of Olof Palme, see *PSK Bulletin* no. 6, November 1996.

17 *Statewatch* 7, no. 1 (January–February 1997).

18 Ibid., for an extended discussion on this.

19 See *Lobster* magazine no. 32 (December 1996), for its comment on the *Mail on Sunday* report.

20 Linked directly to the British security services (MI6 in the early 1970s, MI5 after that). See *Lobster* nos. 16 (1988) and 19 (1990) for information on Paul Wilkinson and see also *Lobster* nos. 10 (1986), 14 (1987) and others for a fuller account of the whole murky area. Wilkinson is an erstwhile colleague of far-right "terrorist experts" such as Brian Crozier and Maurice Tugwell. Subscribe to *Lobster* c/o Robin Ramsay (Dept W), 214 Westbourne Ave., Hull HU5 3JB (website: https://www.lobster-magazine.co.uk/shop).

21 On April 22, 1997.

22 İsmail Beşikçi, *Selected Writings: Kurdistan and Turkish Colonialism* (London: Kurdistan Solidarity Committee, 1991).

23 Ibid.

24 Ibid.

25 It may have been an oversight but I noted that none of the six Israeli writers was listed as having "knowingly and willingly consent[ed] to the publication of the *Mini Freedom of Expression* booklet."

26 From press releases by the Freedom of Thought initiative.

27 From the introduction to the *Mini Freedom of Expression* booklet.

28 Only as I understand it, as a layperson.

29 This involved students unfurling a banner in parliament.

30 A pseudonym adopted by the writer.

31 Famous Turkish musician and composer; former journalist; a leading human rights activist over the last three decades.

32 Amnesty International, "Turkey: No Security Without Human Rights," news release no. EUR 44/084/1996, September 30, 1996, https://www.amnesty.org/en/documents/eur44/084/1996/en.

33 *Kurdistan Information Bulletin* no. 34, January 1997. Just over four weeks after the event, on April 16, Yurdatapan was detained at Istanbul Airport then held at the anti-terror branch of police headquarters.

34 Ibid.

35 An introduction to his work: İsmail Beşikçi, *Selected Writings: Kurdistan and Turkish Colonialism* (London: Kurdistan Solidarity Committee, 1991).

Em Hene!

1   It is worth noting that Italian politicians of the left were open in their support of the Kurdish people, and in the mid-1990s a major conference took place in Rome, attended by members of the Kurdish Parliament-in-Exile.

2   Amnesty International, *Political Killings by Governments* (London: Amnesty International Publications, 1983).

3   Ibid.

4   *Statewatch* 7, nos. 4 & 5 (July–October 1997).

5   General Ahmet Çörekçi, quoted in an Amnesty International briefing entitled "Turkey: No Security without Human Rights," news release no. EUR 44/084/1996, September 30, 1996, https://www.amnesty. org/en/documents/eur44/084/1996/en.

6   See *The Kurdistan Report* no. 27 (August 1989) for Hatip Dicle's report on this example of Turkish "contra-guerrilla activity."

7   If not for *Selected Writings: Kurdistan and Turkish Colonialism*, the little booklet put out by the KSC-KIC in 1991 in London, we would have nothing at all.

8   Crozier returned the compliment, describing Stone as "renowned Oxford historian."

9   *Lobster* no. 17 (1988), the essay "Brian Crozier, the Pinay Circle and James Goldsmith," quotes at length from *Der Spiegel* no. 37 (1982) in an article called "Victory for Strauss." See also "The Pinay Circle and Destabilisation in Europe," *Lobster* no. 18 (1989).

10 Ibid.

11 Former MI5 agent Cathy Massiter, on why she "had been required to resign from MI5"; see Paul Foot, *Who Framed Colin Wallace?* (London: Macmillan, 1989).

12 See "Covert Operations in British Politics 1974–78," *Lobster* no. 11 (April 1986). Note also John La Rose's reference to Kitson in my interview with him which can be found in my own *Selected Interviews* (thi wurd).

13 For the extended discussion of this, see Crozier's *A Theory of Conflict* (London: Hamish Hamilton, 1974), the chapter on "The Problem of Subversion."

14 Yaşar Kemal in his "Kurdistan in Turkey," in *A People without a Country: The Kurds and Kurdistan*, ed. Gerard Chaliand (London: Zed Press, 1980); see also Crozier's *Free Agent: The Unseen War 1941–1991* (London: HarperCollins, 1993).

15 *Sunday Times*, October 17, 1971.

But What Is It They Are Trying to Express?

1   A talk written for a PEN event that took place at the Scottish Poetry Library, June 15, 2016.

2   *Report on Detainment of Gültan Kişanak & Fırat Anlı, Co-Mayors of Diyarbakır* (Diyarbakır, Turkey: Diyarbakır Metropolitan Municipality, 2016), https://www.ft.dk/samling/20161/almdel/URU/bilag/29/1681413.pdf.

3   Latif Tas, Nadje Al-Ali and Gültan Kişanak, "Kurdish Women's Battle Continues against State and Patriarchy, Says First Female Co-mayor of Diyarbakir," *openDemocracy*, August 12, 2016, https://www.opendemocracy.net/en/kurdish-women-s-battle-continues-against-state-and-patriarchy-.

4   Ibid.

5   Ayla Akat, Latif Tas and Nadje Al-Ali, "Kurds and Turks Are at the Edge of a Cliff," *openDemocracy*, November 2, 2016, https://www.opendemocracy.net/en/kurds-and-turks-are-at-edge-of-cliff.

Who's Kidding Who?

1   H.C. Armstrong, *Grey Wolf: Mustafa Kemal; An Intimate Study of a Dictator* (London: Arthur Barker Ltd., 1932), 293, 311.

2   Ibid., 317.

3   Ibid., 317.

4   Ibid., 325.

5   Ibid., 326.

6   Ibid., 304.

7   See "Sykes-Picot Agreement 1916" and "The Proclamation of Baghdad March 11, 1917" at Global Policy Forum, "British Colonialism and Repression in Iraq," accessed March 14, 2023, https://www.globalpolicy.org/iraq-conflict-the-historical-background-/36418.html.

8   Gerard Chaliand, ed., *A People without a Country: The Kurds and Kurdistan* (London: Zed Press, 1980).

9   Giles Milton, "Winston Churchill's Shocking Use of Chemical Weapons," *Guardian*, September 1, 2013, https://www.theguardian.com/world/shortcuts/2013/sep/01/winston-churchill-shocking-use-chemical-weapons.

10 Ibid.

11 For an introduction to this, check out "14 men executed in Kilmainham Gaol" at the Century Ireland project: https://www.rte.ie/centuryireland/index.php/articles/14-men-executed-in-kilmainham-gaol.

12 See Global Policy Forum, "British Colonialism and Repression in Iraq."

13 Gertrude Bell, "Excerpts from the Letters of Gertrude Bell," Global Policy Forum, accessed March 14, 2023, https://archive.globalpolicy.org/security/issues/iraq/history/1922gbell.htm.

14 "Gertrude Bell," profile for *Icons*, BBC, accessed March 14, 2023, https://www.bbc.co.uk/programmes/profiles/373njzqGJGr5py89Z QpMnxH/gertrude-bell.

15 Ibid.

16 Ibid.

Nobody Can Represent a Grieving Family

1 In recent years there has been interest in this racist killing from within the establishment, and the murdered man is named as Axmed Abuukar Sheekh. During the campaign his name was spelled Ahmed Shekh. People involved in the campaign included friends and acquaintances of the victim. I developed this essay from talks and pieces written during the campaign itself, and believe it a mark of respect to retain the original spelling of the name of the young man who died so tragically.

2 The boy was Ahmed Ulla. See *Murder in the Playground: The Burnage Report*, with Ian Macdonald, Reena Bhavnani and Lily Khan (London: Longsight Press, 1989).

3 For more on the murder of Pat Finucane, see the later essay "Arise Ye Torturers-to-the-Crown."

The Evidence Provides the Pattern. The Pattern *Reveals* the Crime.

1 This and the following quotations are from the pamphlet *The New Cross Massacre Story: Interviews with John La Rose* (London: Alliance of the Black Parents Movement, Black Youth Movement and Race Today Collective, 1984).

2 In December 1988.

3 See my essay "Attack not Racist, say British State," in *"And the Judges Said…": Essays* (London: Secker & Warburg, 2002), which refers to a 1989 *Guardian* article regarding the case of "Ramesh K." and the abuse meted out to him and his family: David Rose, "Bitter Questions of Racial Violence," *Guardian*, December 13, 1989.

4 *Independent*, October 13, 1990.

5 "Opening Statement on Behalf of Suresh Grover and the Monitoring Group," Undercover Policing Inquiry, November 9, 2020, https://www.ucpi.org.uk/wp-content/uploads/2020/11/20201109-Opening_Statement-The_Monitoring_Group-SGrover.pdf.

6 See my essay "Attack not Racist, say British State," in *"And the Judges Said…"*

Pernicious Fabrications

1   Jenny Bourne, "The Political Legacy of Blair Peach," *Institute of Race Relations*, April 23, 2009, https://irr.org.uk/article/the-political-legacy-of-blair-peach.

2   See the accounts on Ballymurphy and Derry in "Arise Ye Torturers-to-the-Crown" later in this book.

3   Black History Month Editorial Team, "The Mangrove Nine—We Remember the Protest 50 Years Ago in Notting Hill Gate," *Black History Month*, June 6, 2021, https://www.blackhistorymonth.org.uk/article/section/civil-rights-movement/the-mangrove-nine-we-remember-the-protest-50-years-ago-in-notting-hill-gate.

4   Riaz Phillips, "For the Mangrove Nine, the Crucible of Resistance Was a Restaurant," *Eater London*, November 20, 2020, https://london.eater.com/21579077/mangrove-restaurant-history-notting-hill-small-axe-steve-mcqueen.

5   See his autobiography, *Free Agent*.

6   David Teacher, *Rogue Agents: The Cercle and the 6I in the Private Cold War 1951–1991*, 2015, "1977–1980—Election Fever," https://powerbase.info/index.php/Rogue_Agents_-_1977-1980_-_Election_Fever. See pages 58–59 for more on Brian Crozier, in my essay "Em Hene!"

7   For a full account of this see *Southall: The Birth of a Black Community*, by the Campaign Against Racism and Fascism (London: Institute of Race Relations, 1981).

8   See the introduction to Campaign Against Racism and Fascism, *Southall*. Note that the *Daily Telegraph* is a supporter of the right-wing Tory Party.

9   Ibid.

10 Commissioner Sir David McNee; see Paul Lewis, "Partner of Man Killed by Met Officers Calls for Investigation to Be Made Public," *Guardian*, June 12, 2009, https://www.theguardian.com/politics/2009/jun/12/blair-peach-police-investigation-death.

11 Bourne, "The Political Legacy of Blair Peach."

12 "National Front (UK)," Wikipedia: The Free Encyclopedia, last modified January 1, 2023, https://en.wikipedia.org/wiki/National_Front_(UK).

A Notorious Case

1   Michael Mansfield, *Memoirs of a Radical Lawyer* (London: Bloomsbury, 2009), 124.

2   "Biography of Nelson Mandela," Nelson Mandela Foundation, accessed March 14, 2023, https://www.nelsonmandela.org/content/page/biography.

3 Iyiola Solanke, *Making Anti-Racial Discrimination Law: A Comparative History of Social Action and Anti-Racial Discrimination Law* (London: Routledge, 2009).

4 "Student Murder Charges Are Dropped: Teenagers Freed as CPS Finds Insufficient Evidence to Provide a Realistic Prospect of Conviction for 'Racially Motivated' Attack," *Independent*, July 29, 1993, https://www.independent.co.uk/news/uk/student-murder-charges-are-dropped-teenagers-freed-as-cps-finds-insufficient-evidence-to-provide-a-1487933.html.

5 Information on the Monitoring Group may be had at https://tmg-uk.org/about-us.

6 See my essay "Attack not Racist, say British State," in *"And the Judges Said ...": Essays* (London: Secker & Warburg, 2002), which refers to a 1989 *Guardian* article regarding the case of "Ramesh K." and the abuse meted out to him and his family: David Rose, "Bitter Questions of Racial Violence," *Guardian*, December 13, 1989.

7 From a campaign press release which I had in my possession when I wrote an essay on the case back in the late 1990s, and is now part of my archive.

8 Somewhere inside, the Kurdish politician Kani Yılmaz was in solitary confinement during this time.

9 See Mansfield, *Memoirs of a Radical Lawyer*, and Doreen Lawrence, *And Still I Rise: Seeking Justice for Stephen* (London: Faber & Faber, 2006).

10 Lisa O'Carroll, "Stephen Lawrence's Parents Thank Daily Mail for 'Going Out on a Limb,'" *Guardian*, January 4, 2012, https://www.theguardian.com/media/2012/jan/04/stephen-lawrence-parents-daily-mail.

11 Ian Cobain and Rob Evans, "Jack Straw to Be 'Denied Knighthood and Peerage' under Jeremy Corbyn," *Guardian*, February 9, 2016, https://www.theguardian.com/politics/2016/feb/09/jack-straw-denied-knighthood-peerage-jeremy-corbyn.

12 "Straw Announces Inquiry into Lawrence Murder," Politics 97, BBC, 1997, http://www.bbc.co.uk/news/special/politics97/news/07/0731/lawrence.shtml.

13 Macpherson of Cluny, Scotland's twenty-seventh Hereditary Chief of Clan Macpherson.

14 For an idea of the hostile reaction Macpherson received, see Nick Hopkins, "Time to Move On, Says Macpherson," *Guardian*, February 18, 2000, https://www.theguardian.com/uk/2000/feb/18/lawrence.ukcrime1.

15 "Straw Announces Inquiry into Lawrence Murder."

16 Targeted minorities will include Irish and other European peoples, as a function of particular situations faced by the State.

17   Hopkins, "Time to Move On, Says Macpherson."
18   "Full Text of Jack Straw's Statement to Parliament," *Guardian*, February 24, 1999, https://www.theguardian.com/uk/1999/feb/24/lawrence.ukcrime1.
19   As a result of the Macpherson Inquiry and the repeal of the old "double-jeopardy" ruling, one of the "five white murderers" who had escaped a finding of guilt was later retried and found guilty. For more on this see Joshua Rozenberg, "Change in Double Jeopardy Law Led to Gary Dobson's Retrial," *Guardian*, January 3, 2012, https://www.theguardian.com/law/2012/jan/03/double-jeopardy-change-law-retrial.
20   This was how they were described in the report of the Macpherson Inquiry, which can be found as "The Stephen Lawrence Inquiry: Report of an Inquiry by Sir William Macpherson of Cluny" at https://assets.publishing.service.gov.uk/government/uploads/system/uploads/attachment_data/file/277111/4262.pdf.
21   Stephen Wright, "The Mail's Victory: How Stephen Lawrence's Killers Were Finally Brought to Justice Years after Our Front Page Sensationally Branded the Evil Pair Murderers," *Daily Mail*, January 3, 2012, https://www.dailymail.co.uk/news/article-2080159/Stephen-Lawrence-case-How-killers-finally-brought-justice.html.
22   Paul Dacre, "A Glorious Day for Justice: How the Mail's Monumental Risk Could Have Put Editor Paul Dacre in Court … but Instead Did 'A Huge Amount of Good and Made a Little Bit of History,'" *Daily Mail*, January 4, 2012, https://www.dailymail.co.uk/news/article-2081934/Stephen-Lawrence-murder-How-Mails-risk-did-huge-good.html.

Murder in the Line of Duty

1   See page 111.
2   Sam Volpe, "'She Is a Martyr': 25 Years on, Joy Gardner's Mother Is Still Fighting for Justice after Death in Custody," *Ham & High*, July 26, 2018, https://www.hamhigh.co.uk/news/21356353.she-martyr-25-years-joy-gardners-mother-still-fighting-justice-death-custody.
3   "Death of Joy Gardner," Wikipedia: The Free Encyclopedia, last modified January 8, 2023, https://en.wikipedia.org/wiki/Death_of_Joy_Gardner, citing Karen Evans, *Crime Prevention: A Critical Introduction* (London: SAGE Publications, 2011).
4   Institute of Race Relations, *Deadly Silence: Black Deaths in Custody* (London: Institute of Race Relations, 1991).
5   Liz Smith, "Britain: Report Alleges Assaults on Immigration Detainees," *World Socialist Web Site*, April 18, 2005, https://www.wsws.org/en/articles/2005/04/asyl-a18.html.
6   Volpe, "'She Is a Martyr.'"
7   "Death of Joy Gardner," *Wikipedia*.

8   John Austin-Walker.

9   Trevor Rayne, "'The Kurds Don't Vote for Me': The Kurds and Britain," *Revolutionary Communist Group*, March 18, 2016, https://www.revolutionarycommunist.org/middle-east/me/4287-tk180316.

10   For fuller information on this and others see Simon Hattenstone, "We Cannot Take Them at Their Word," *Guardian*, August 18, 2005, https://www.theguardian.com/politics/2005/aug/18/media.pressandpublishing.

11   "CPS Announces No Action against Officers Responsible for Death of Shiji Lapite," *Inquest*, June 4, 1998, https://www.inquest.org.uk/no-cps-action-against-shiji-lapite-death-officers.

12   Ibid.

13   See my essay "Attack not Racist, say British State," in *"And the Judges Said ...": Essays* (London: Secker & Warburg, 2002), which refers to David Rose, "Bitter Questions of Racial Violence," *Guardian*, December 13, 1989.

14   "Death of Oluwashijibomi Lapite," Wikipedia: The Free Encyclopedia, last modified November 25, 2020, https://en.wikipedia.org/wiki/Death_of_Oluwashijibomi_Lapite, citing a 2000 report by the Committee for the Prevention of Torture.

15   Martin Bright, "The Film That Refuses to Die," *Guardian*, August 12, 2001, https://www.theguardian.com/uk/2001/aug/12/filmnews.film.

16   Michael Mansfield, *Memoirs of a Radical Lawyer* (London: Bloomsbury, 2009), 130–31.

17   Kent Kiehl and Julia Lushing, "Psychopathy," Scholarpedia: The Peer-Reviewed Open-Access Encyclopedia, last modified May 14, 2014, http://www.scholarpedia.org/article/Psychopathy.

18   Mikey Powell Campaign, "Family Vigil Marks 10 Years since Controversial Custody Death," 4WardEver.UK, May 9, 2005, https://web.archive.org/web/20221028150420/https://4wardeveruk.org/cases/adult-cases-uk/police-restraint-2/brian-douglas.

19   "New Wayne Douglas Inquest Ruled Out," *BBC News*, July 30, 1998, http://news.bbc.co.uk/2/hi/uk_news/142385.stm.

20   For further information see "New Wayne Douglas Inquest Ruled Out."

21   mudlark121, "Today in London's History: Ibrahima Sey Unlawfully Killed by Ilford Police, 1996," Rebel History Calendar (blog), Past Tense, March 16, 2016, https://pasttenseblog.wordpress.com/2016/03/16/today-in-londons-history-ibrahima-sey-unlawfully-killed-by-ilford-police-1996.

22   Ibid. The incident took place in March 1996; see *Statewatch* 7, no. 6 (November–December 1997) for a report on the inquest.

23   Ibid.

24 The argument makes use of medical evidence relating to deaths in custody and police restraining techniques to make the case. More on this can be found at Amnesty International, "United Kingdom: Death in Custody of Ibrahima Sey," news release no. EUR 45/015/1996, October 11, 1996, https://www.amnesty.org/en/documents/eur45/015/1996/en.

25 mudlark121, "Ibrahima Sey Unlawfully Killed by Ilford Police."

26 "UK Proposals," *Statewatch* 5, no. 4 (July–August 1995), https://www.statewatch.org/media/documents/subscriber/protected/sw5n4.pdf.

27 For a fuller account see Harmit Athwal, "'Accidental Death' during Immigration Raid, Says Inquest Jury," *Institute of Race Relations*, March 11, 2003, http://www.irr.org.uk/news/accidental-death-during-immigration-raid-says-inquest-jury.

28 Ibid.

29 "The Rt Hon Lord Michael Howard CH KC," biography on Gov.uk, accessed March 14, 2023, https://www.gov.uk/government/people/lord-howard-of-lympne.

30 Ian Cobain and Rob Evans, "Jack Straw to Be 'Denied Knighthood and Peerage' under Jeremy Corbyn," *Guardian*, February 9, 2016, https://www.theguardian.com/politics/2016/feb/09/jack-straw-denied-knighthood-peerage-jeremy-corbyn.

31 Rob Evans and Paul Lewis, "Police 'Smear' Campaign Targeted Stephen Lawrence's Friends and Family," *Guardian*, June 24, 2013, https://www.theguardian.com/uk/2013/jun/23/stephen-lawrence-undercover-police-smears.

32 "Stephen Lawrence's Mother Suggests Police Should Close Murder Inquiry," *Telegraph*, April 7, 2018, https://www.telegraph.co.uk/news/2018/04/07/doreen-lawrence-police-should-honest-state-stephens-murder-probe.

33 Evans and Lewis, "Police 'Smear' Campaign."

34 Mandy Rhodes, "Interview with Jack Straw," *Holyrood*, July 1, 2013, https://www.holyrood.com/inside-politics/view,interview-with-jack-straw_5722.htm.

Arise Ye Torturers-to-the-Crown

1 "David McNee," Wikipedia: The Free Encyclopedia, last modified October 9, 2022, https://en.wikipedia.org/wiki/David_McNee.

2 Kehinde Andrews, "Forty Years on from the New Cross Fire, What Has Changed for Black Britons?," *Guardian*, January 17, 2021, https://www.theguardian.com/world/2021/jan/17/forty-years-on-from-the-new-cross-fire-what-has-changed-for-black-britons.

3 Virgillo Hunter, "The New Cross Fire (January 18, 1981)," *Black Past*, June 9, 2019, https://www.blackpast.org/global-african-history/

the-new-cross-fire-january-18-1981. John La Rose was chairman of the New Cross Massacre Action Committee.

4   Ibid.

5   "New Cross Massacre Campaign," George Padmore Institute, accessed March 14, 2023, https://www.georgepadmoreinstitute. org/collections/new-cross-massacre-campaign-1980-1985. For further detail on the New Cross Massacre and related information visit https://www.georgepadmoreinstitute.org/collection/ new-cross-massacre-campaign.

6   Andrews, "Forty Years on from the New Cross Fire."

7   This was an interview I conducted with John La Rose back in 1993; see "An Interview with John La Rose," in *"And the Judges Said ...": Essays* (London: Secker & Warburg, 2002). For more on John La Rose go to https://www.georgepadmoreinstitute.org/about.

8   James Hughes, "Frank Kitson in Northern Ireland and the 'British Way' of Counterinsurgency," *History Ireland*, January/ February 2014, https://www.historyireland.com/volume-22/ frank-kitson-northern-ireland-british-way-counterinsurgency.

9   See report by the *Punjabi Times* of May 1, 1979, cited in *Southall: The Birth of a Black Community*, by the Campaign Against Racism and Fascism (London: Institutue of Race Relations, 1981).

10 Bob Mitchell and Ed Moloney, "The Cairo Gang, the Force Research Unit and ... Rupert Murdoch," *openDemocracy*, December 20, 2012, https://www.opendemocracy.net/en/opensecurity/cairo-gang-force-research-unit-and-rupert-murdoch.

11 For more information, see Marc Parry, "Uncovering the Brutal Truth about the British Empire," *Guardian*, August 18, 2016, https:// www.theguardian.com/news/2016/aug/18/uncovering-truth-british-empire-caroline-elkins-mau-mau, and on detention camps see "List of British Concentration Camps during the Mau Mau Uprising," Wikipedia: The Free Encyclopedia, last modified November 15, 2022, https://en.wikipedia.org/wiki/List_of_British_ concentration_camps_during_the_Mau_Mau_Uprising.

12 "Kikuyu Hammered on the Anvil," *Daily Nation* (Kenya), April 15, 2004.

13 John McGhie, "British Brutality in Mau Mau Conflict," *Guardian*, November 8, 2002, https://www.theguardian.com/uk/2002/ nov/09/3.

14 "Kikuyu Hammered on the Anvil."

15 For a full account, see Machua Koinange, "My Encounter with the Man Who Shot Dedan Kimathi," *Standard*, February 18, 2014, https:// www.standardmedia.co.ke/special-reports/article/2000095871/ my-encounter-with-the-man-who-shot-dedan-kimathi.

16 Ibid.

17   Royals and guests ate breadcrumb-battered fish and french-fried potatoes on plates of the finest silver, followed by custard and dumpling served in Chinese bowls of unknown antiquity.

18   Rosie Waites, "The Moment a Princess Became a Queen," *BBC News*, February 6, 2012, https://www.bbc.co.uk/news/magazine-16795006.

19   "Kikuyu Hammered on the Anvil."

20   Ibid.

21   R.T. Paget, 513 H.C. Deb. (March 31, 1953) col. 1112, https://api.parliament.uk/historic-hansard/commons/1953/mar/31/kenya-massacre-uplands-1.

22   "Kikuyu Hammered on the Anvil."

23   For example, Barbara Castle MP.

24   530 H.C. Deb. (July 22, 1954) cols. 1575–639, https://api.parliament.uk/historic-hansard/commons/1954/jul/22/kenya.

25   Reginald Paget was the MP; R.T. Paget, 513 H.C. Deb. (March 31, 1953) col. 1109, https://api.parliament.uk/historic-hansard/commons/1953/mar/31/kenya-massacre-uplands-1.

26   "Reginald Paget, Baron Paget of Northampton," Wikipedia: The Free Encyclopedia, last modified November 29, 2022, https://en.wikipedia.org/wiki/Reginald_Paget,_Baron_Paget_of_Northampton.

27   R.T. Paget, 513 H.C. Deb. (March 31, 1953) col. 1110, https://api.parliament.uk/historic-hansard/commons/1953/mar/31/kenya-massacre-uplands-1.

28   "Erich von Manstein," Wikipedia: The Free Encyclopedia, last modified January 1, 2023, https://en.wikipedia.org/wiki/Erich_von_Manstein.

29   Ibid., citing Ronald Smelser and Edward Davies, *The Myth of the Eastern Front: The Nazi-Soviet War in American Popular Culture* (Cambridge: Cambridge University Press, 2008).

30   Ibid., citing Smelser and Davies, *The Myth of the Eastern Front*.

31   "Ian Henderson," WikiSpooks, last modified May 2, 2022, https://wikispooks.com/wiki/Ian_Henderson.

32   "British Officer Henderson, Known as the Butcher of Bahrain, Dies," *Islam Times*, April 16, 2013, https://www.islamtimes.org/en/news/254601/british-officer-henderson-known-as-the-butcher-of-bahrain-dies.

33   Ibid.

34   See "Ian Henderson," *WikiSpooks*.

35   Amnesty International, "UK: Amnesty International Welcomes Investigation into Henderson's Role in Torture in Bahrain," news release no. EUR 45/003/2000, January 7, 2000, https://www.amnesty.org/en/documents/EUR45/003/2000/en.

36   In the words of George Galloway MP.

37 "Ian Henderson (Police Officer)," Wikipedia: The Free Encyclopedia, last modified November 19, 2022, https://en.wikipedia.org/wiki/Ian_Henderson_(police_officer).

38 "Ian Henderson," *WikiSpooks.*

39 Jamie Merrill, "Government Refuses to Release Details of Relationship with Authoritarian Bahrain," *Independent,* March 10, 2015, https://www.independent.co.uk/news/uk/politics/government-refuses-release-details-relationship-authoritarian-bahrain-10099197.html.

40 "Frank Kitson," Wikipedia: The Free Encyclopedia, last modified January 7, 2023, https://en.wikipedia.org/wiki/Frank_Kitson.

41 Mitchell and Moloney, "The Cairo Gang, the Force Research Unit and ... Rupert Murdoch."

42 Fern Lane, "Bloody Sunday: The Revelations Continue," *An Phoblacht,* September 26, 2002, https://www.anphoblacht.com/contents/9234.

43 Laura Friel, "Bloody Sunday: So Who Was Guilty?," *An Phoblacht,* August 27, 2010, https://www.anphoblacht.com/contents/228.

44 For a fuller account of this see Stephen Dorril and Robin Ramsay, *SMEAR! Wilson & the Secret State* (London: Fourth Estate, 1991).

45 See his acknowledgements in *Low Intensity Operations: Subversion, Insurgency & Peacekeeping* (London: Faber & Faber, 1971).

46 "Kitson and Counter-Revolution!," *News Line,* February 4, 2021, https://wrp.org.uk/features/kitson-and-counter-revolution-2.

47 Kitson believed this; see *Low Intensity Operations*, 13.

48 Kitson, *Low Intensity Operations*, 24.

49 Hughes, "Frank Kitson in Northern Ireland."

50 See the Ballymurphy Massacre site for eyewitness accounts: http://www.ballymurphymassacre.com/cms/massacre.

51 See the site of the families' campaign at https://mcgurksbar.com/tag/general-sir-frank-kitson. See also for a fuller account https://mcgurksbar.com/tag/collusion.

52 "McGurk's Bar Bombing," Wikipedia: The Free Encyclopedia, last modified December 7, 2022, https://en.wikipedia.org/wiki/McGurk%27s_Bar_bombing#cite_ref-30.

53 Adam Ramsay, "Bloody Sunday and How the British Empire Came Home," *openDemocracy,* March 15, 2019, https://www.opendemocracy.net/en/opendemocracyuk/bloody-sunday-british-empire.

54 Friel, "Bloody Sunday."

55 "Kincora Boy's Home Scandal: South African Intelligence 'Secretly Backed Loyalist Paramilitary Group Tara,'" *Belfast Telegraph,* April 15, 1996, https://www.belfasttelegraph.co.uk/news/northern-ireland/kincora-boys-home-scandal-south-african-intelligence-secretly-backed-loyalist-paramilitary-group-tara/28385497.html.

56 There is a great deal of information available online; attested and unattested. Books are useful here: Chris Moore, *The Kincora*

Scandal: Political Cover-Up and Intrigue in Northern Ireland (Dublin: Marino Books, 1996); Paul Foot on the Colin Wallace Affair: *Who Framed Colin Wallace?* (London: Macmillan, 1989).

57 "Kincora Boy's Home Scandal."

58 See *Village* magazine's coverage of the Kincora scandal at https://villagemagazine.ie/tag/kincora.

59 The Ulster Defence Association, formed in 1971. Mitchell and Moloney, "The Cairo Gang, the Force Research Unit and … Rupert Murdoch."

60 Ed Moloney and Bob Mitchell, "The Force Research Unit—How It Began," *The Broken Elbow* (blog), January 4, 2013, https://thebrokenelbow.com/2013/01/04/the-force-research-unit-how-it-began.

61 Mitchell and Moloney, "The Cairo Gang, the Force Research Unit and … Rupert Murdoch."

62 Hughes, "Frank Kitson in Northern Ireland and the 'British Way' of Counterinsurgency."

63 Ibid.

64 See page 102 for further information.

65 Description for *War School*, episode 1, "Kitson's Class," aired January 9, 1980, on BBC One, accessed March 14, 2023, https://genome.ch.bbc.co.uk/92978256315f457bb62d5c72a6fa99ba.

66 Seumas Milne, "During the Miners' Strike, Thatcher's Secret State Was the Real Enemy Within," *Guardian*, October 3, 2014, https://www.theguardian.com/commentisfree/2014/oct/03/miners-strike-thatcher-real-enemy-within-extremism.

67 This was the phrase Thatcher used to describe the left in general, even at one point the British Labour Party.

68 Russell Malloch, "The Order of the British Empire (Part Four): 1957 to 1993," *The Gazette*, accessed March 14, 2023, https://m.thegazette.co.uk/all-notices/content/101117.

69 "Frank Kitson," *Wikipedia*.

70 Rory Carroll, "Ministers Reject Calls for Public Inquiry into Pat Finucane Murder," *Guardian*, November 30, 2020, https://www.theguardian.com/uk-news/2020/nov/30/ministers-reject-call-for-public-inquiry-into-pat-finucane.

71 Henry McDonald, "Pat Finucane Murder 'Caused by British Infiltration Policy', Court Told," *Guardian*, May 11, 2015, https://www.theguardian.com/uk-news/2015/may/11/pat-finucane-murder-belfast-high-court.

72 "Royal United Services Institute for Defence Studies," Powerbase: Public Interest Investigations, last modified August 28, 2016, https://powerbase.info/index.php/Royal_United_Services_Institute_for_Defence_Studies.

73 "Jeremy Blackham," Powerbase: Public Interest Investigations, last modified August 22, 2013, https://powerbase.info/index.php/ Jeremy_Blackham, citing "Labour Party Conference," SourceWatch, last modified August 21, 2008, https://www.sourcewatch.org/index. php?title=Labour_Party_conference.

74 See for example "Risk, Threat and Security: The Case of the United Kingdom," Powerbase: Public Interest Investigations, last modified November 4, 2010, https://powerbase.info/index.php/ Risk,_Threat_and_Security:_The_Case_of_the_United_Kingdom.

75 "Collusion and Cover-Up," McGurk's Bar Massacre website, accessed March 14, 2023, https://web.archive.org/web/20200928131250/ http://mcgurksbar.com/collusion.

76 Kitson, *Low Intensity Operations*, 24.

77 Known in law as the "Hitler had a nice moustache" argument.

78 Owen Bowcott, "Bloody Sunday Timeline: From 1972 Killings to Charges against Soldier," *Guardian*, March 14, 2019, https://www. theguardian.com/uk-news/2019/mar/14/bloody-sunday-timeline- from-1972-killings-to-charges-against-soldier.

79 Stephen Knight, *The Brotherhood: The Secret World of the Freemasons* (London: Grafton Books, 1988), 17, available at https://erenow.net/ common/the-brotherhood-the-secret-world-of-the-freemasons/18. php.

80 Simon Winchester, "Amid the Tears and Cheers, a Full Stop to Britain's Colonial Experience in Northern Ireland," *Guardian*, June 15, 2010, https://www.theguardian.com/uk/2010/jun/15/ derry-bloody-sunday-northern-ireland.

81 Friel, "Bloody Sunday."

82 Lane, "Bloody Sunday."

83 Winchester, "Amid the Tears and Cheers."

84 "Bloody Sunday: Decision Not to Prosecute 15 Former Soldiers Upheld," *Sky News*, September 29, 2020, https://news.sky.com/ story/bloody-sunday-decision-not-to-prosecute-15-former-soldiers- upheld-12085093.

85 Lesley-Anne McKeown, "Widow Sues Army's Top Officer over 1973 Paramilitary Killing," *Belfast Telegraph*, April 28, 2015, https://www. belfasttelegraph.co.uk/news/northern-ireland/widow-sues-armys- top-officer-over-1973-paramilitary-killing/31175867.html.

86 Kevin Mullan, "Bloody Sunday Families Continue Justice Fight after PPS Decides to Discontinue Proceedings against Soldier F," *Derry Journal*, July 2, 2021, https://www.derryjournal.com/news/crime/ bloody-sunday-families-continue-justice-fight-after-pps-decides- to-discontinue-proceedings-against-soldier-f-3294728.

87   Anthony Neeson, "Ballymurphy Families Speak of Pain," *Irish Echo*, September 24, 2021, https://www.irishecho.com/2021/9/ballymurphy-families-speak-of-pain.

Home Truths

1   For more on this see "Swearing In and the Parliamentary Oath," UK Parliament, accessed March 14, 2023, https://www.parliament.uk/about/how/elections-and-voting/swearingin.

2   "Work of the House of Lords," UK Parliament, accessed March 14, 2023, https://www.parliament.uk/business/lords/work-of-the-house-of-lords.

3   In particular the lines on Reginald Paget and Frank Kitson, pages 141–42 or thereabouts.

A Brief History

1   See *De Jure Regni apud Scotos* (*The Powers of the Crown in Scotland*) by George Buchanan (published in 1579). Buchanan advocates the limited powers of the Monarch and the people's right to get rid of a bad one. He tutored King James VI, who was strongly opposed to such skepticism. At one stage Buchanan had to face the Portuguese inquisition. His work greatly influenced European thought for a couple of hundred years, and had a seminal impact on founder members of the American Constitution.

2   "The Principal Acts of the General Assembly of the Free Church of Scotland, Act IV—Act anent Loyal and Dutiful Address to Her Majesty the Queen (No 4 of Class II)," Free Church of Scotland, May 2015, https://freechurch.org/wp-content/uploads/2021/06/2015-Acts-of-Assembly-for-Website-2018.pdf.

Selected Bibliography

Armstrong, H.C. *Grey Wolf: Mustafa Kemal; An Intimate Study of a Dictator.* London: Arthur Barker Ltd., 1932.

Beşikçi, İsmail. *Selected Writings: Kurdistan and Turkish Colonialism.* Kurdistan Solidarity Committee, 1991.

Chaliand, Gerard, ed. *A People without a Country: The Kurds and Kurdistan.* London: Zed Press, 1980.

Fernandes, Desmond. *The Kurdish and Armenian Genocides: From Censorship and Denial to Recognition?* Spånga, Sweden: Apec Förlag, 2007.

Hitti, Philip K. *History of the Arabs: From the Earliest Times to the Present.* London: Macmillan, 1963.

Hourani, A.H., and S.M. Stern, eds. *The Islamic City: A Colloquium.* Oxford: Bruno Cassirer Ltd., 1970.

Miley, Thomas Jeffrey, and Frederico Venturini, eds. *Your Freedom and Mine: Abdullah Öcalan and the Kurdish Question in Erdoğan's Turkey.* Montreal: Black Rose Books, 2018.

Öcalan, Abdullah. Three pamphlets published by International Initiative Editions, 2013: *Democratic Confederalism, Liberating Life: Women's Revolution, War and Peace in Kurdistan.*

Rizgar, Baran. *Learn Kurdish: A Multi-Level Course in Kurmanji.* London: Lithosphere Print & Production Network, 1996.

Van Bruitnessen, Martin. *Agha, Shaikh and State: The Social and Political Structures of Kurdistan.* London: Zed Books, 1992.

Index

Page numbers in *italic* refer to illustrations. "Passim" (literally "scattered") indicates intermittent discussion of a topic over a cluster of pages.

Africa, 57–58. *See also* Kenya; South Africa
Amnesty International, 30, 41, 45, 49, 67, 154
Anlı, Fırat, 70–71, 75
asbestos-related terminal disease, 24–26
assassination by British State, 67, 136, 146
Ata, Ayla Akat, 77
Atatürk, Mustafa Kemal, 64, 79–82
Austin-Walker, John, 37, 54

Bahrain, 144–45
Ballymurphy massacre, 1971, 147–48, 156
BBC, 1–2, 85, 152, 156
Belgium, 37
Bell, Gertrude, 84, 85
Beşikçi, İsmail, 6–7, 23, 36–37, 41–52 passim, 55–56, 60, 67, 73
black communities: UK, 24, 25, 98–104 passim, 105–35 passim, 178
Blackham, Jeremy, 155

Blair, Tony, 131–32
Bloody Sunday, Derry, Northern Ireland, January 30, 1972, 148–51 passim, 156–59
British State. *See* UK
Buchanan, George, 67, 172, 224n1 (Brief History)

Celts, hatred of, 13–14
censorship: Turkey, 32–34 passim, 51, 57, 71
Ceylan, Münir, 40–41, 44–45, 48
Churchill, Winston, 83–85
colonial policing, 136–59, 178
Connolly, James, 87, 89
Conservative Party (UK), 100–101, 104, 113, 164
counterterrorist legislation: UK, 38–39
Crentsil, Joseph, 129–30
criminalisation: of black people, 98, 117; of Kurds, 66; of the PKK, 78
Crozier, Brian, 58, 59, 100

democratic rights and human rights, 49
demonstrations, protests, etc., 27, 86–90 passim, 119; colonial India, 136; Derry, 148; labour movement, 28; London, 93, 99, 101–2, 125–26, 134–35, Turkey, 1, 6, 45, 46; Scotland, 87–88
Denmark, 37
Derry massacre, January 30, 1972. *See* Bloody Sunday, Derry, Northern Ireland, January 30, 1972
Dicle, Hatip, 55
Douglas, Brian, 124–25
Douglas, Wayne, 125

Elizabeth II, Queen of Great Britain, 139–40, 143–44, 153, 162
Erdal, Pelin, 46
Erdoğan, Aslı, 73, 74
Erdoğan, Recep Tayyip, 72, 76, 77

Farhi, Moris, 41, 44
Finucane, Pat, 89, 150, 153–54
France, 9, 60, 64; Sykes-Picot Agreement, 83

Gàidhlig, 9, 11, 173
Galloway, George, 38
Gardner, Joy, 119–21, 128
Gareau-Des Bois, Louise, 44
Germany: Turkish relations, 8, 9, 31, 37, 54–56 passim, 65
Great Britain. *See* UK
"Great Leader" notion, 61–62, 67
Greece: Öcalan and, 8, 9
Güçlükonak massacre, 1995, 47

hate crimes, racially motivated. *See* racially motivated crimes
Havers, Michael, 149
Heath, Edward, 145–46, 156

Henderson, Ian, 138–39, 143–44
Howard, Michael, 38, 120, 121, 128, 131
human rights and democratic rights. *See* democratic rights and human rights

immigrants and asylum seekers: UK, 119–31, 155
India, 83, 136, 172
Iran, 24, 34, 64, 67–68
Iraq, 24, 30, 34, 64, 82–85
Ireland, 83, 174. *See also* Northern Ireland
Istanbul University, 45, 50
Italy, 31, 211n1; Öcalan and, 8, 9, 52, 65

Jallianwala Bagh massacre (Amritsar massacre), 136
James I, King of England, 10, 13–14, 140, 170, 171, 173, 224n1 (Brief History)
John, Gus, 88

"Kafka Trial" (Turkey), 42–44
Kemal, Yaşar, 5–6, 42, 43–44
Kenya: British colonial occupation, 136–45 passim, 150
Kimathi, Dedan, 138, 140
Kışanak, Gültan, 70–71, 75–76
Kitson, Frank, 58–59, 135–58 passim
Kurdistan (word), 34, 63
Kurdistan Workers' Party (PKK), 1–9 passim, 23, 37, 40, 51, 55, 57, 63–67 passim, 160; massacre allegations, 47, 55
Kurds, 1–9 passim, 23–24, 30–78 passim, 121–22, 179

labour movement: UK, 24–28 passim, 86, 89, 152–53, 164

Labour Party (UK), 99–100, 113,
131, 133, 141–42, 164, 178–79
languages, 20; Gàidhlig, 9, 11,
173; Kurmanji, 34, 36, 63,
68; repression of, 11, 34–36
passim, 63, 82; Standard
English, 175–76
Lapite, Shiji, 122–23
La Rose, John, 135, 136–37
Lawrence, Doreen, 132
Lawrence, Neville, 112–13
Lawrence, Stephen, 105–20
passim, 126, 132, 150
Leedom-Ackerman, Joanne, 46,
50
libraries: Turkey, 33–34
Lloyd of Berwick, Anthony John
Leslie Lloyd, Baron, 38–39, 60
Lockheed Martin UK, 16–17

Macpherson Inquiry (UK),
113–17, 132
Macpherson, William, 113, 117,
132
Mandela, Nelson, 106–8, 150
Mansfield, Mike, 110
Manstein, Erich von, 143
massacres: India, 136; Northern
Ireland, 147–51 passim,
156–59. See also New Cross
Massacre Action Committee
Mayhew, Patrick, 38
McCann, Joe, 158
McGrath, William, 150
McGurk's Bar massacre,
December 4, 1971, 148, 156
McNee, David, 102, 103
Metropolitan Police (London),
97, 98, 101–3, 109, 122, 151–52;
killings by, 119–33 passim;
New Cross fire investigation,
134
Miletus, 15, 18

miners and mining: UK, 13, 14,
151–53 passim
Mosaddeq, Mohammad, 67
Murdoch, Rupert, 151

National Front (UK), 101, 104
National Union of Miners (UK),
13
NATO, 9, 37, 56
Nelson, Brian, 150
New Cross Massacre Action
Committee, 134, 135
Northern Ireland, 12–15 passim,
39, 99, 147–50, 156–59, 170, 171,
178; Finucane, 89, 150, 153–54

Öcalan, Abdullah, 7–9 passim,
41, 51–56 passim, 61–65
passim, 69, 77–78, 121–22
Organisation of Revolutionary
Kurdish Youth (DDKO), 36
Öztürk, Ünsal, 6–7, 44, 47–48

Paget, Reginald Thomas, 142–43
Palestinians, 24
Palme, Olof, 38
Parliament (UK), 4, 99–100,
115, 135, 146, 162–67 passim;
exclusion of Catholics, 14;
Kenya discussion, 141–42, 143;
Straw, 132, 133; Yılmaz, 121
Peach, Blair, 97, 102–4 passim,
122, 154
PEN, 30, 41–49 passim, 78
People's Democratic Party (HDP)
(Turkey), 76–77
Pinay Circle, 58
PKK. See Kurdistan Workers'
Party (PKK)
police, London. See
Metropolitan Police (London)
Police Scotland, 2–4
press repression: Turkey, 32, 42

Protestantism, 14–15, 171, 174; Kitson, 147, 156
protests. *See* demonstrations, protests, etc.

Queen Elizabeth II. *See* Elizabeth II, Queen of Great Britain

race relations, 22–23, 155. *See also* racism
racism, 20–21, 26, 93–104 passim, 114–15, 177–78; colonial Kenya, 140–43 passim; in policing, 119–33 passim; racially motivated crimes, 92–97, 105–18, 134–35; racial profiling, 4–5; Scotland, 86–91 passim
Roman Catholics and Catholic Church: British State and, 14–15, 174
Russian Revolution, 83

Santiago, Soledad, 47–48
Scotland, 86–91 passim, 160, 170–74; national police, 2–4; "Scottish culture," 21, 22; Scottish-Kurdish parallels, 33, 69; Scottish National Party, 164; "Scottish solution," 7
Scottish Gaelic. *See* Gàidhlig
Scottish Trades Union Congress, 45
Sekhon, Kuldip Singh, 93–97 passim
Sey, Ibrahima, 126–28
Shekh, Ahmed, 86, 88
Skinner, Dennis, 38
South Africa, 150
Stone, Norman, 58, 60
Straw, Jack, 54, 113, 115, 117, 131–32, 133
student movements: Turkey, 45, 56, 65

Siziba, Kwanele, 130–31

Thatcher, Margaret, 99–100, 103, 108
Tkachenko, Alexander, 46, 50
torture: Bahrain, 144; colonial Kenya, 137, 138; Turkey, 30–31, 40, 59, 71
Tory Party (UK). *See* Conservative Party (UK)
Tuffy, Mark, 124–25
Türkali, Vedat, 45, 47, 179
Turkey, 1–9 passim, 23–24, 52–78 passim, 121, 161; Atatürk, 64, 79–82; freedom of expression, 5–9 passim, 30–51 passim, 56, 60, 72–74 passim; tourists, 15–16, 30, 57, 65–66; UK model for, 80–81
Tuzo, Henry, 154

UK, 57–60 passim, 86–91 passim, 98–104, 134–69; Bahrain, 144–45; Elizabeth II, 139–40, 153; India, 83, 136, 172; Iran, 67–68, 136; Iraq, 64, 82–85; Jurisdiction (Conspiracy and Incitement) Bill (1997), 38; Kenya, 136–45 passim, 150; Lloyd Report, 38–39; MI5, 58, 121, 123, 150, 153; model for Turkey, 80–81; New Cross fire, January 18, 1981, 134–35; racially motivated crimes, 92–97, 105–18; Yılmaz incarceration, 37–38, 54. *See also* Northern Ireland; Parliament (UK); Scotland
Uzun, Mehmed, 8

Waciuri, Kimathi wa. *See* Kimathi, Dedan
Wales: Plaid Cymru, 164
Wallace, Colin, 39

Westminster Parliament. *See*
   Parliament (UK)
Widgery, John Passmore, Baron,
   156–57
Wilford, Derek, 156
Wilkinson, Paul, 39, 60

Yağmurdereli, Eşber, 47
Yildiz, Firsat, 1
Yılmaz, Kani, 37–38, 54, 121–22
Yurdatapan, Şanar, 6–7, 46, 50,
   50
Yurtçu, Ocak Işık, 44

Zana, Leyla, 55

About the Author

James Kelman was born in Glasgow, June 1946, and left school in 1961. He travelled about and worked at various jobs. He lives in Glasgow with his wife, Marie, who has supported his work since 1969.

ABOUT PM PRESS

PM Press is an independent, radical publisher
of books and media to educate, entertain, and
inspire. Founded in 2007 by a small group of
people with decades of publishing, media, and
organizing experience, PM Press amplifies the
voices of radical authors, artists, and activists.
Our aim is to deliver bold political ideas and vital stories to people from
all walks of life and arm the dreamers to demand the impossible. We
have sold millions of copies of our books, most often one at a time, face
to face. We're old enough to know what we're doing and young enough
to know what's at stake. Join us to create a better world.

PM Press
PO Box 23912
Oakland, CA 94623
www.pmpress.org

PM Press in Europe
europe@pmpress.org
www.pmpress.org.uk

FRIENDS OF PM PRESS

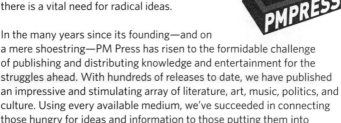

These are indisputably momentous times—the financial system is melting down globally and the Empire is stumbling. Now more than ever there is a vital need for radical ideas.

In the many years since its founding—and on a mere shoestring—PM Press has risen to the formidable challenge of publishing and distributing knowledge and entertainment for the struggles ahead. With hundreds of releases to date, we have published an impressive and stimulating array of literature, art, music, politics, and culture. Using every available medium, we've succeeded in connecting those hungry for ideas and information to those putting them into practice.

Friends of PM allows you to directly help impact, amplify, and revitalize the discourse and actions of radical writers, filmmakers, and artists. It provides us with a stable foundation from which we can build upon our early successes and provides a much-needed subsidy for the materials that can't necessarily pay their own way. You can help make that happen—and receive every new title automatically delivered to your door once a month—by joining as a Friend of PM Press. And, we'll throw in a free T-shirt when you sign up.

Here are your options:

- **$30 a month** Get all books and pamphlets plus a 50% discount on all webstore purchases

- **$40 a month** Get all PM Press releases (including CDs and DVDs) plus a 50% discount on all webstore purchases

- **$100 a month** Superstar—Everything plus PM merchandise, free downloads, and a 50% discount on all webstore purchases

For those who can't afford $30 or more a month, we have **Sustainer Rates** at $15, $10 and $5. Sustainers get a free PM Press T-shirt and a 50% discount on all purchases from our website.

Your Visa or Mastercard will be billed once a month, until you tell us to stop. Or until our efforts succeed in bringing the revolution around. Or the financial meltdown of Capital makes plastic redundant. Whichever comes first.

DEPARTMENT OF ANTHROPOLOGY & SOCIAL CHANGE

Anthropology and Social Change, housed within the California Institute of Integral Studies, is a small innovative graduate department with a particular focus on activist scholarship, militant research, and social change. We offer both masters and doctoral degree programs.

Our unique approach to collaborative research methodology dissolves traditional barriers between research and political activism, between insiders and outsiders, and between researchers and protagonists. Activist research is a tool for "creating the conditions we describe." We engage in the process of co-research to explore existing alternatives and possibilities for social change.

Anthropology and Social Change
anth@ciis.edu
1453 Mission Street
94103
San Francisco, California
www.ciis.edu/academics/graduate-programs/anthropology-and-social-change

God's Teeth and Other Phenomena

James Kelman

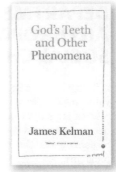

ISBN: 978-1-62963-939-0 (paperback)
　　　 978-1-62963-940-6 (hardcover)
$17.95/$34.95　 368 pages

Jack Proctor, a celebrated older writer and
curmudgeon, goes off to residency where he
is to be an honored part of teaching and giving
public readings but soon finds that the atmosphere of the literary world
has changed since his last foray into the public sphere. Unknown to
most, unable to work on his own writing, surrounded by a host of odd
characters, would-be writers, antagonists, handlers, and members
of the elite House of Art and Aesthetics, Proctor finds himself driven
to distraction (literally in a very tiny car). This is a story of a man
attempting not to go mad when forced to stop his own writing in order
to coach others to write. Proctor's tour of rural places, pubs, theaters,
and fancy parties, where he is to be headlining as a "Banker Prize winner,"
reads like a literary version of *This Is Spinal Tap*. Uproariously funny,
brilliantly philosophical, gorgeously written, this is James Kelman at his
best.

James Kelman was born in Glasgow, June 1946, and left school in 1961.
He traveled and worked various jobs, and while living in London began
to write. In 1994 he won the Booker Prize for *How Late It Was, How Late*.
His novel *A Disaffection* was shortlisted for the Booker Prize and won the
James Tait Black Memorial Prize for Fiction in 1989. In 1998 Kelman was
awarded the Glenfiddich Spirit of Scotland Award. His 2008 novel *Kieron
Smith, Boy* won the Saltire Society's Book of the Year and the Scottish
Arts Council Book of the Year. He lives in Glasgow with his wife, Marie,
who has supported his work since 1969.

"God's Teeth and Other Phenomena *is electric. Forget all the rubbish
you've been told about how to write, the requirements of the marketplace
and the much vaunted 'readability' that is supposed to be sacrosanct. This is
a book about how art gets made, its murky, obsessive, unedifying demands
and the endless, sometimes hilarious, humiliations literary life inflicts on
even its most successful names.*"
—Eimear McBride, author of *A Girl is a Half-Formed Thing* and *The Lesser
Bohemians*

Between Thought and Expression Lies a Lifetime: Why Ideas Matter

Noam Chomsky & James Kelman

ISBN: 978-1-62963-880-5 (paperback)
       978-1-62963-886-7 (hardcover)
$19.95/$39.95   304 pages

"The world is full of information. What do we do when we get the information, when we have digested the information, what do we do then? Is there a point where ye say, yes, stop, now I shall move on."

This exhilarating collection of essays, interviews, and correspondence—spanning the years 1988 through 2018, and reaching back a decade more—is about the simple concept that ideas matter. They mutate, inform, create fuel for thought, and inspire actions.

As Kelman says, the State relies on our suffocation, that we cannot hope to learn "the truth. But whether we can or not is beside the point. We must grasp the nettle, we assume control and go forward."

Between Thought and Expression Lies a Lifetime is an impassioned, elucidating, and often humorous collaboration. Philosophical and intimate, it is a call to ponder, imagine, explore, and act.

"*The real reason Kelman, despite his stature and reputation, remains something of a literary outsider is not, I suspect, so much that great, radical Modernist writers aren't supposed to come from working-class Glasgow, as that great, radical Modernist writers are supposed to be dead. Dead, and wrapped up in a Penguin Classic: that's when it's safe to regret that their work was underappreciated or misunderstood (or how little they were paid) in their lifetimes. You can write what you like about Beckett or Kafka and know they're not going to come round and tell you you're talking nonsense, or confound your expectations with a new work. Kelman is still alive, still writing great books, climbing.*"
—James Meek, *London Review of Books*

"*A true original. . . . A real artist. . . . It's now very difficult to see which of [Kelman's] peers can seriously be ranked alongside him without ironic eyebrows being raised.*"
—Irvine Welsh, *Guardian*

Keep Moving and No Questions

James Kelman

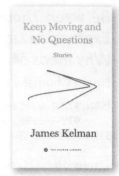

ISBN: 978-1-62963-967-3 (paperback)
        978-1-62963-975-8 (hardcover)
$17.95/$29.95   288 pages

James Kelman's inimitable voice brings the
stories of lost men to light in these twenty-
one tales of down-on-their-luck antiheroes
who wander, drink, hatch plans, ponder existence, and survive in an
unwelcoming and often comic world. *Keep Moving and No Questions* is a
collection of the finest examples of Kelman's facility with dialog, stream-
of-consciousness narrative, and sharp cultural observation. Class is
always central in these brief glimpses of men abiding the hands they've
been dealt. An ideal introduction to Kelman's work and a wonderful
edition for fans and Kelman completists, this lovely volume will make
clear why James Kelman is known as the greatest living modernist writer.

*"Kelman has the knack, maybe more than anyone since Joyce, of fixing
in his writing the lyricism of ordinary people's speech. . . . Pure aesthete,
undaunted democrat—somehow Kelman manages to reconcile his two
halves."*
—*Esquire*

All We Have Is the Story: Selected Interviews (1973–2022)

James Kelman

ISBN: 979-8-88744-005-7 (paperback)
      979-8-88744-006-4 (hardcover)
$24.95 / $39.95   352 pages

Novelist, playwright, essayist, and master of the short story. Artist and engaged working-class intellectual. A proud husband, father, and grandfather as well as committed revolutionary activist.

From his first publication (a short story collection *An Old Pub Near the Angel* on a tiny American press) through his latest novel (*God's Teeth and other Phenomena*) and work with Noam Chomsky (*Between Thought and Expression Lies a Lifetime*—both published on a slightly larger American press), *All We Have Is the Story* chronicles the life and work—to date—of "Probably the most influential novelist of the post-war period." (*The Times*)

Drawing deeply on a radical tradition that is simultaneously political, philosophical, cultural, and literary, James Kelman articulates the complexities and tensions of the craft of writing; the narrative voice and grammar; imperialism and language; art and value; solidarity and empathy; class and nation state; and, above all, that it begins and ends with the story.

"One of the things the establishment always does is isolate voices of dissent and make them specific—unique if possible. It's easy to dispense with dissent if you can say there's him in prose and him in poetry. As soon as you say there's him, him, and her there, and that guy here and that woman over there, and there's all these other writers in Africa, and then you've got Ireland, the Caribbean—suddenly there's this kind of mass dissent going on, and that becomes something dangerous, something that the establishment won't want people to relate to and go Christ, you're doing the same as me. Suddenly there's a movement going on. It's fine when it's all these disparate voices; you can contain that. The first thing to do with dissent is say 'You're on your own, you're a phenomenon.' I'm not a phenomenon at all: I'm just a part of what's been happening in prose for a long, long while." —James Kelman from a 1993 interview

The Art of Freedom: A Brief History of the Kurdish Liberation Struggle

Havin Guneser with an Introduction by Andrej Grubačić and Interview by Sasha Lilley

ISBN: 978-1-62963-781-5 (paperback)
      978-1-62963-907-9 (hardcover)
$16.95/$39.95   192 pages

The Revolution in Rojava captured the imagination of the left, sparking a worldwide interest in the Kurdish Freedom Movement. *The Art of Freedom* demonstrates that this explosive movement is firmly rooted in several decades of organized struggle.

In 2018, one of the most important spokespersons for the struggle of Kurdish Freedom, Havin Guneser, held three groundbreaking seminars on the historical background and guiding ideology of the movement. Much to the chagrin of career academics, the theoretical foundation of the Kurdish Freedom Movement is far too fluid and dynamic to be neatly stuffed into an ivory-tower filing cabinet. A vital introduction to the Kurdish struggle, *The Art of Freedom* is the first English-language book to deliver a distillation of the ideas and sensibilities that gave rise to the most important political event of the twenty-first century.

The book is broken into three sections: "Critique and Self-Critique: The rise of the Kurdish freedom movement from the rubbles of two world wars" provides an accessible explanation of the origins and theoretical foundation of the movement. "The Rebellion of the Oldest Colony: Jineology—the Science of Women" describes the undercurrents and nuance of the Kurdish women's movement and how they have managed to create the most vibrant and successful feminist movement in the Middle East. "Democratic Confederalism and Democratic Nation: Defense of Society Against Societycide" deals with the attacks on the fabric of society and new concepts beyond national liberation to counter it. Centering on notions of "a shared homeland" and "a nation made up of nations," these rousing ideas find deep international resonation.

Havin Guneser has provided an expansive definition of freedom and democracy and a road map to help usher in a new era of struggle against capitalism, imperialism, and the State.

Beyond State, Power, and Violence

Abdullah Öcalan
with a Foreword by Andrej
Grubačić
Edited by International Initiative

ISBN: 978-1-62963-715-0
$29.95   688 pages

After the dissolution of the PKK (Kurdistan Workers' Party) in 2002, internal discussions ran high, and fear and uncertainty about the future of the Kurdish freedom movement threatened to unravel the gains of decades of organizing and armed struggle. From his prison cell, Abdullah Öcalan intervened by penning his most influential work to date: *Beyond State, Power, and Violence*. With a stunning vision of a freedom movement centered on women's liberation, democracy, and ecology, Öcalan helped reinvigorate the Kurdish freedom movement by providing a revolutionary path forward with what is undoubtedly the furthest-reaching definition of democracy the world has ever seen. Here, for the first time, is the highly anticipated English translation of this monumental work.

Beyond State, Power, and Violence is a breathtaking reconnaissance into life without the state, an essential portrait of the PKK and the Kurdish freedom movement, and an open blueprint for leftist organizing in the twenty-first century, written by one of the most vitally important political luminaries of today.

By carefully analyzing the past and present of the Middle East, Öcalan evaluates concrete prospects for the Kurdish people and arrives with his central proposal: recreate the Kurdish freedom movement along the lines of a new paradigm based on the principles of democratic confederalism and democratic autonomy. In the vast scope of this book, Öcalan examines the emergence of hierarchies and eventually classes in human societies and sketches his alternative, the democratic-ecological society. This vision, with a theoretical foundation of a nonviolent means of taking power, has ushered in a new era for the Kurdish freedom movement while also offering a fresh and indispensible perspective on the global debate about a new socialism. Öcalan's calls for nonhierarchical forms of democratic social organization deserve the careful attention of anyone interested in constructive social thought or rebuilding society along feminist and ecological lines.

Building Free Life: Dialogues with Öcalan

Edited by International Initiative

ISBN: 978-1-62963-704-4 (paperback)
        978-1-62963-764-8 (hardcover)
$20.00/$49.95   256 pages

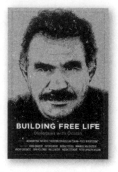

From Socrates to Antonio Gramsci, imprisoned philosophers have marked the history of thought and changed how we view power and politics. From his solitary jail cell, Abdullah Öcalan has penned daringly innovative works that give profuse evidence of his position as one of the most significant thinkers of our day. His prison writings have mobilized tens of thousands of people and inspired a revolution in the making in Rojava, northern Syria, while also penetrating the insular walls of academia and triggering debate and reflection among countless scholars.

So how do you engage in a meaningful dialogue with Abdullah Öcalan when he has been held in total isolation since April 2015? You compile a book of essays written by a globally diverse cast of the most imaginative luminaries of our time, send it to Öcalan's jailers, and hope that they deliver it to him.

Featured in this extraordinary volume are over a dozen writers, activists, dreamers, and scholars whose ideas have been investigated in Öcalan's own writings. Now these same people have the unique opportunity to enter into a dialogue with his ideas. *Building Free Life* is a rich and wholly original exploration of the most critical issues facing humanity today. In the broad sweep of this one-of-a-kind dialogue, the contributors explore topics ranging from democratic confederalism to women's revolution, from the philosophy of history to the crisis of the capitalist system, from religion to Marxism and anarchism, all in an effort to better understand the liberatory social forms that are boldly confronting capitalism and the state.

Contributors include: Shannon Brincat, Radha D'Souza, Mechthild Exo, Damian Gerber, Barry K. Gills, Muriel González Athenas, David Graeber, Andrej Grubačić, John Holloway, Patrick Huff, Donald H. Matthews, Thomas Jeffrey Miley, Antonio Negri, Norman Paech, Ekkehard Sauermann, Fabian Scheidler, Nazan Üstündağ, Immanuel Wallerstein, Peter Lamborn Wilson, and Raúl Zibechi.